PRIZE POSTERS

Sale No. 2

to be held at auction
SUNDAY, NOVEMBER 10, 1985
at 11 a.m. precisely
at
HOTEL CONTINENTAL
505 North Michigan Avenue
Chicago, Illinois 60611

EXHIBITION:
FRIDAY AND SATURDAY,
NOVEMBER 8 and 9
from 11 a.m. to 9 p.m.

This sale organized and
catalogue written by
Jack Rennert

Assisted by
Ms. Alexandra Corn

POSTER AUCTIONS INTERNATIONAL, INC.
37 Riverside Drive, New York, N.Y. 10023
Telephone: (212) 787-4000.
Cable: POSTERS, NEW YORK

Exclusive book trade distribution by:
Gibbs M. Smith, Inc./Peregrine Smith Books
P.O. Box 667/Layton, Utah 84041
ISBN 0-87905-223-6

Contents

Automobile Posters—to 1914	1-31
Automobile Posters—post 1914	32-62
Important Reference Works and Albums	63-65
Poster Stamp Collection	66
American Posters	67-93
More Recent American Posters	94-98
British Posters	99-115
Dutch Posters	116-126
French Posters—to 1914	127-242
French Posters—post 1914	234-315
German Posters	316-350
Italian Posters	351-359
Spanish Posters	360-364
Swiss Posters	365-392
Bibliography	
Conditions of Sale	

ACKNOWLEDGMENTS

I am grateful for the many individuals who have given their full support and assistance to this second sale of Poster Auctions International. First and foremost, our thanks go to the 51 consignors in six countries who entrusted their finest works to us.

Our staff in New York, most especially my associate, Ms. Alexandra Corn, and also Ms. Terry Shargel and Mr. Chester Collins, were helpful in all aspects of the auction, from editorial and administrative work to the substantial logistical effort involved in bringing this sale to Chicago.

Ms. Beverly Kimes, an authority on automotive history, graciously shared her fount of knowledge with us.

Ms. Rachel Isola ably handled matters in Paris.

In the production of the catalogue, I was fortunate to be able to call on the talents and devotion of fine craftsmen, most of whom have labored on a variety of publishing projects for me for many years: Bill Aller handled the photography in New York and David Lyles the Chicago assignments; Harry Chester Associates, and especially Alexander Soma of their staff, was in charge of design; Brandy Young expedited the typography; Offset Plates did its always superb job in the film and plating; Robert Mauriello of Jalor Color took charge of the color separations and the results show he cares very much; Sanford Graphics provided their usual expert and careful printing and Harold Zigman and his crew make it all very pleasant as well; Sam Goldman at Publishers Book Bindery wrapped it all up with his experienced touch.

To all of them and all the others, many thanks for a job well done.

—Jack Rennert.

Please note the Conditions of Sale on last 2 pages.

© Copyright 1985 Poster Auctions International, Inc. All rights reserved. Printed in the United States of America.

AUTOMOBILE POSTERS – to 1914

The automobile, much like the bicycle at its start, promised a new dimension of freedom, but unlike its two-wheeled counterpart, it was, at its inception, a vehicle for the wealthy. And if the manufacturer was to distinguish his car from another, he had to resort more often to appeals to the class consciousness of his clientele than to the mechanical innovations of his car.

"On both sides of the Atlantic, advertisements for cars capitalized on the upper-class connotations as a selling point. Ads featured elegantly tailored figures, with elite breeds of dogs in tow. Footmen hold open the car door; chauffeurs take riders for a leisurely spin. Sometimes chic and wealth are joined by sex appeal as advertising ploys. Handsome, well-dressed men behind the wheel of a motorcar are often the focus of admiring feminine glances." (Automobile & Culture, p. 47).

"One might say that automobile advertising, by 1914, was oriented in two directions, each playing on a facet of human nature: on the one hand, one associates the automobile with speed, adventure and escape; on the other hand, one wishes for a symbol of status, comfort and elegance." (Auto & Publicité, p. 32).

These two tendencies, speed and elegance, are well illustrated in this collection of automobile posters. And the artists represented here used an inexhaustible range of clever and creative devices in their designs, many of them inspired by the complex nature of the automobile itself.

Design techniques seen here range from distorted proportions and exaggerated perspectives (35,59),or simplified forms and strong colors (6, 60), to detailed representations (30) or a mixture of various mediums, from photography (53) to needlepoint (36). Designers used attractive models (26), clever characters (17) and even stars of the racing circuit (58).

The images in these posters sell sport, speed and danger (5, 59), entertainment, comfort and leisure (42), elegance and class (7, 24), as well as dependability and practicality (15, 34).

"(These) creators of posters for (automobiles) were not only great commercial artists, but also educators of the eye who knew how to bring advanced aesthetic ideas to the larger public." (Auto & Publicité, p. 44). This is well reflected in this unique collection of eye-pleasing automobile images.

ANON.
1. Morieux.
37 x 50¾ in/94 x 128.9 cm
Affiches Kossuth, Paris
Cond B+/ Horizonal crease through lower right image; small tears and stains at paper edges.
Many of the earliest automobile builders followed issues of illustrated scientific journals and magazines, copying automobile designs from the available reproductions of drawings, diagrams and models. As these early designs were relatively simple, they could easily be duplicated. Already equipped with factories, many manufacturers, ranging from makers of umbrella ribs and plumbing equipment to manufacturers of bicycles, such as Morieux, eagerly sought to capitalize on the viable new invention. It was not until later that automobile manufacturers, suffering from stiff competition, managed to experiment with and improve upon the basic designs. Woman in sporty red dress, auto and text in red, ground in tan and details primarily in green.
Est: $600-800.

2. Pneumatiques Anglo-American. 1899.
37 x 50⅞ in/94 x 129.3 cm
Imp. Kossuth, Paris
Cond A–/ Small tears and stains, largely in margins
Tires tossed from hot-air balloons are reached for by eager hands below. Colors are light blue, green and orange.
Est: $400-500.

3. Cycles Terrot Automobiles. c. 1900.
45¾ x 61¼ in/116.4 x 158.1 cm
Imp. P. Vercasson, Paris
Cond B+/ Small tears in margins; folds show in background; colors excellent
Bibl: Meisterplakate, 251
The Terrot firm started in the 1890s in Dijon, making bicycles; at the turn of the century they also began to manufacture automobiles. The chain, which this poster features, was used as late as 1910 on high-powered racing cars and evolved from the earlier belt drive. As automobile engines were improved and vehicles began to operate much faster, the more secure chain was used to replace the belt, a device which would slip easily at fast speeds. And it is speed which is emphasized here, with the festively frocked automobilist tooting her horn and gesturing at the train she has just raced and beat through the tunnel. Terrot used the same idea in an earlier poster, designed by Tamagno, in which one of its bicycles also comes out of the tunnel ahead of the train. Green and yellow predominate; lettering is red.
Est: $700-900.

4

5

7

6

9

HUGO D'ALESI (1849-1906)
For other work by d'Alesi, see 131.

4. Gladiator. c. 1903.
62-3/8 x 91½ in/158.5 x 232.4 cm
Imp. Cornille & Domicile, Paris
Cond A / Small tears in margins only.
Bibl: Auto Show I, 17

The Gladiator bicycle firm was founded in 1891 by Aucoc and Darracq. By 1896, when the automobile fever had already swept through France and England, a British group acquired Gladiator and joined it with Clement, another bicycle manufacturer, with the idea of producing automobiles. The first model was a 4-HP, single-cylinder car with the engine mounted horizontally on a tubular frame. Unfortunately, since the combined operations used Clement's works, buyers complained that the Gladiator looked exactly like the better known Clement. To remedy the problem, several models were built instead at the Austin works in England in which the owners were also financially involved. These models, in turn, looked exactly like Austins. Finally, in 1910, the company was bought back from the British by Vinot & Deguingand, and the manufacturing was moved to Puteaux/Seine. Now the Gladiators looked like Vinots! By 1920, the company gave up the uneven struggle altogether. In this early two-sheet poster, an exchange of flowers from male bicyclist to female auto passenger brings the two arms of the firm together. Red automobile on country road, the Pyrenees rising purple and blue in the background.
Est: $800-1000.

H. BEHEL
5. Georges Richard Automobiles & Cycles. 1901.
48-4/8 x 75 in/123.4 x 190.5 cm
Imp. Camis, Paris
Cond B / Some tears and creasing, largely in text areas; restored hole in clover upper right; staining in text at top; colors and image excellent.
Bibl: Auto Show, I, 11; Auto & Publicité, 23; Phillips I, 42

Georges Richard was another bicycle manufacturer who, in 1897, turned his bicycle shop in Ivry-Port into an auto plant. Pictured here is one of their early, robust automobiles, a typical voiturette patterned after the Benz line. By 1901, the belt drive was being replaced by the modern shaft drive, allowing the automobile to travel much faster with a 2-cylinder, 7½ HP engine. And indeed the emphasis is on speed in this poster, as the auto kicks up dust, the driver thrusts his head forward and the passenger tucks her head against the wind, holding onto her hat as her cape flies out behind her. In 1902, the year after this poster, Richard teamed up with Brasier, an engineer with a superior design; the automobile was known as the Richard-Brasier. In 1904 and 1905, the car designed by Brasier won the Gordon Bennett Trophy for France, making his name so famous that the car was from then on known simply as the Brasier. It was manufactured until 1930. The poster design is an impressionistic rendering in fresh colors: auto in yellow, text in red. The lovely border includes the trademark of the company, the four-leaf clover.
Est: $600-800.

LUCIEN BERNHARD (1883-1972)
For other work by Bernhard, see 323.

6. Adler. 1913.
18½ x 13½ in/69 x 34.2 cm
Hollerbaum & Schmidt, Berlin (not shown)
Cond B+/ Small tear at top right paper edge; two small blue stains at left corners; colors and image excellent. Framed.
Bibl: DFP-II, 236 (var); Wember, 91 (var)

The Adler was an extremely advanced automobile. The man behind it, Heinrich Kleiyer, went to the United States to learn American production methods. On his return to Frankfurt, in 1880, he set up a business importing American bicycles and when he was no longer able to import a large enough quantity, began manufacturing his own bicycles under the name "Herold". An enterprising businessman, Kleiyer also founded the German branch of Dunlop tires and began supplying wire wheels to Carl Benz. The name "Herold" was changed in the 1890s to "Adler", the German word for eagle, with its more aggressive logo. The company went into automobile production in 1900, attracting customers far and wide, including Kaiser Wilhelm II. The car was sturdy and highly successful in reliability trials and long distance events which were sponsored by the aristocracy. Among the famous fine craftsmen who worked for Adler were the engineer Edmund Rumple, and the renowned German architect Walter Gropius, who was hired at one time to design the automobile's chassis. The company stopped operation in 1939. The shadow of the Adler auto and the eagle logo are in royal blue, light blue and black, with the lettering in red. In this smaller format, the artist's name does not appear.
Est: $800-1000.

LEONETTO CAPPIELLO (1875-1942)
For other works of Cappiello, see 39, 137-141, 253-256.

7. Automobiles Charron. c. 1906.
49½ x 76¾ in/125.6 x 185 cm
Imp. P. Vercasson, Paris
Cond B−/ Some tears and creasing, largely at folds; colors excellent.
Bibl: Auto Show I, 30; Poulain, p. 38 (preliminary drawing).
Manufactured between 1901 and 1930 at Puteaux, the Charron was at first known as CVG, based on the names of its three founders, former racers of Panhard cars: Charron, Voigt and Girardot. Fernand Charron, who won the first Gordon Bennett cup in a car of his own design in 1900, eventually took over the company and manufactured large, comfortable—and expensive—sedans. The closed cab shown in the poster was the natural evolution from carriage design—it was very popular with the aristocracy as it exudes elegance and luxury. All this is reinforced by Cappiello's design, showing an elegant lady addressing her driver before entering the cab. The frame around the image, including the title plate, suggests that the Charron automobile is a masterpiece.
Est: $1500-1800.

See color plate 1.

CELLERIS.
8. Goodrich.
46 x 61¼ in/117 x 155.5 cm
Imp. B. Arnaud, Paris
Cond B / Some tears at paper edges; folds show; colors and image excellent.
A most amusing poster for the tire company founded in 1870 in Ohio by Dr. Benjamin F. Goodrich: the brave goose testifies to the suppleness of the Goodrich tire as it rolls over his feathered back—softer than goose down? His friends comment, "My dear, what suppleness." Colors are blue, yellow and green, with red lettering.
Est: $600-800.

E. CELOS
9. Darracq. c. 1905.
85⅜ x 54½ in/216.7 x 138.4 cm
Imp. Kossuth, Paris
Cond B−/ Folds show, with related tears; staining in image; colors very good.
Bibl: Auto Show I, 23 (color; var)
Alexander Darracq started in 1891 with the Gladiator bicycle, which he sold to British interests in 1896. In the same year he established a car works in Suresnes and started producing several lines of inexpensive, reliable cars, which were sold all over the world. The first New York City taxicab fleet was, in fact, made up of a number of Darracqs in 1901. But the company's reputation was made with its racing cars and it was given a real boost in the sales race when a Darracq, driven by the famous engineer and driver Victor Heméry, won the second Vanderbilt Cup on Long Island in 1905, the only international auto race in the United States during this period. This is a most fascinating design: The shadow of the Darracq in purple on bright yellow beach, green, blue and pink horizon is framed with lavendar border. The automobile is apparently faster than its shadow, "Plus vite que l'objectif!" The sentence is a tip-on, covering the phrase "Plus vite que Kodak". (*See* Auto Show I, 23.) The camera manufacturer must have objected.
Est: $800-1000.

PHILIPPE CHAPELLIER
10. Phares Ducellier. 1908.
62¾ x 47⅝ in/159.3 x 121.1 cm
Cond B / Some tears, largely at folds; colors and image excellent.
Bibl: Bibliothèque Nationale, Vol. IV, p. 284.
Cyclopean headlights were either acetylene or oil-powered before the turn of the century. Electric lights were not introduced to the gasoline-run automobiles until 1912. The geese shown in this amusing design do not relish being run over by the onrushing car and are grateful for the Ducellier headlight which saves them. Their otherwise occupied owners remain oblivious to the near accident. The countryside is rendered in subtle colors with dark outlines—blue, green and brown predominate, with text in yellow.
Est: $700-900.

E. CLOUET
11. Exposition de Locomotion Automobile. 1895.
35¾ x 50 in/90.8 x 127 cm
Imp. J. Kossuth, Paris
Cond B−/ Folds show; tears and losses along folds; colors very good
Bibl: Auto Show I, 1; Auto & Publicité, 34
The Paris-Bordeaux race and the concurrent exhibition for which this poster was designed occurred in 1895. It was the first purely speed automobile race, as previous races had been run as much for reliability as for speed, with prizes actually awarded for safety and reliability. The first organized automobile race, from Paris to Rouen, was sponsored by the newspaper *Le Petit Journal* as a circulation builder in 1894. The following year, when the Count de Dion and other automobile enthusiasts insisted on a speed race, the newspaper withdrew its support, fearing bad publicity from their competition should many accidents occur. The committee thus formed by the Count de Dion and his friends in order to organize and sponsor the race became known as the Automobile Club de France (l'A.C.F.). The autos entered in the race were exhibited at the Champ de Mars before and after the event. The race started at the Arc de Triomphe, ran to Bordeaux and then back again to Paris. The poster shows a Belle Epoque model holding a French flag and revealing a view of Bordeaux at lower left and of the Paris site of the Auto show, with the Eiffel Tower at right. Woman in red and purple, background in multiple colors, including yellow, green, orange, purple and blue, with text in varied colors. One of the very first automobile exhibitions ever held. Rare!
Est: $1000-1200.

13

16a

15

16b

14

17

18

CHARLES DETAVAT
12. G. Fouillaron.
50⅞ x 37⅛ in/129 x 94.2 cm
Cond B / Some tears and creasing, largely at paper edges; text banner at bottom.
Shortly after the turn of the century, innovation was all important in successfully marketing automobiles. The industry was by then highly competitive and a gimmick or gadget could provide a critical sales tool. The Fouillaron had, in fact, an interesting marketing feature, a transmission innovation that allowed the driver to control the car with infinitely variable gears. The cars were small; the 7 models in their catalogue in 1905 offered between 6 and 24-HP engines, from a single cylinder up to 4. The company, with the help of this innovation, lasted for a relatively long time, going out of business after fifteen years of automobile manufacturing in 1914. The poster announces a 2-seater with 6-HP at 4,250 francs and a 4-seater with 8-HP at 5,250 francs.
Est: $500-600.

FERNAND FERNEL (1872-c. 1934)
13. Auto Panel. c. 1905.
45½ x 8⅜ in/105.5 x 21.4 cm
Cond A. Framed.
A parade of automobiles, motorbikes and motorcycles in red, yellow and brown, by an illustrator who frequently drew bicycles, cars and airplanes.
Est: $200-250.

GASTON SIMOES DE FONSECA (1874-)
14. 12e Salon de l'Automobile. 1910.
47⅛ x 63⅛ cm/119.8 x 160.4 cm
Imp. E. L. Martinez, Paris
Cond B / Folds show, some related tears; unobtrusive 7 in. tear into bottom image
Bibl: Auto Show I, 40
Annual automobile shows, usually held in the fall, were the social event of the year for motoring enthusiasts. Royalty were often included in the high-society crowds which attended in full regalia to celebrate the automobile—the "aristocrat's plaything"—an upperclass product in a class-conscious society. Even wealthy Americans would travel to Paris for the exhibitions where automobiles could be bought or ordered. And it is a most festive auto show at the Grand Palais that we see here: A twilight scene in lavender with light festooned Grand Palais in bright yellow and orange, lettering in yellow and green. DeFonseca, a Portuguese artist born in Rio de Janeiro, started out as a designer and restaurateur in Paris around the turn of the century, winning the bronze medal at the Salon des Artistes Français in 1914. His only other known poster, also in 1910, was for a shoe polish.
Est: $1200-1500.

LEONHARD F. W. FRIES
15. Brennabor. c. 1914.
36 x 27 in/68.6 x 91.5 m
Cond B- / Three large tears; colors and image excellent. Framed.
The Brennabor was built between 1908 and 1934 in Brandenburg, Germany. The automobile started with a 3-wheel motorbike and went on to the 4-cylinder models that became highly popular for their durability and reliability in the years just before World War I. Later, in the 1920s, Brennabor built various 6- and 8-cylinder touring sedans. Touted in the poster as "The most reliable car", it was the standard, middle-class German touring car of the period. In good weather, these automobiles afforded their owners great pleasure and mobility, but in bad weather even short distance travel could be most miserable. The folding top could, of course, be raised and stretched over the automobile

a   b   c   19

20

with some difficulty, but the side curtains of isinglass that were then drawn leaked terribly and fogged up in the humidity leaving them a rather impractical means of protection. The Berlin artist, Fries, has rendered the automobile in grey with red upholstery and details in yellow. The lettering is in blue and background in black.
Est: $1300-1500.

GAMY
16. Two Renault prints.
Mabileau & Co., Paris
Cond A / P.
a. Renault 1911.
25⅛ x 14½ in/63.8 x 36.2 cm
Turquoise and brown.
b. Renault racing cars. 1913.
35½ x 17⅝ in/90.2 x 44.8 cm
Sparkling pastel colors.
Renault was founded in 1899. By 1911, it was the best selling car in France, its popularity won, to a great extent, on the track. Both Louis and Marcel Renault began racing their cars at the turn of the century (Marcel was, in fact, killed in the Paris-Madrid race of 1903). The Renault was even imported and raced in the United States, scoring major successes in the 24-hour grinds—the popular non-stop automobile races. It is probable that Gamy was in fact Marguerite Montaut, wife of the automobile artist, Ernest Montaut (1879-1909). Her nickname was Magy; all Gamy-signed works date after Montaut's death.
Est: $400-500. (2)

GEORGES GAUDY (1872-   )
17. Automobile Club de Belgique. 1898.
36¼ x 49⅞ in/92 x 126.8 cm
O. de Rycker, Bruxelles
Cond B/ Folds show, some related tears; small ink stain in image; colors excellent.
Bibl: DFP-II, 1047, Color Pl. XXIV; Auto Show I, 6; II, 1; Belgique Sportives, 72; Automobile & Culture, p. 41 (color)

"An 1898 poster by Georges Gaudy announces the Course Bruxelles, an auto race sponsored by the Automobile Club of Belgium. Painter, magazine illustrator, accomplished cyclist, and race car driver, Gaudy put Father Time behind the wheel of a fast-moving auto, his cloak, snowy hair, and beard whipped by the wind. . . . Gaudy seems to be suggesting that modern speed alters the traditional notion of time." (Automobile & Culture, pp. 37-39). In this race against time, Father Time is in red robe, auto in navy blue, background is navy blue and light green. Rare.
Est: $800-1000.

JULES-ALEXANDRE GRUN (1868-1934)
For other work by Grun, see 170.

18. Gobron Automobiles. 1911.
45 x 60 in/114 x 152.3 cm
Cond B/ Some tears in background upper right; colors and image excellent.
Bibl: Auto Show II, 36; Phillips III, 449; PAI-I, 211
In 1903, Gustave Gobron severed his partnership with Eugène Brillié and began manufacturing automobiles under his own name. (Brillié went on to build trucks.) This 1911 poster, though rendered with a great deal of artistic license, shows an early closed auto in which a limousine top was simply fixed to the top of an opened car. Gobron went out of business with the stock market crash. Grun gives us a bright yellow Gobron sedan with happy travelers soaring into the blue sky.
Est: $1000-1200.

19. Three Auto Advertisements.

JOSEPH CHRISTIAN LEYENDECKER (1874-1951)
For other Leyendecker works, see 80-83.

a. Collier's. 1906.
10 x 14⅛ in/25.8 x 35.8 cm
Cond B+/ Tear and related creases in lower margin; some rippling. Framed.
Light red automobile, drawing in brown. Madison Square and its old Garden are seen in the background.
b. Pierce Arrow. 1909.
7¼ x 10¾ in/18.5 x 27.3 cm
Cond B/ Creasing in image. Framed.
Bibl: Schau, p. 84
Couple going to theatre in Pierce Arrow—a portrait of the American leisure class in soft colors: yellow, lavender and brown. The Pierce Arrow was one of the most prestigious automobiles made in the United States during the pre-World War I period. It was one of the three famed "P's"—Peerless from Cleveland, Packard from Detroit, and Pierce Arrow from Buffalo. The car's engine was so quiet that it was used by rum runners during prohibition to power their boats. The company folded during the depression.

J. J. GOULD
For other works by Gould, see 77-79.

c. Country Life in America. 1908.
8⅞ x 12¾ in/22.5 x 32.4 cm
Cond A-/ Diagonal crease at top right corner. Framed.
Monochrome magazine advertisement.
Est: $600-800. (3)

GEORGES MEUNIER (1869-1942)
20. Ader Automobiles. 1903.
62⅛ x 42¼ in/157.7 x 107.3 cm
Imp. Chaix, Paris
Cond B/ Some tears in lower right corner margin and at left and right paper edges; slight creasing in image; image and colors excellent.
Bibl: DFP-II, 595; Auto Show I, 18; Meunier, 38; Auto & Publicité, 16; Phillips II, 396
Designer Clement Ader was originally a telephone company engineer. In the 1890s, he tinkered with the idea of building an aircraft, and constructed a steam-powered contraption which however remained firmly on the ground. He then went on to build a more practical automobile, and designed an 8-HP V-twin engine which he put into production at Levallois-Perret in 1900. The automobile graduated to 12-HP in 1902 and 16 a year later, but sales were not good and the company went out of business in 1907. This delightful poster by Meunier shows a confrontation between automobile and animal on a one-lane bridge—where new challenges old—a frequent theme in early automobile advertising. Pastel colors suggest that this is a twilight rendezvous.
Est: $700-900.

21. Two automobile prints. c. 1902.
Each: 18¼ x 26⅞ in/46.4 x 68.3 cm
Imp. Chaix, Paris
Cond A
Two whimsical scenes involving lovers and autos. One is titled "Moto-Flirt" and the other "Moto-Fuite" (Motor-Escape). Meunier's early posters and prints show the influence of Chéret, his chief at the printing firm of Chaix. His role there is simply described by Maindron as "attaché à la maison Chaix en qualité de dessinateur." (p. 91). With the Ader poster and these two prints we begin to see the development of a more personal style.
Est: $250-300. (2)

MISTI (Ferdinand Mifliez, 1865-1923)
22. Cleveland Car. c. 1900.
41 x 115½ in/103.7 x 193.4 cm
Imp. P. Vercasson, Paris
Cond B-/ Folds show; a 17 in. tear into image background at upper right; small tears at paper edges; colors excellent.
Elmer A. Sperry of Cleveland was instrumental in establishing the electric street railway in that city. His early inventions in the 1890s included the electric arc lamp and electrically operated mining equipment, with which he made his fortune. He built his first electric carriage in 1898 and in 1899 he contracted with the Cleveland Machine Screw Company to manufacture his automobile for him. The resulting Cleveland Car had lamps operated by push button and a single lever for

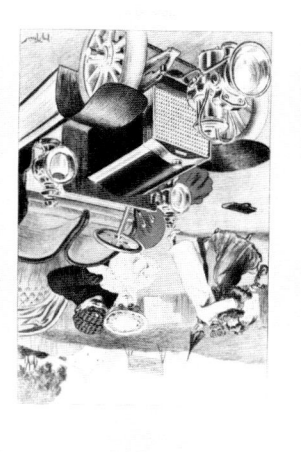

21

27

22

23

24

controlling the movement of the automobile. The lever was moved sideways to indicate direction, pushed downward for speed and pulled upward to remove the current and apply the brakes. The automobile was ultimately known as the Sperry in the United States and was exported under the name "Cleveland Car". Misti, in this long two-sheet poster, shows an evening ride in the electric car beneath a midnight blue sky with shooting stars, figures in black with yellow highlights, lettering in red.
Est: $800-1000.

PAL (Jean de Paléologue, 1860-1942)
For other works by Pal, see 201-207.

23. Salon du Cycle et Automobile. 1897.
36¾ x 50 in/93.3 x 127 cm
Caby & Chardin, Paris
Cond B/ Some tears and losses, largely at paper edges
Bibl: Auto Show 1, 3; Auto & Publicité, 35
For an exhibition of autos and bicycles at the Palais des Machines on the Champ de Mars. Model, wearing headpiece with winged wheel ornament, holds auto in one hand, bicycle in the other. She is dressed in red, the Palais is blue, sky and lettering in yellow.
Est: $600-800.

EDWARD PENFIELD (1866-1925)
For other works of Penfield, see 84-90.

24. The Great Arrow. c. 1905.
10 x 14½ in /25.4 x 36.8 cm
Cond A. Framed.

Of all the prestige cars in the United States, none enjoyed more reputation over a longer period of time than the Pierce Arrow. The car was the brainchild of one George N. Pierce, a Buffalo tinkerer who built bicycles and birdcages in his spare time. His first vehicle, which he called the Pierce Motorette, appeared in 1901, and it was a humble affair with a 3-HP De Dion motor. The name Arrow was used in 1903 for the first time, and Pierce began to cater to the upper crust. By 1914, his was the largest standard car built in America, with a 6-cylinder motor. There was plenty of snob appeal: In the 1910s, when women wore large hats, the roof bulged in the back to accommodate them; and the name never appeared on the grille as other cars' names did (except on one 1928 model) because the idea was that one should be able to recognize it without having to be told. The great American painter, illustrator and posterist, Edward Penfield, created this exceptional advertisement for the company, showing an elegant group leaving the theatre in their Arrow, the city aglow in the background.
Est: $800-1000.

See color plate 2.

BENJAMIN RABIER (1869-1939)
25. Belle Jardinière. 1907.
52 x 82½ in/132.1 x 209.6 cm
Imp. Chaix, Paris
Cond B-/ Tears and staining at folds; colors very good.
Bibl: Auto & Publicité, 62
As early as 1908, automobiles could travel at speeds of up to 40 or 50 miles per hour. The warmth of one's clothing was all important and a new fashion industry grew up around the automobile. In this charming scene for the automobile clothes being sold at the Belle Jardinière department store, a family arrives at a country inn. It is treated in cartoon style, with flat colors and sparse details. Solid, primary colors: red, blue, green and yellow predominate.
Est: $400-500.

GEORGES ROCHEGROSSE (1859-1938)
26. Xme Salon de l'Automobile. 1907.
45¾ x 95¾ in/116.1 x 243.2 cm
Imp. J. Barreau, Paris
Cond B/ Some small tears; folds show, with some related tears; colors excellent
Bibl: Auto Show I, 39
A two-sheet poster of impressive size and design. Dramatic colors include plum, red, gold and dark green. The Grand Palais in the background is surrounded by hundreds of horseless carriages and an invitation is extended by the lovely, seductive model who personifies the splendor of the exhibition.
Est: $1200-1500.

TH. SCHORK
27. Excelsior.
38⅞ x 28⅝ in/98.8 x 72.7 cm
Hollerbaum & Schmidt, Berlin
Cond B-/ Several large vertical tears and creases, largely unobtrusive; restored losses at upper corners; small tears, mostly at paper edges; colors excellent.

In this poster for Excelsior tires, three tire-bearing vehicles converge—a red automobile, grey motorcycle and black bicycle—on a road through mountainside caverns and at the site of a curiously located advertisement. Naturalistic colors include lush blues and greens in the scenery, grey, olive green and black for the cavern interior. Artist's name is an approximation.
Est: $600-800.

EMILE SEVELINGE
28. Circuit des Ardennes. c. 1903.
Daytime scene: 25¼ x 17¼ in/64.1 x 43.9 cm
Nighttime scene: 25¼ x 19⅜ in/64.1 x 59.3 cm
Cond A
Baron de Crawhez, featured in these two prints (only the "daytime" version is illustrated here) was an aristocrat and sportsman who, above all, was an automobile enthusiast. The Circuit des Ardennes, the first important automobile race organized by the Automobile Club de Belgique (1902) was first conceived by the Baron; he won the race in 1903 in his 70-HP Panhard. The last Circuit des Ardennes race was held in 1907.
Est: $200-250. (2)

TAMAGNO
29. Peugeot.
47¼ x 62⅞ in/120 x 159.8 cm
Affiches Camis, Paris
Cond B/ Folds show slightly; crease at top, largely in margin; small tears at paper edges; colors excellent
For the Paris Exposition of 1889, Armand Peugeot had Leon Serpollet build him a steam car. The automobile was a miserable failure, but while attending the exposition Armand took notice of the gasoline powered automobile of Gottlieb Daimler and insisted that his engineer manage a ride in the car. Later, Emile Levassor, Daimler's representative in France, agreed to supply Peugeot with Daimler built engines. The Peugeot auto was successful from the beginning, with the base of a wealthy factory and fine engine. It won many races and was, prior to World War I, one of France's most popular and most successful automobiles. In Tamagno's design, the red Peugeot in the foreground drives along with a colorful pack of Peugeot bicycles streaming from the huge factory in the background. A lion, the Peugeot trademark, roars above the scene. Text in yellow, blue-green border.
Est: $600-800.

WALTHER THOR (1870-1929)
30. Voiturette Lion. c. 1908.
85¾ x 53⅜ in/217.9 x 135.6 cm
Imp. Elleaume, Paris
Cond B / Some tears and creases at folds; restored loss at bottom left paper edge; colors excellent.
By 1905, the question raised at any auto race was never who would win the race, but which Peugeot would win the race. When a family feud occurred between Armand Peugeot and his young second cousin Robert, Armand split from the family company and began manufacturing under the name "Société Anonyme de Peugeot Automobiles". Clearly, he did not wish to abandon the highly successful family name altogether. Robert, in turn, continued to manufacture under the name "Les Fils de Peugeot Frères" and further distinguished his automobiles from those of Armand by calling them Voiturettes Lion or "Lion Peugeots". Within a few years, Armand returned to the family business. The lion was therefore adopted as the company's logo. Thor's object-poster is in red, yellow and green with a decorative border. Michelin tires are also advertised.
Est: $1000-1200.

AUTOMOBILE POSTERS – Post-1914

32   a   b   33

35   34

CHARLES TICHON
31. Gladiator.
15 1/8 x 22 3/8 in/38.4 x 56.8 cm
Imp. Kossuth, Paris
Cond A−/ Small unobtrusive tears at paper edges.
Gladiator automobile and bicycle are seen side by side in a pastel country scene; lettering and auto in red.
Est: $400-500.

ANON.
32. Das Lied einer Nacht. 1932.
36 1/2 x 54 7/8 in/94.8 x 139.4 cm
Offsetdruck August Scherl, Berlin
Cond B−/ Folds show, with some related tears and restorations; colors excellent.
Mercedes, in the early 1930s, was the fastest production car in the world. It was certainly the perfect get-away car for the beleaguered superstar who sought to escape his public in a 1932 film starring Jan Kiepura. Mercedes is generally considerd to be the prototype of the truly modern car; it was the first to have an all-steel frame and an engine designed for high performance under all conditions. The Mercedes was built with these specifications by Daimler. But the person who urged Daimler to build such a vehicle was a far-sighted tycoon, Emil Jellinek, an Austrian of Czech origin who served in the diplomatic service for his country in Nice (one of the auto racing capitals of Europe), and one of the early automobile enthusiasts. With his wealth, he acquired a seat on the board at Daimler, and urged Daimler to build a thoroughly innovative car. Jellinek entered the prototype in a race in Nice, but because the name Daimler was licensed to a manufacturer in France he could not use it there, and instead, gave the car the name of his eldest daughter, Mercedes. The car won in Nice in two categories (1901), and thus the name acquired a wide notoriety. Never one to argue with success, Daimler chose to continue to use the name Mercedes, retaining the name Daimler only for commercial vehicles. After the merger with Benz, in 1926, it was known as Mercedes-Benz. In this film poster, the car is red, with a colorful country background scene; text in yellow.
Est: $1500-1800.

33. Two Buick Posters.
a. 26 3/8 x 40 in/66.9 x 101.7 cm
Cond A
Flat colors: Buick is grey and black, carrying a colorfully clothed family; blue green and black background; tree blossoms stand out in fiery red and orange. Artist's monogram at left.
b. 24 x 37 3/4 in/61 x 95.8 cm
Cond B+/ Small tear at upper right corner; light foxing in upper image.
Family outing in a Buick with pastel blue, green and pink predominant, lettering in dark green. Artist's initials lower right: H.W.
In 1899, David Dunbar Buick sold his plumbing business and began producing gasoline engines primarily for farming and marine equipment—by 1903, Buick had designed and built his first automobile. After a series of bad partnerships and superfluous experimentations he finally began production of the Buick automobile with the help of a far more clever businessman, William C. Durant. Within three years of entering into his partnership with Durant in 1904, Buick's automobile succeeded so spectacularly that the company was selling some 8,000 cars a year. David Dunbar Buick, however, left the company in 1908, disgruntled by the frantic pace of the automobile industry. That very same year, Durant, using the Buick as a cornerstone, incorporated the company as General Motors—later adding Cadillac, Oldsmobile, and Oakland (Pontiac). While Durant went on to make a fortune and the Buick became one of the best selling

36

37

38

39

cars in the United States, the man for whom it was named went from one poor venture to another and eventually died in poverty.
Est: $800-1000. (2)

34. Chevrolet. 1938.
48⅛ x 38 in/123.2 x 96.5 cm
Cond C+/ Some tears and staining; folds show; colors and image very good.
Among the pioneer users of the truck were Macys and Gimbels. As early as 1895, these companies began importing Benz delivery cars to the United States, testing them as a replacement for the sluggish horse and wagon. It was World War I, however, that firmly established the truck and created an enormous impetous for truck manufacturing. Chevrolet began manufacturing trucks at this time, as did Ford, with whom it encountered vigorous competition. The increasing demand for large trucks forced companies to develop special chassis as well as other specialty features. In the United States, for example, where a farm family could afford only one vehicle, the convertible, as it was then known, came into popular use: the truck bed used to carry produce during the week could be replaced with seats on Sunday for taking the family to church. The French import stamp indicates that this poster, printed in the United States, was used for the French market. There's a great deal of impact in this strong image with text in bold stencil type to further emphasize the ruggedness of the truck. Colors are red, ochre and grey.
Est: $400-500.

35. La Buire. 1922.
46 x 61¼ in/116.8 x 155.8 cm
Joseph-Charles, Paris
Cond B+/ Some restored tears at upper left, largely in margin and at horizontal folds; image and colors excellent.
Bibl: Auto & Publicité, 74
La Buire was started in Lyons in 1904, when a company named Chantiers de la Buire, which had produced cars for the manufacturer Sepollet, decided it could do just as well on its own. La Buire was never interested in racing; it was a good, solid middle-class car that scored its major wins in fuel consumption tests. In this excellent design, we get the sharp perspective of the gleaming white La Buire against background of mountain scenery in flat, bright colors: red road; mountains green, lavender, blue; sky light blue; trees purple, and lettering in yellow. "Belle ligne" indeed.
Est: $1000-1200.

See color plate 3.

36. Come Home to Ford. c. 1974.
74 x 28¾ in/188 x 73 cm
Macnaughton Lith. Co., Secaucus, N.J. (not shown)
Cond A
At a time when foreign cars were beginning to make a real inroad into the American market, Ford's New Jersey dealers embarked on a campaign to get car buyers to "Come Home to Ford," reminding them of the heritage and tradition based on the Model-T Ford. It was also a time in which American folkart, including needlepoint, was on the ascent and so the use of that craft to convey this message—in a 30-sheet billboard as well as this smaller format—was most appropriate.
Est: $200-250.

ADRIEN BARRERE (1877-1931)
37. Buick Marquette. 1929.
45⅛ x 61 in/114.5 x 155 cm
Imp. 26 Rue Philippe de Girard, Paris
Cond C+/ Tears and creasing, largely at paper edges and text area; colors excellent.
The Marquette was to Buick what the LaSalle was to Cadillac and the Viking was to Oldsmobile—a less expensive spin-off designed to enter a new segment of the automobile market. The stock market crash in 1929 ruined the Marquette which had been introduced only a short while before; after 35,007 cars had been built, its manufacture was abruptly halted. This is a most unusual poster design by Barrère, better known for his film and theatrical posters drawn in caricature style, with flat colors and broad treatments. In this French poster for the American car, the flowers are bright pink, orange, yellow and light blue, behind a beige automobile. A very late and very rare work of Barrère.
Est: $1300-1500.

G. BOURDIER
38. Renault. 1929.
61⅝ x 46 in/156.5 x 117 cm
La Fregate-T. Burnand, Paris
Cond A-/ Unobtrusive folds and tears at paper edge. Framed.
Bibl: Phillips III, 354
By 1913 Renault had 5,000 employees building 10,000 cars a year. Renault has always been among the most popular cars in France. It was, however, a caravan of these cars in World War I (hinted at in this poster) that made the company beloved to the French people. On September 7, 1914, the French General Gallieni commandeered 1,000 Renault taxi cabs from the Paris streets to close a hole in the Marne line opened by the attacking Germans. This was the first concerted use of the automobile in warfare and preceded the tank by several years. The car is blue; background is yellow.
Est: $800-1000.

40

41

42

LEONETTO CAPPIELLO (1875-1942)
For other works of Cappiello, see 7, 137-141, 253-256.
39. Peugeot. 1925.
46¾ x 63 in/118.9 x 160.2 cm
Devambez, Paris
Cond B−/ Tears and creasing in bottom text area; folds show; colors excellent
Bibl: Cappiello, 316
The boat tail, a design featured on automobiles of the 1920s, resulted in what was considered to be one of the raciest of the roadster type models. It was also highly impractical, as the odd-pointed shape at back left no room for storage. In this powerful poster by Cappiello, the Peugeot lion roars above the sporty green automobile, spotlighted by the blue, white and red aura emanating from it.
Est: $700-900.

JEAN CARLU (b. 1900)
For other works by Carlu, see 257-266.
40. Phares Marchal.
21¼ x 32 ⅝ in/54 x 82.8 cm
Cond A. Framed.
Maquette of the 1924 poster repainted in 1985 by Carlu. Gouache and colored pencil on board. This interesting advertisement for the Marchal auto headlights —"your eyes in the night"— is a cubist design which combines flat shapes and fractured lines: an automobile silhouette and the silhouette of a human head are joined to form a pair of eyes, creating a brightly lit field of vision. Colors include vivid blues and purples at top, text in contrasting red.
Est: $1800-2000.

A.M. CASSANDRE (1901-1968)
For other works of Cassandre, see 267-278.
41. Triplex. 1931.
30¼ x 46 in/76.8 x 117 cm
Alliance Graphique, Paris
Cond A−/ Unobtrusive small tear in upper background; image and colors excellent. Framed.
Bibl: Brown & Reinhold, 54, Pl. 25; Cassandre, p. 41 (var); Cassandre/Japan, 41 (color); Weill, 340; Avant Garde, 160; Word & Image, p. 80; Poulain, p. 183; Phillips I, 112; III, 378; PAI-I, 273
Poulain gives an appreciation of the ingenuity of Cassandre's design for this poster for automobile safety glass – a most difficult subject to convey under any circumstances: "In adapting the avant-garde art to the language of the walls, Cassandre transformed the style of the poster. In Triplex, he borrows forms and composition from a cubism that he tempers with a noble and restrained purism, and from Bauhaus he takes his typography, putting them all together into an

43

original synthesis. Master of symbols, he gives the viewer the subtle pleasure of discovering, on second look, that the arms of the steering-wheel symbolize a road crossing, thus justifying the intense look of the eyes.' (p. 182).
Est: $3000-3500.

A. CHAZELLE
42. Amilcar. 1933.
47 x 62¾ in/119.7 x 159.4 cm
Imp. H. Chachoin, Paris
Cond B+/ Several unobtrusive tears at paper edges; an 8-in. tear into text top center; colors and image excellent.
The small Amilcar was one of the sportiest French automobiles of the 1920s, the dream car of every young French couple of more limited means. It was also during the 1920s that the Ritz Bar became *the* watering-hole in Paris and many a Rolls Royce would line the street in front of the grand hotel. When Horace Chase, a wealthy young American, pulled up to the Ritz in his stylish but small Amilcar, he was playfully nicknamed "Mr. Sidecar"— his tiny automobile bearing a closer resemblance to the one-wheeled cars attached to the sides of motorcycles than to the grand limousines outside the hotel. Chase would often ask

44

Frank, the bartender, to mix him a special drink that was popular at home in Florida – Bacardi, lemon and brandy. Frank mixed the drink and after its immediate success dubbed it the Sidecar. By 1930, Amilcar was prosperous enough to also produce larger touring cars, but the Depression hit the company hard and by 1939 it went out of business. Bold flat colors add to the impact of this poster, showing a fashionable family on an outing to the shore. Note that the driver is on the right—during this period the buyer could pick the location of the wheel.
Est: $1200-1500.
See color plate 4.

ANDRE GIRARD
43. Peugeot. 1930.
45¾ x 60¾ in/116.1 x 154.4 cm
Cond B−/ Some largely unobtrusive tears in image; rippling in background; upper left corner restored.
The poster, showing three speeding Peugeot models, indicates that they were all tested at Montlhéry, the famous autodrome about fifteen miles from Paris which was opened in 1924, not only for racing cars, but for testing them. Automobiles in black and grey race along blue, white and red track.
Est: $700-900.

45

a

b 47

46

48

GASTON GORDE
44. Concentrum Hydrogazo.
31⅛ x 46½ in/79 x 118.1 cm
Editions Gaston Gorde, Grenoble
Cond B+/ Unobtrusive tears at top center and bottom left paper edge; image and colors excellent.
A very strong deco image with two Atlas-type figures, probably representing the two special car oils, launching the cars and trucks into space. Colors are red, yellow and black. The words at top, "Power! Energy! Economy!" describe the poster as well as the product. Gorde was both a printer and designer; this is his most dynamic work.
Est: $600-800.

GEO HAM (1900-1972)
Ham, whose real name was Georges Hamel, devoted his whole career as painter and illustrator to automobiles and airplanes. Poulain calls him the "graphic historian of automobile and air races between the two wars and up to the 1960s." Probably more than any other artist, he was able to catch the feeling and speed of these races through line and perspective, so that the viewer felt he had the same seat as the spectator at the event.

45. Grand Prix de l'A.C.F. 1937.
44½ x 48⅜ in/112.8 x 122.8 cm
Cond B / Folds show; some small related tears; colors excellent
Bibl: Poulain, p. 163 (color; gouache)
Ham gives us the powerful image of a red racing car on a brown track. Fast strokes and a strong diagonal composition dramatize the dangerous speeds as an automobile reaches a curve and races up the bank of the track.
Est: $1800-2000.

46. Midget Racing. 1954.
63 x 46⅞ in/160 x 119.1 cm
Imp. de la Renaissance
Cond B / Folds show; some largely unobtrusive tears and losses at paper edges and folds; colors excellent.
Midget racing was enormously popular, especially in the United States, prior to World War II. The cars were fairly inexpensive and perfect for young sporting blades to race in. The event was indeed very devil-may-care and many an Indianapolis-500 driver got his start in this swashbuckling endeavor. Ham's lithograph shows a jumble of racing cars drawn with bold, lively strokes, bright colors and exaggerated composition, the driver in far foreground capturing the wild spirit of dirt track racing.
Est: $1200-1500.

HARLING
47. Two Boston Auto Show posters.
a. Boston Auto Show. 1916.
14 x 21¼ in/35.4 x 54 cm
Cond B-/ Restored hole and related tears in image; some restored tears at edges; color and image very good.
A Deco image with grey silhouette border, car in light red.
b. ANON. Boston Auto Show.
13¼ x 21¼ in/33.5 x 54 cm
F.E. Dodge, Providence, R.I.
Cond B-/ Restored hole and related tear in image center; on heavy stock.
Evening drive: brown-grey with light yellow text.
Est: $400-500. (2)

LUDWIG HOHLWEIN (1874-1949)
For other works of Hohlwein, see 331-338.
48. Automobil-und Motorrad-Rennen. 1928.
33½ x 41⅜ in/85.1 x 105.1 cm
Hermann Sonntag & Co., Munchen
Cond B+/ Very unobtrusive tears; colors and image excellent.
Bibl: Hohlwein/Stuttgart, 276 (var)
A powerful Hohlwein image for an Automobile and Motorcycle race sponsored by the Auto Club of Munich.
Est: $1200-1500.

See color plate 8.

49

50

52

53

51

HORMAN
49. Humber Super Snipe.
39⅜ x 30 in/100.2 x 76 cm
Cond B / Vertical center fold shows; tear at paper
edges; colors excellent

Thomas Humber started his bicycle company in 1868 and went into car manufacturing about thirty years later. The Humber was the typical middle-class automobile of the English. It was the solid, bread-and-butter model for a rather staid and conservative manufacturer, similar to the Buick in the United States. During World War II, however, these sturdy automobiles served valiantly and the successful Super Snipe which appeared shortly after the war had a built-in reputation in a market of grateful Britons. The Super Snipe was manufactured through the 1960s. Humber discontinued it after Chrysler bought into the company in 1970 and the Humber name all but disappeared by 1976. In this fine poster, the gleaming white auto speeds by, seemingly racing the airplane in the sky at left. Photo-realist treatment captures high gloss and sparkling chrome; colors are white, brown and bright blue, with lettering in light green.
Est: $600-800.

ALEXIS KOW (1901-1978)
50. Salmson. c. 1929.
42¼ x 62 in/107.5 x 157.5 cm
Imp. J.E. Goosens, Lille-Paris
Cond B / Restored loss at upper right corner;
unobtrusive tear at upper left; colors and
image excellent.

Salmson was originally a manufacturer of water-cooled radial airplane engines—and the poster boasts that the car has the precision of these airplane motors. Their first automobiles appeared in 1921, and graduated from flimsy cyclecars to sports cars to elegant luxury sedans. During the 1920s the Salmson, like the Amilcar, was known as a fine, sporty machine. In 1925, Salmson won 76 races and set 14 speed records for its class. It continued to be a competitive and winning car throughout the 1920s, but the fun-spirited Salmson ended with the stock market crash in 1929; from then on the company concentrated on practical and long-lasting sedans. In 1957, the firm was bought out by Renault, home-based in the same town of Billancourt/Seine. For 40 years, Russian-born Kow created smart and sleek automobile print advertisements and posters. Here there is an effective use of strong, flat colors with black and yellow automobile with orange and green headlights on black background, the Salmson insignia flashed above.
Est: $800-1000.

See color plate 8.

51. La Voiture Française. 1939.
46¾ x 63 in/118.8 x 160 cm
Editions Steff
Cond B-/ Restorations largely in border; colors
excellent
Bibl: Kow, p. 159; Phillips II, 330

This poster, published by L'Action pour la Prospérité Française, makes the point very clear: "The French Automobile is the world's best for the French road." And in case the protectionist message doesn't get through, the French road is painted blue, white and red.
Est: $800-1000.

PIERRE LOUYS
52. Citroen. 1925.
61⅝ x 87⅛ in/156.5 x 121.3 cm
Imp. Chaix, Paris
Cond B-/ Folds show; several tears and a restored
loss in image at right; colors excellent.
Bibl: Auto Show II, 50

It was Andre Citroen who introduced mass production to France in 1919. Previous to that time, mass production was known only in the United States where Henry Ford had originated the moving assembly line in 1913. Ford had reduced the amount of time needed to build a single chassis from 12½ hours to one hour and 33 minutes and began the mass production of the Model T. The idea of the assembly line had occurred to Ford when he saw one used for meat carcasses at the Swift meat packing plant in Chicago. The idea was a profitable one when the wealthy Citroen, who had been a munitions maker during World War I and was left with a large factory and few orders after the war, introduced it to France. Like other large manufacturers, he recognized the potential in directing his capability toward the production of automobiles. In this large, colorful poster for the B-12 model, four fashionable women are on a Chateau tour in their Citroen.
Est: $800-1000.

JOSEF MULLER-BROCKMANN (b. 1914)
53. Schutzt das Kind! 1953.
35⅝ x 50¼ in/90.5 x 127.6 cm
Lithographie & Cartonnage AG, Zurich
Cond A
Bibl: Swiss Posters, 53.21; Muller-Brockmann, 158;
Margadant, 176
Muller-Brockmann is one of the most influential graphic

artists of the post-World War II period. His style ranges from geometric abstractions to largely typographic treatments, but, in many ways, he is most effective in communicating his message in the poster medium when he uses photographic techniques. This is evident in his famous Anti-Noise poster of 1960 and especially in this classic photo-offset poster sponsored by the Automobile Club of Switzerland: "Protect the Child!" Describing how "photography more and more frequently and skillfully took over the function of the objective, impartial and informative communication of situations, people and objects" in posters of the twenties, the artist explains the reason: "An untouched photograph shows the picture of reality, the actual facts. People and objects are verifiable. For this reason, factual photography is objectively and informatively the most authentic and is superior to all other possibilities of graphic representation." (Muller-Brockmann, p. 120). There is a bright yellow band at bottom, with smaller text in red. Image (from a photograph of Ernst A. Heiniger) is black-and-white.
Est: $400-500.

CARLO NICCO (1883-   )
54. Carburatore Eureka.
39-3/8 x 54-3/4 in/100 x 139 cm
A. Cotta, Torino
Cond B-/ Tears and losses largely in margins and at folds; colors excellent.
A green devil shoots a red automobile through his bow in a stark demonstration of the explosive speed and force produced by the Eureka carburetor. Text in yellow and blue, background black, border in blue.
Est: $1000-1200.

ROGER PEROT (1908-1976)
55. Marchal. 1927.
38-5/8 x 58-1/4 in/98.1 x 147.9 cm
Hachard, Paris
Cond B / Several tears in image, largely unobtrusive; image and colors excellent
Bibl: Auto Show I, 66; Phillips I, 488; II, 481
Bold image for Marchal automobile headlights: a stylized figure flashes light into path of car. Blue background, blue figure, yellow light beam, black text band, with green lettering. Marchal has created the "perfect light" and Pérot the perfect poster to show it off.
Est: $700-900.

J. RAMEL.
56. Circuit International—Nice. 1949.
25-1/8 x 39-1/4 in/63.8 x 99.8 cm
Imp. A.D.I.A., Nice
Cond A-/ Unobtrusive tears in upper right corner margin; colors and image excellent
At the turn of the century, the city of Nice was the residence of the motoring aristocracy and each year hosted a "Semaine Automobile" (Automobile Week). The glamorous motoring sport would take place along the famous Promenade des Anglais. It is such an event that is seen in this 1949 poster: a speeding red car in foreground with bright, lemon-yellow ground and blue details; lettering in red and black text area at bottom.
Est: $300-400.

BURTON RICE
57. Mobiloil. 1926.
50 x 37-7/8 in/126.9 x 96.3 cm
Les Affiches Lutetia, Paris

Cond B / Folds show; some small tears at folds; colors and image excellent.
Poster for Mobil motor oil's French market instructs drivers to choose the correct oil for their car and to change that oil every 1500 km (900 miles) in summer and every 750 km (450 miles) in winter. In 1926 the Mobil logo was a gargoyle (not yet the winged horse of later years). In this effective poster, a helpful attendant in yellow coveralls services the automobile of an attractive, oil-conscious young woman. Image is framed by green and grey border similar to a point of purchase display; car is blue, woman in green, yellow and red beneath tree, with leaves in same fall colors and black background.
Est: $800-1000.

YVES THOS.
58. Brabham.
45-1/8 x 61-1/8 in/114.7 x 155.2 cm
Chabrillac, S.A., Toulouse
Cond A-/ Restored (2x14 in) loss of white paper background at lower right corner.
Jack Brabham was the first Australian ever to win a championship and the first driver anywhere to win in a car of his own manufacture. The Brabham racing car has been in existence only since 1962, when he gave up active racing and started his own production. It is a small but exclusive business, producing only about 300 custom-made racers per year. In 1966 and 1967 his racing cars won the world championship of Formula One racing. The Brabham remains a major power in Grand Prix auto racing to this day. The champion driver Graham Hill is seen at the wheel in this photo-offset

lithograph—a painterly treatment of a red racing car in motion.
Est: $150-200.

RENE VINCENT (1879-1936)
For other works of Vincent, see 309-311.
René Vincent was one of the first citizens to have a driver's permit in France. When he built his home in the fashionable 16th arrondisement of Paris in 1911, it was one of the first houses in that city to have an automobile garage built in. These are only small indications of the total enthusiasm for the automobile displayed by this great painter, illustrator and posterist. Described by Weill, "René Vincent, a fashion illustrator, was, even more, an automobile fanatic. His posters for *Salmson, Peugeot, Motobloc* and *Bugatti* are masterpieces of refinement." (p. 195). The world of high fashion and high living permeates his work, with striking women often embellishing the product. He lived a life as elegant as the individuals who people his posters. Jean Cocteau called him "the most refined individual I ever met."

59. Peugeot. 1919.
47¼ x 63⅛ in/120.1 x 160.3 cm
Imp. Draeger, Paris
Cond B+/ Small unobtrusive tears; folds barely visible; image and colors excellent.
Bibl: Auto Show I, 46; Auto & Publicité, 66; Phillips I, 597; II, 589.
In 1913, Peugeot developed the classical racing engine layout—twin cam shafts operating four inclined valves per cylinder— and every modern racing car engine designed since that time has been a variation on that theme. The speeding Peugeot racing car seen in this poster dominated motor sports for many years, and due to the break in designing of such cars during World War I, would have been very similar to the prototypical Peugeot racing car of 1913. In 1913, when Jules Goux won the Indianapolis-500 in a Peugeot, he astonished the attending Hoosiers—at each pit-stop he refueled his car with gasoline and refueled himself with a drink of champagne! In this most dramatic of all Vincent posters, the exaggerated perspective emphasizes power and speed. The strong diagonal lines forming the shadow of automobile on ground combined with the white clouds emanating from the wheels make this rare poster a most striking one as well.
Est: $4000-5000.

See color plate 5.

60. Bugatti. 1930.
38¼ x 54½ in/97.1 x 138.4 cm
Imp. Joseph-Charles, Paris
Cond B+/ Small tears at top and bottom paper edges; folds very unobtrusive; image and colors excellent. Framed.
Bibl: Auto Show I, 69 (color); Die Bugattis, E67
Ettore Bugatti built some of the most fabulous automobiles in history. Between 1924 and 1927 alone these sleek machines won 1,800 races and the wealthy young enthusiasts made it the most sought after car in Europe. Though his automobiles were very expensive, what set Bugatti apart from other designers was his unique ability as an artist—his automobiles were like sculptures, his engines like jewels. As an engineer, he was imperious and, yet, an incredible aesthete, and when he became successful was predictably more than a little bit arrogant. When Bugatti, for instance, built his famous Royale, the grandest single model automobile ever built (only six were constructed), King Zog of Albania went to him directly to purchase one of the highly prized vehicles. Bugatti, however, refused to sell him the car as the King's table manners were deemed atrocious. And Vincent's design is up to challenge, giving us a design as grand as the car portrayed: A sleek, deco image, including an elegant yellow and black T46-Bugatti, striped hub caps and sparkling chrome details racing across a black stripe, lettering in orange and background in white. It is a design which is at once understated and yet perfect and perfectly appropriate in every line and detail. Extremely rare!
Est: $5000-6000.

See color plate 6.

61

59

60

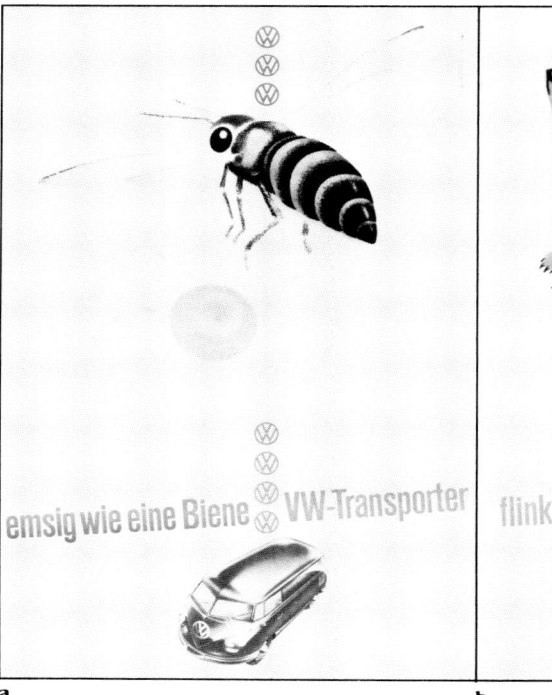
a

b

62

PL 1   **Leonetto Cappiello**   No. 7

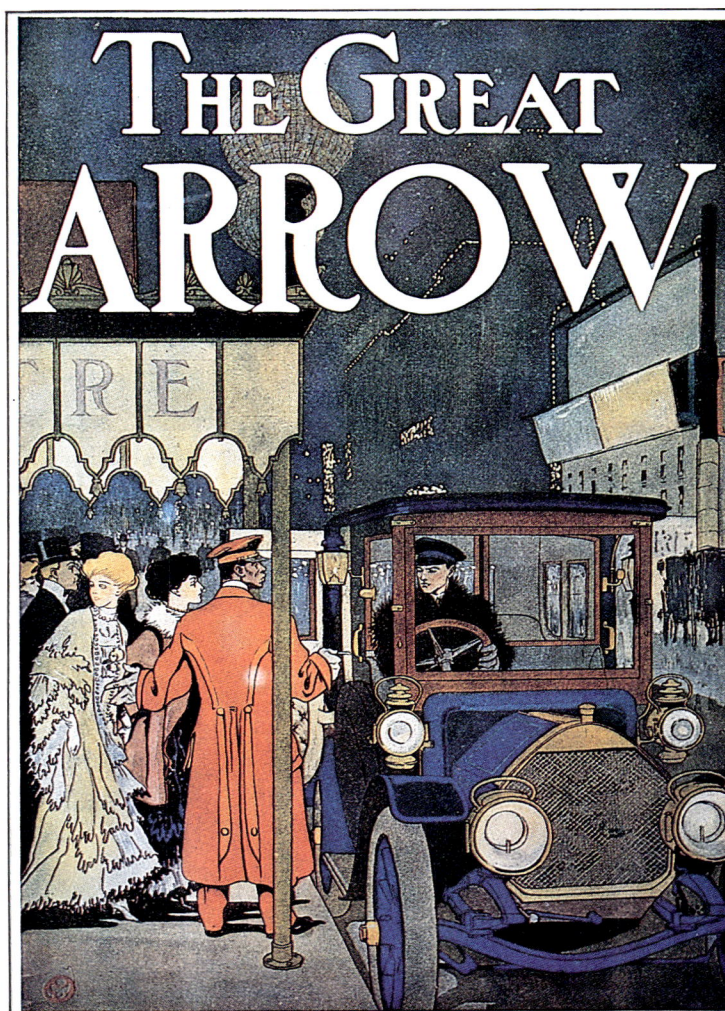

PL 2   **Edward Penfield**   No. 24

PL 3   **Anon.**   No. 35

PL 4   **A. Chazelle**   No. 42

PL 5 — René Vincent — No. 59

PL 6 — René Vincent — No. 60

PL 7 — Ludwig Hohlwein — No. 48

PL 8 — Alexis Kow — No. 50

PL 9　　　　　　　Anon.　　　　　　　No. 67

PL 10　　　　　　Will Bradley　　　　　No. 72

PL 11　　　　　　　Brien　　　　　　　No. 102

| PL 12 | Tom Purvis | No. 113 |

| PL 13 | Albert Hemelman | No. 122 |

| PL 14 | Frank Newbould | No. 112 |

61. Au Bon Marché. 1930.
137⅝ x 91¼ in/349.6 x 231.9 cm
Imp. Duval et Bedos, Paris
Cond A−/ Some staining at paper edges.
Bibl: Auto Salon II, 55 (color; var); Phillips II, 591 (var)
This 13-foot long, 6-sheet billboard for the Bon Marché department store of Paris, depicts the "Concours d'Elégance," an event peculiar to the 1920s and 1930s. Though the Concours was primarily an automobile show and contest, fashionable and well-heeled women would dress as elegantly as possible, embellishing their cars in order to attract the attention of the judges. A magnificent dog, often groomed as well as the automobiles themselves, added the final touch. In this smartest of all the many Bon Marché posters he executed, Vincent shows two such fashionably dressed women in front of their automobile, one in blue, white and green stripes, the other in red; the automobile is grey, the whippet is white. (The same design was also printed as one-sheet poster.)
Est: $2000-2500.

W.H. ZIMMERMANN
62. Two Volkswagen posters.
32 x 46⅞ in/81.4 x 119.1 cm
Cond A
a. VW-Transporter.
Graphopress, Stuttgart
Bee and daisy in yellow and brown, text in green, VW logo in blue, wagon in black-and-white. Text indicates that the Volkswagen van is busy as a bee.
b. Volkswagon-Fox.
Elsnerdruck, Berlin
Tan fox, VW logo in blue, text in green, car is black-and-white. "Quick as a fox" is the message. Volkswagens originated with the rise of Hitler who wanted to become (among other things) the Henry Ford of Germany. His plans called for one Volkswagen ("people's car") for every German. Though World War II foiled Hitler's plan, Volkswagen continued manufacturing during the war and developed an amphibious model for use in warfare. On February 17, 1972, the Volkswagen Beetle broke the production record of the Model-T Ford (1908-1927) of 15,007,033 units of an individual model. By 1979, when the Beetle was officially discontinued, over 19,000,000 had been manufactured. Developing countries, including Brazil, Mexico and Nigeria, continued to build the rugged little Beetles into the 1980's. Both posters are produced by photo-offset.
Est: $200-250. (2)

IMPORTANT REFERENCE WORKS AND ALBUMS

63

63. Les Maitres de l'Affiche. 1896-1900.
12⅜ x 15¾ in/31.5 x 40 cm
Published by Librairie Chaix, Paris
All 256 plates.
Bound in five volumes.
Includes all the text: Preface to each volume by Roger-Marx.
With original Paul Berthon-designed covers!
Est: $13000-15000.

64. L'Estampe Moderne.
12 x 16 in/30.7 x 41 cm
All 100 plates, in 2 volumes, with decorative floral period binding.
Published by Imprimerie Champenois, Paris, from 1897 to 1899.
Each plate has a tissue overlay with commentary on the work. Almost all these lithographs were commissioned especially for this series and they include the works of Donnay, Evenepoele, Rassenfosse, Louis Rhead (2), H. Meunier, Lepere, Leandre, Berchmans, DeFeure, Mucha (2), Grasset, Helleu, Ibels, Robbe, Roedel, Steinlen and Willette.
Est: $9000-10000.

65. Three Classic Poster Reference Works.
Three volumes in matching hardcover binding.
a. Les Affiches Illustrées, by Ernest Maindron. Published by H. Launette, Paris, 1886. The rare first volume: 160 pages, 62 black/white plates, plus 20 color plates of Chéret posters. Size: 9 x 12½ in. Limited edition of 525 copies.
b. Les Affiches Illustrées 1886-1895, by Ernest Maindron. Published by G. Boudet, Paris, 1896. 256 pages, size 9 x 12½ in. 64 splendid color reproductions; 102 posters reproduced in black/white. In a limited, numbered edition of 1,025 copies. Probably the single most important reference work in the field of poster art; the text (French) is erudite and enthusiastic, the reproductions sumptuous and plentiful. Contains the most complete listing of Chéret's posters (882) prior to the recent updating by Broido.
c. Les Affiches Etrangères Illustrées. This classic contains 210 pages, size 8⅝ x 12¼ in. 62 posters reproduced in magnificent color plates by Chaix; 150 in black/white. Published by G. Boudet, Paris, in 1897. Posters from Germany, England, Austria, Belgium, USA and Japan; articles by Bauwens, Hayashi, LaForgue, Meier-Graefe and J. Pennell. Text in French. Color cover design by Rassenfosse. One of 1,050 numbered copies.
Est: $2500-3000. (3)

64

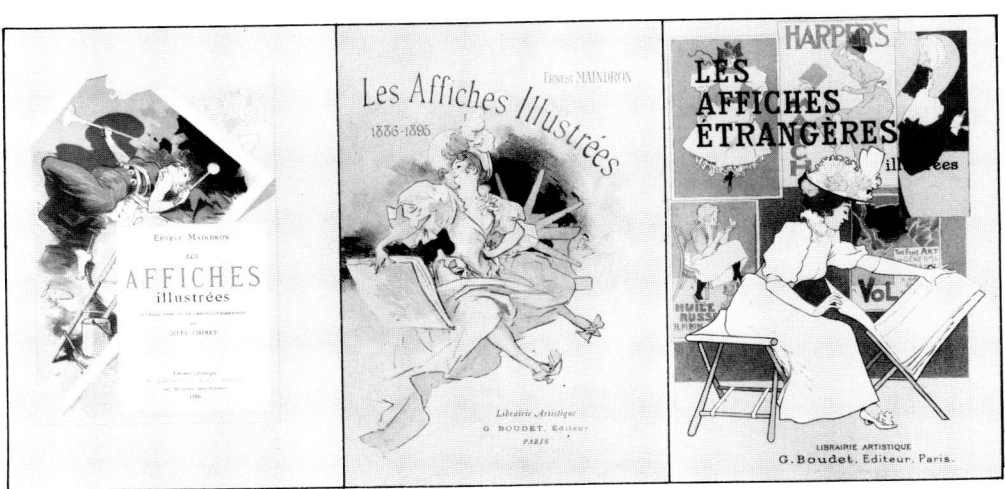
a b c
65

A UNIQUE COLLECTION OF 9,000 POSTER STAMPS

66. This collection, in excellent condition, is in 14 albums. The stamps are arranged by subject matter; three of the albums are of foreign stamps, the rest American.

Poster stamps, an esoteric rarity among collectibles, are stamps that do not serve to pay postage, but to carry an advertising message. The commonly known use of them today is in Christmas seals, but in their heyday, between 1890 and 1940, thousands of companies and organizations routinely affixed them to their correspondence and circulars, as an added medium of communication.

While they flourished, poster stamps were traded and valued much like postage stamps, and hundreds of collector clubs sprang up all over the world. Philatelists refer to them as "Cinderellas." Subsequently, there was a decline in activity which still lingers, but, as is the case with many collectibles of real value, a stirring of renewed interest appears to be in the making.

In proof, Poster Auctions International proudly offers one of the largest collections of its type, consigned to us by a prominent Midwestern numismatist who, in more than 30 years of collecting, has meticulously amassed a comprehensive cross section of poster stamps, both foreign and domestic, in virtually all categories in which they were ever applied. A majority of these stamps date prior to 1920 – adding to their interest and value.

As miniature posters, many poster stamps were, in fact, simply reductions of large-sized posters of the day. But the vast majority of the stamps in this unique collection were designed specifically as stamps.

To give an indication of the range of these images, here are some of the highlights:

A group of stamps for the Chicago World's Fair, 1933, and the New York World's Fair, 1939
A collection of stamps of early film stars: Charlie Chaplin, Joan Crawford, Tom Mix, Lillian Gish, etc.
City stamps for major cities (New York, Chicago, San Francisco, etc.) and smaller towns with catchy phrases such as "Sheboygan Makes It," and "Eugene—City of Radiation."
Collection of stamps from Paris 1900 Exposition, and the Pan American Exposition in Buffalo, 1901.
Two stamps for Mucha's 1896 classic, "Job." The only known impressions!
Rare collection of poster stamps by Edward Penfield for Hart, Schaffner and Marx; many other fashion poster stamps.
Chicago 500-mile International Auto Race of 1915; and many other automobile advertising stamps.
A large collection of poster stamps relating to the printing industry; some of the most beautiful in the collection are by printers of poster stamps, including Strobridge. Some depict printing process, some show collectors, others are simply decorative.
Stamps calling for women's suffrage in Idaho, Colorado, Wyoming and Utah (1915).
American advertising poster stamps for Elgin Watches, Dutch Boy Paint, Gold Medal Flour, Bell Telephone, Edison Lighting, Bloomingdale's (the department store offers house dresses for 88¢).
An extremely rare poster stamp advertising ham with a 1915-1916 calendar pad miraculously attached to it!
A collection of Olympic poster stamps dating from 1906 to the 1950's, as well as large numbers of sports-related images.
Transportation poster stamps, including airplane travel and expositions, railroad companies, shipping lines.
Poster stamps by European poster artists, many reproducing actual posters: Hohlwein, Klinger, Erdt, Maier, Von Stuck, Mucha, etc.
Political and war stamps from both sides of the conflict, including samples of German vitriolic hate campaign ("Gott strafe England!"—"May God punish England!").
Est: $22000-25000.

AMERICAN POSTERS

67   Front   Back   69

68

70   71

ANON.

67. Perfect Tea. c. 1895.
34⅞ x 71½ in/88.6 x 181.6 cm
Cond B+/ Some slight creasing and staining.
Image is watercolor on paper; text is wood engraving with some hand-coloring. The Japanese woman is flanked by bird and floral border, with text banners top and bottom. No doubt an American artist sought to copy the popular Japanese woodcuts and watercolors of that period and he succeeds precisely because he departs from that style sufficiently—heavier brush strokes and harsher color contrasts—to make a most striking poster.
Est: $700-900.

See color plate 9.

68. M. Hommel. c. 1895.
26¾ x 20⅜ in/67.8 x 51.9 cm
Wittemann Litho. Co., New York
Cond A−/ Small unobtrusive stains and light foxing; image excellent.
For an American liquor manufacturer who boasts the highest award for American champagnes at the 1893 World's Columbian Exposition held in Chicago. Bottles of champagne, vermouth and brandy frame a view of the factory in Sandusky, Ohio. Fine lithography in subtle earth tones, with details in gold and silver.
Est: $600-800.

69. Pabst Extract Calendar. 1910.
7¼ x 35⅞ in/18.4 x 91.1 cm
J. Ottmann Lith. Co., New York
Cond B / Several small tears at paper edges; colors and image excellent.
"American Girl" calendars were very popular at the beginning of the century and this one, for Pabst Brewing Company's Pabst Extract, is one of the most appealing of all. The lithography is first-rate, with colors given a velvety quality, heightened by gold. On the reverse is the calendar for 1911, with a good deal of text to convince us that Pabst Extract, "an article of medicine—not an alcoholic beverage—Strengthens the Weak, Builds up the Overworked, Conquers Dyspepsia, Relieves Insomnia, Assists Nursing Mothers." The artist's name is unfortunately not decipherable.
Est: $600-800.

70. Inman Bros. Flying Circus.
25⅛ x 37¾ in/63.9 x 95.9 cm
Cond A
Two early planes, a Boeing and a Ford, are featured in this poster for the Inman Bros. Flying Circus. In addition to rides on the airplanes, there is the added attraction of a 4000 ft. parachute jump. The fact that there is a "collection taken for the jumper" is somewhat ominous. Colors are solid red, blue, yellow, green and black.
Est: $300-400.

WILLIAM H. BRADLEY (1868-1962)

Bradley was a brilliant and prolific artist, illustrator, publisher and printer. He made many posters for literary journals, some of them his own, including the *Inland Printer*, *Harper's*, *St. Nicholas*, *The Chap-Book*, *Century*, and *Bradley: His Book*. He was to become art director of *Colliers*, *The Century* and *Good Housekeeping*. In an article on Bradley in the October 1898 issue of *The Poster*, S.C. de Soissons concludes: "In our times, when there is such a great distance between useful and artistic, when the art driven out from everyday useful objects retreats more and more to the museums, and has no connection with life, the artistic posters made by Bradley are one of the links between the beautiful and the practical."

71. The Chap Book. 1895.
14⅛ x 21¼ in/36 x 54 cm
Cond A−/ Small tears and losses in margins; image excellent paper.
Bibl: DFP-I, 155; Margolin, p. 106; Hiatt, p. 301; Price, p. 153; Keay, p. 16; Affiches Etrangères, p. 157; Maitres, 136; Phillips II, 96.
Of the five Chap-Book posters he designed, this is the only one in black-and-white. And it is a romantic, graceful, yet striking design that heightens one's curiosity for the "ballads, tales and histories" to be found in the pages of this magazine. The influence of Art Nouveau and Aubrey Beardsley, whose drawings were just reaching America through *The Yellow Book*, is clearly visible. Price commented that "his black and white shows clever massing and a pleasing grace of line governed by a much greater restraint in feeling than ever appeared in Beardsley's drawings." (p. 162).
Est: $1000-1200.

WILL BRADLEY (continued)

72. Bradley—His Book. 1896.
29⅛ x 41⅞ in/73.9 x 106.4 cm
Cond B−/ Some tears and restored holes at folds and at paper edges; colors excellent. Framed.
Bibl: DFP-I, 174; Margolin, p. 101 (color); Phillips II, 97 (color); III, 172
The November issue of this short-lived magazine which Bradley designed, wrote and printed, announced that "The Kiss" would be "the first of a series of posters engraved on wood by Will Bradley." It is his most magnificent work and demonstrates how well he knew the possibilities of wood engraving. We are given a romantic, pre-Raphaelite vision in a decorative style with gothic text revealing Bradley's fascination with the work of William Morris. Extremely rare!
Est: $3000-3500.

See color plate 10.

73. A Few Commercial Designs/Bradley—His Book. 1896.
Plates: 9⅛ x 11¾ in/23.2 x 29.8 cm
Poster: 8⅝ x 19⅝ in/21.7 x 49.7 cm
Published by: The Wayside Press, Springfield, Mass.
Cond A / Plates in excellent condition; jacket torn at spine; poster in excellent condition; horizontal center fold.
Bibl: (Poster) DFP-I, 171; Margolin, p. 116; Reims, 1132; Keay, p. 27; Phillips III, 170
Bound set of fifteen color plates. Title plate signed in ink, numbered "fourteen" and inscribed "To Edmond Sagot Esq." (Sagot was the leading poster dealer of Paris). From an edition of 215 copies, most designs reprinted from *Bradley—His Book*. The inserted poster is a special impression (color variant) of the June 1896 *Bradley—His Book*.

Late in 1894 Bradley moved to Springfield, Massachusetts to work as a freelance designer, accepting additional commissions for commercial designs for manufacturers of bicycles, paper, etc. A year later he established the Wayside Press and began publishing *Bradley—His Book*.
Est: $2000-2500.

HOWARD CHANDLER CHRISTY (1873-1952)

74. Join the Marines. 1915.
30⅛ x 40⅛ in/76.5 x 102 cm
Cond B+/ Small tears at paper edges; staining at upper left corner; image excellent
Bibl: Theofiles, 62
The great American painter and illustrator did several recruiting posters in which a uniformed young lady charms us into enlisting in one of the armed services. Here she is in blue, with marines in khakis landing at lower left; text in blue and red. The English writers Hardie and Sabin noted in 1920: "The (American) recruiting posters in particular have a freedom of design, a vigour and grip, which really tell. For when America came into the War, she started to hustle with all the feverish pent-up energy characteristic of the race. Posters like Christy's . . . show a vigour and freshness which our official British recruiting posters never possessed. There was an air of glad youth in them which came like a Spring wind over our war-weary spirits." (pp. 34-35). Theofiles rates this poster "scarce."
Est: $600-800.

75. I Want You for the Navy. 1917.
27 x 41¼ in/68.5 x 104.7 cm
Forbes, Boston
Cond A
Bibl: Barnicoat, p. 239 (color); Phillips I, 160
From the alluring to the seductive. . . . Christy's Navy recruiter makes a more persuasive case than the traditional Uncle Sam. Tan background; lettering in red and blue.
Est: $600-800.

NEMHARD N. CULIN

76. New York World's Fair. 1937.
28¼ x 39¾ in/71.7 x 101 cm
Cond B−/ Losses and stains in margins; three restored holes in image center; unobtrusive 12 in. tear into image at top left.
This is the poster that announced the upcoming World's Fair in New York. We are given a futurist image in grey, green and brown; text in blue and orange. It's a twilight evening view, with effective aerial perspective and dramatic lighting of the Fair's symbol.
Est: $400-500.

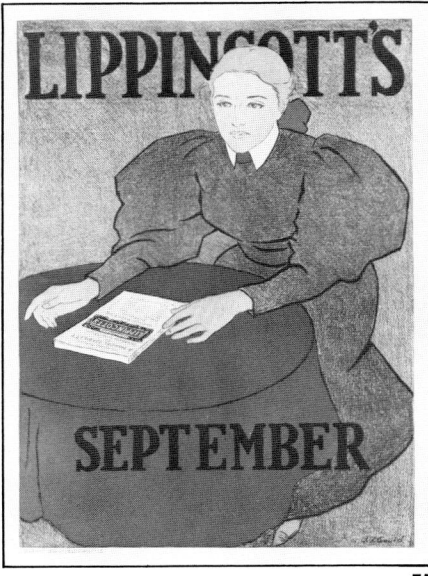
77

78

79

a b

81
a b

J.J. GOULD

Gould took over the task of designing the posters for *Lippincott's* after Carqueville's departure. His style is often compared to Penfield's—but it's high quality rather than imitation which comes to mind. Gould's series for *Lippincott's* is as distinguished as that of Penfield's for *Harper's*; Gould used flat color planes effectively, and his placards can be said to be more poster-like. One of his tricks was to thrust the head of his subject into the lettering of *Lippincott's*. This somehow works: it adds impact to the appeal of his subjects. Unfortunately, little is known of his life.

77. Lippincott's. September. 1896.
14½ x 20 in/36.7 x 50.7 cm
Cond A–/ Small tears in margins; colors and image excellent.
Bibl: DFP-I, 252; Phillips I, 256; III, 192 (color)
One of the very best of the Lippincott's posters of Gould. A lovely girl in green is seated at red table, lettering in blue.
Est: $500-600.

78. Lippincott's. December. 1896.
12¾ x 15½ in/32.3 x 38.8 cm
Cond B / Folds show; small tears at bottom corners; trimmed to borderline; colors excellent
Bibl: DFP-I, 225; Margolin, p. 83; Phillips III, 194
Couple seated on streetcar; young women glances at the viewer while her older companion peruses an issue of *Lippincott's* with a seemingly relevant feature article on "The Chase of an Heiress" by Christian Read.
Est: $500-600.

79. Lippincott's for March. 1897.
14⅛ x 17⅛ in/35.8 x 43.5 cm
Cond A.
Bibl: DFP-I, 259
Stern, old woman in dark brown clutching a book is contrasted against the attractive and animated young woman in green seated next to her, a copy of *Lippincott's* in her hand. Text in orange. An obvious message appealing to the youthful element of the leisure class.
Est: $500-600.

JOSEPH CHRISTIAN LEYENDECKER (1874-1951)

Michael Schau's fine book on this prolific illustrator is worth quoting: "As America begins to rediscover the rich heritage of its decorative and commercial artists and illustrators, the art of J.C. Leyendecker is again emerging. Leyendecker developed as a major graphic arts talent around the turn of the century and proceeded to become America's most popular illustrator. His fine reputation—the product of hundreds of pictures and several decades—had already begun to fade in the late forties, during the last years of his life, but with the revised interest in the work of the great illustrators, Leyendecker's brilliance is receiving renewed recognition." (Schau, p. 13).

80. Two magazine covers:
a. Saturday Evening Post. 1908.
10¼ x 13½ in/25.8 x 34.2 cm
Cond A/ Framed.
Bibl: Schau, p. 171
Magazine cover with text verso. Light orange, blue and brown.
b. Success, August. 1902.
9½ x 13¼ in/24.1 x 33.6 cm
Cond A / Framed.
Bibl: Schau, p. 163
Pastel colors, reproduction of oil painting.
Est: $400-500. (2)

81. Two Colliers sports prints. 1904.
Cond A / Framed.
a. The Football Player
9½ x 10¾ in/24 x 27.3 cm
b. The Hurdler.
10 x 10¼ in/25.3 x 26 cm
Est: $300-400. (2)

J.C. LEYENDECKER (continued)

82. Two Arrow Collars advertisements.
a. Arrow Collars Cluett Shirts. 1910.
12-3/4 x 20-7/8 in/32.4 x 53 cm
Cond A−/ Unobtrusive horizontal center fold. Framed. Colors are light orange, brown and black. Fashionable men in range of styles and variety of fabrics: stripes, plaids and solids.
b. Arrow Collars and Shirts.
21-3/4 x 14 in/55.2 x 35.1 cm
Cond B+/ Vertical center fold with staple holes visible; light staining. Framed.
Bibl: Schau, p. 108 (color; maquette)
Dapper gentlemen chat on floral-patterned sofa in this two-page *Saturday Evening Post* advertisement. Colors are light orange, brown and black.

"In 1905, Leyendecker received what became his most important commercial art assignment. He was hired to do advertisements by Cluett, Peabody & Co., Inc., manufacturers of Arrow brand detachable shirt collars. . . . Over the next twenty-five years, the 'Arrow Collar Man' became the symbol of fashionable American manhood. As surely as Charles Dana Gibson created a prototype of the elegant young woman, Leyendecker, through the Arrow ads, defined the ideal of the American male: a dignified, clear-eyed man of taste, manners, and quality." (Schau, p. 28).
Est: $600-800. (2)

83. America Calls. c. 1917.
28-1/8 x 41 in/71.2 x 104.1 cm
U.S. Navy Publicity Bureau, N.Y.
Cond B / Tears and faint staining at paper edges; 7 in. tear at top right edge; colors and image excellent.
Bibl: Theofiles, 51.

Leyendecker was commissioned to do posters during both World War I and II. Here, a sailor and "Liberty" clasp hands, her arm resting symbolically on his shoulder. Colors are red, white and blue.
Est: $600-800.

EDWARD PENFIELD (1866-1925)
For other work by Penfield, see No. 24.

Penfield is America's premier posterist. For a ten-year period, from 1891 to 1901, he was an art director at Harper's and from 1893 he produced a series of monthly posters for its magazine. These were largely used as in-store displays for bookshops as well as newsstands. Most are deliciously irrelevant; all are interesting. The series became immediately popular with collectors.

In the catalogue of the Penfield exhibition held last year at The Hudson River Museum in Yonkers, New York, Walker Penfield, his son, gives us a good description of the artist's method: "After preliminary sketches had fixed the subject and layout of the poster, he would make a master drawing in black ink with pen and brush, mostly the latter. He would then color this in with watercolor. The next step would be to lay tracing paper over this master drawing, using a different piece for each color and painting in the appropriate areas in black ink. Each of these pieces of tracing paper became the diagram for one or another of the zinc plates. He made considerable use of 'spatter,' often that on one plate would cover some of the areas of another. Thus green would be produced from the blue and yellow plates. He went into the pressroom and mixed and blended the inks for a poster run, staying with the pressman until the presses settled down and the poster prints were coming out just as father desired them to." (Penfield, p. 11)

88

89

90

87

84. Harper's. January. 1895.
12¾ x 17⅞ in/32.5 x 45.4 cm
Cond A−/ Some faint staining at bottom paper-edge and upper right corner.
Bibl: DFP-I, 340; Phillips III, 248
Harper's readers greet each other on a winter day; colors are yellow, orange, blue and green.
Est: $400-500.

85. Two Harper's Posters.
a. Harper's. March. 1895.
13⅝ x 18⅞ in/34.4 x 47.9 cm
Cond B+/ Small tear at right paper edge; slight creasing in image; colors excellent. P.
Bibl: DFP-I, 342; Margolin, p. 30
Woman with rabbit displays Penfield's sense of humor.
b. Harper's. April. 1896.
13¼ x 17¾ in/33.6 x 45.2 cm
Cond B / Small tears at paper edges; tiny loss at lower left corner; colors and image excellent.
Bibl: DFP-I, 355; Phillips I, 470; II, 473; III, 256.
Colors are orange, green, gray-green and black.
Est: $600-700. (2)

86. Two Harper's Posters.
a. Harper's. February. 1895.
12⅜ x 18 in/31.5 x 45.1 cm
Cond B−/ Horizontal fold visible; small tears and staining image and at paper edges; colors excellent.
Bibl: DFP-I, 341; Phillips I, 465
Man in gold coat mails a valentine in a bright orange mail box as woman in dark blue glances over his shoulder. Background in bright cobalt blue, lettering in dark blue and orange.

b. Harper's. March. 1896.
10¾ x 18¼ in/27.3 x 46.4 cm
Cond B / Small unobtrusive tears at paper edges; restored loss at lower left corner; horizontal crease; colors excellent.
Bibl: DFP-I, 354; Phillips III, 255.
Woman in navy blue on tan background; orange text panel with blue lettering.
Est: $500-600. (2)

87. Harper's. May. 1896.
11¾ x 17¾ in/29.7 x 45.1 cm
Cond A−/ Faint tape stain at bottom left corner, P.
Bibl: DFP-I, 356; Penfield, p. 6; Margolin, p. 67
Woman with cats on grey background; cats in white, orange and black. Like Steinlen, Penfield often used a cat in his designs—"well-drawn and business-like cats they are" declares Rogers (p. 88). Price, full of praise for Penfield's style, singles out this poster: "Of this whole (Harper's) series, the May poster, of the girl with the two Angora cats has, perhaps, the greatest and most lasting charm. Its quaint originality and again the absolute informality of its subject and the extraordinary simplicity of its treatment make it a poster that one remembers for years after it has been put away." (pp. 235-36).
Est: $500-600.

88. Harper's. June. 1897.
18½ x 14¼ in/47 x 36.2 cm
Cond B / Folds show slightly; tear at top center; restored losses at upper corners; colors and image excellent.
Bibl: DFP-I, 379, Color Pl.XX; Phillips III, 263 (color)
Green background, orange rocking chair, woman in beige, text in brown and red roses on the arm of the chairs.
Est: $600-700.

89. Harper's. July. 1897.
19⅛ x 14 in/48.5 x 35.5 cm
Cond B+/ Small stain at upper left; folds show; colors excellent.
Bibl: DFP-I, 380; Margolin, p. 69; Penfield, p. 8 (color); Phillips II, 475
A fine portrait of the leisure class. The couple sits on deck chairs; woman in red cape, plaid blankets in red, yellow and black. A splendid combination of patterns and textures. Price states that this is one of the many posters in this series that "tell their story and suggest as well the various pleasant pursuits of pleasant people." (p. 235). Possibly Penfield himself was on a summer cruise and sent this design from London, as indicated below his signature.
Est: $600-700.

90. Harper's. January. 1899.
19¼ x 11⅜ in/48.9 x 28.9 cm
Cond B−/ Vertical center fold, restored tears largely at paper edges; colors excellent.
Bibl: DFP-I, 397; Penfield, p. 4 (color)
Man wrapped in furs rides crimson sleigh; crimson text on light green background.
Est: $500-600.

WEIMER PURSELL (1906-1974)
Born near Memphis, Pursell studied at the Chicago Art Institute and went on to a long and distinguished career in illustration and advertising art. He was a member of the "27 group" of illustrators and designers in Chicago. His World War II posters were exhibited at the Museum of Modern Art. His work epitomizes some of the best Art Deco designs to be found in any American artist's output.

91. Western-Winchester. 1955.
27¾ x 42⅜ in/70.6 x 107.5 cm
Cond A−/ Small tears in top margin
The squirrel, although probably not the hunter's target, gives us the animals' view of the impending danger in the forest, in lovely fall coloring. In 1955, the fact that the squirrel is merely an observer was apparently enough to mitigate the menace of the scene so that the design could be used as an advertisement for a weapon. One wonders if today the same image might offend the viewers' sensibilities.
Est: $400-500.

WILLY G. SESSER
92. Illinois Centennial. 1918.
27½ x 41 in/69.8 x 104.2 cm
Illinois Litho. Co., Chicago
Cond B / Unobtrusive tear through figure's head; some tears at bottom paper edge; colors excellent.
Poster celebrating the 21st state's centennial; frontiersman framed by the American flag clutches a corner of it in one hand and a rifle in the other (a spirit recently repopularized). The Illinois capitol building stands in the background. The image is drawn with the rough and rugged element of a woodcut.
Est: $400-500.

More recent American Posters

MARTIN D. GLANZMAN
93. Hockey at Madison Square Garden.
42½ x 83¾ in/108 x 212.7 cm
Cond B / Folds show.
By superimposing one figure on the other, Glanzman, in the manner of Paul Colin, gives us a vivid image of fast-paced action. A 2-sheet poster with solid shapes and lines in yellow and red, text in yellow, background in bright blue.
Est: $500-600.

ROY LICHTENSTEIN (b. 1923)
94. Lincoln Center Film Festival. 1966.
29½ x 45 in/75 x 114.2 cm
Cond A / P.
Bibl: Lincoln Center, 22 (color); Modern American Poster, 170 (color)
This is one of the best of the List-sponsored Lincoln Center posters and avoids the abstract irrelevance of so many of the others. It is also one of the best posters of this most popular painter (along with his Aspen Winter Jazz poster of 1967), giving us a brightly colored Pop Art image that evokes the excitement of the old Art Deco movie palaces. Approximately 500 copies were printed.
Est: $400-500.

BEN SHAHN (1898-1969)
95. Two World War II Posters. 1942.
U.S. Government Printing Office, Washington
Cond B / Folds show; some related tears; colors excellent.
"In (his posters) for the war effort, Shahn used his skill as an illustrator to create memorable, bold designs that are notable for their incorporation of the painter's direct brushwork into images as arresting as the polished forms of Kauffer and Cassandre, but with more passion and personal engagement" (Word & Image, p. 62).
a. We French Workers Warn You.
40⅛ x 28⅜ in/102 x 72 cm
Bibl: Shahn, 143 (color); Phillips I, 531; Takashimaya, 234 (color)
Shahn's first war poster, it is a warning to Americans: "We French workers warn you . . . defeat means slavery, starvation, death." On the wall is an "Official Vichy Decree."
b. This is Nazi Brutality.
38¼ x 28¼ in/97 x 71.7 cm
Bibl: Shahn, 144 (color); Word & Image, p. 91; Internationale Plakate, 686; Phillips II, 531; Takashimaya, 233 (color)
Another poster issued by the Office of War Information where Shahn was a resident artist for a year. The ticker-tape spells out clearly "the enormity of the Nazi crime against the citizens of Lidice, Czechoslovakia" and gives this chilling announcement the power and immediacy that makes it so effective.
Est: $400-500. (2)

BRIEN
102. East Coast.
49⅞ x 39¾ in/126.6 x 109 cm
Haycock Press, London
Cond A
A most striking and unusual design for the London & North Eastern Railway, promoting travel to the East Coast of England and its beaches. It is a colorful beach scene in watercolor—stylized figures form a pattern of sculptured Deco forms. Layers of transparent colors include magenta, aquamarine, yellow and green on sandy beach. The couple in foreground is no doubt consulting "The Holiday Handbook" which is being offered by the LNER.
Est: $1000-1200.

See color plate 11.

H. RUSSELL FLINT
103. Chester.
49⅞ x 40 in/126.4 x 101.5 cm
Bemrose & Sons, Ltd.
Cond A−/ Unobtrusive vertical center fold; colors excellent.
Painterly sidewalk view of Chester captures flavor of old and new—flower vendors and old architecture contrasted with modern travelers. Buildings in dark red and brown; figures and flowers add colorful details. For the Great Western Railway.
Est: $600-800.

TOM GILFILLAN
104. Fingal's Cave. Staffa.
49⅞ x 40 in/126.6 x 101.5 cm
John Horn Limited, Glasgow
Cond B / Vertical center fold; tears into border at bottom right and into lower left paper edge; colors excellent.
Excursion on Macbrayne's Steamers to Fingals' Cave in Scotland. Blue, brown and red predominate, border in tan with brown lettering. Water is so calm that the touch of the gull in the foreground creates a series of ripples. Staffa is a small island in the Inner Hebrides, west of the large island of Mull.
Est: $600-800.

E. McKNIGHT KAUFFER (1890-1954)
Born in Montana, Kauffer studied at the Chicago Art Institute in 1913 and in 1914 moved permanently to London. He was to return to the United States in 1940. For 25 years between the wars, Kauffer created posters for the London Underground and several other companies. "Consistent characteristics (of his posters) are his simplication of form, bold and legible composition, and symbolic imagery used to convey the essence of his subject matter. The 1930s marked the height of Kauffer's success, when his posters were common sights in the 'subterranean picture galleries' of the London 'Tube' " (Avant Garde, p. 199). In his introduction to the English posters section of his new book, Alain Weill indicates: "While France shone between the wars thanks to a few first-quality artists who worked for many clients, the poster situation in Great Britain was characterized by a few large advertisers—the London Underground, the railway companies, Shell-Mex—who could maintain a high level in their campaigns. They provided work for a whole generation of artists, but the only true star to stand out from the lot was E. McKnight Kauffer." (p. 223).

105. London Underground. 1932.
24⅜ x 39¼ in/61.8 x 99.6 cm
Vincent Brooks Day, London
Cond B−/ Restored losses at corners; unobtrusive water and tape stains; colors very good.
Frank Pick, who was in charge of advertising at the London Underground, was one of the most influential people in this field. He often and consistently selected the best artists for his posters and none was used with greater frequency or with better results than Kauffer. Here we get an abstract forest scene in three greens, grey, brown and black, with a quote from Izaak Walton to explain it all.
Est: $400-500.

106. Actors Prefer Shell. 1933.
44⅛ x 29½ in/112.1 x 75 cm
Cond A−/ Tear at right paper edge and at lower left corner margin; colors and image excellent.
Bibl: Purvis, p. 21; Weill, 412; Auto Show II, 77; Kauffer/MOMA, 49.
After the merger of Shell-Mex and B.P. oil companies, Jack Beddington, the publicity director, launched a publicity campaign to persuade the public that "people of all professions prefer Shell." The campaign resulted in an exciting group of posters by artists working in styles that ranged from classicism to surrealism. And in Kauffer's design there are elements of surrealism and cubism in this mask-like image, with colors in red, blue, beige and black.
Est: $700-900.

107. Two Shell Posters.
a. Merchants Prefer Shell. 1933.
44¾ x 29⅞ in/113.7 x 75.9 cm
Cond B / Small tears and some staining at paper edges; colors and image very good
Bibl: Kauffer/MOMA, 48
Stylized hook lifting crate; colors blue, red, brown and black.
b. HANS FEIBUSCH. Architects Prefer Shell.
44 x 29¼ in/117.7 x 74.9 cm
Vincent Brooks, Day & Son, London
Cond B−/ Small tears and staining largely in margins; colors and image very good.

E. McKNIGHT KAUFFER (continued)

Montage of architect's tools, drawing paper and Greek architecture—beige background, yellow, light blue, lettering in brown. This German artist painted figures and still life, primarily in watercolors. He left Germany in the 1930s and made his home in England.
Est: $800-1000. (2)

108. Three BP Ethyl Posters.
44⅜ x 29⅛ in/112.8 x 75 cm
Cond B+/ Small tears or creases at paper edges; colors and image excellent.
a. Ask for BP Ethyl. 1933.
Bibl: Kauffer/MOMA, 46
Text and simple shapes in red, light blue, yellow and black.
b. BP Ethyl Anti-Knock. 1936.
Bibl: Weill, 418; Cooper, p. 52 (color)
This poster was also done as a 48-sheet billboard; it combines photographic image, line and text—Greek sculpture of god and horse and a bolt of lightning before them. Colors are light blue, yellow and black. Cooper comments on this "splendid" poster: "Its strength and dignity in both linear and tonal content gave it a force and directness that made it a memorable and remarkable achievement. Here is a photograph used with admirable effect indeed." (p. 92).
c. BP Ethyl Controls Horse Power, by Garretto. 1934.
Stylized cubistic rendering of man and horse, with man symbolically controlling horse. Colors are tan, yellow and green, with black background.
Est: $1200-1500. (3)

109. Two Shell Posters.
a. Shell. Bodiam Castle. 1932.
44 x 29¾ in/111.7 x 75.6 cm
Vincent Brooks, Day & Son, London
Cond A-/ Small tear in upper right image background; colors excellent
Bibl: Kauffer/MOMA, 44
Dramatic midnight view of Bodiam Castle. Colors are dark blue, green and black. This castle was built in 1386-89 at Battle, the actual site of the 1066 Battle of Hastings, about six miles from that town. It is one of the most romantic of the preserved castles, with a moat so wide that the building seems to rise from an island.
b. Shell. Dinton Castle. 1936.
45 x 29½ in/114.5 x 75.1 cm
Cond A-/ Small tears at paper edges; colors and image excellent
Easel with canvas depicting Dinton Castle near Aylesbury. Green, light green and red predominate.
Est: $700-900. (2)

110. Eno's Fruit Salt. 1924.
19½ x 29⅝ in/49.5 x 75.3 cm
Vincent Brooks, Day & Son, London
Cond B+/ Small tears largely at paper edges; colors excellent.
Bibl: Jones, p. 39 (color); Kauffer/MOMA, 16
Design in solid, bright primary colors (red, blue, yellow and green) with black forming a stylized sun and rooster, to advertise a "fruit salt" which, when taken first thing every morning, will invigorate, refresh and purify the system.
Est: $400-500.

ALFRED LAMBART (1902-)
111. Tynemouth.
25⅛ x 39¾ in/63.7 x 101.1 cm
Ben Johnson & Co., York
Cond A-/ Small tear into top border area; colors and image excellent.
Flat colors, forms reduced to shapes in off-beat colors—lime, olive green, violet, sepia, tan and light blue, with black border. Active beach scene is promoted by the London & North Eastern Railway for its vacation travel to Tynemouth, a seaside resort on the east coast of England in the Northumberland district.
Est: $600-700.

FRANK NEWBOULD (1887-1950)
112. Berlin.
50 x 40 in/127.1 x 101.2 cm
Chorley & Pickersgill Ltd., Leeds
Cond A-/ Folds show slightly; colors excellent.
For the London & North Eastern Railway's twice-daily train to Berlin, Newbould gives us a magnificent image of a pre-war scene at a Berlin sidewalk café. He arrests us not only with superbly delineated characters but with his special use of flat colors in odd, but eye-catching tones, including magenta, teal blue, puce and olive, as well as an effective use of black and beige. Commenting on these LNER posters, Walter Shaw Sparrow concludes: "Posters of this fine order do not implore us to buy season tickets; they invite us, indirectly, to make plans for the (summer) holidays." (p. 36).
Est: $2000-2500.

See color plate 14.

TOM PURVIS (1888-1959)
113. Imperial Airways.
24¾ x 39⅝ in/63 x 100.5 cm
Haycock Press
Cond A-/ Some very unobtrusive tears at paper edges; image and colors excellent.
A strong, graphic image in sharp, flat colors: blue, bright green, yellow, brown and black. It's not clear if the steward is delivering the check or the menu card to the passenger in the airplane lounge, but it's quite clear that there is much "comfort in the air." Purvis,

a

b

c

108

attached to the Glasgow School of Art, wrote a book titled *Poster Progress* and is best known for his posters for the LNER and for Austin Reed clothiers.
Est: $800-1000.

See color plate 12.

114. East Coast by LNER.
39¾ x 50 in/100.8 x 126.8 cm
Haycock Press, Ltd.
Cond B / Small creases and tears primarily at paper edges and at folds; tears in background lower right; colors excellent. P.
For the London and North Eastern Railway, Purvis gives us an image in flat, solid colors. Child in magenta bathing suit drags a presumably inflatable green dragon over his shoulder—at lower right the words "George and the Dragon," a humorous reference to the universal folk theme of St. George, the patron saint of England. Text in grey. As Weill indicates, "Following the Beggarstaffs and Hohlwein, (Purvis) formed his figures solely from masses of color, without outline. The adroitness with which he composed his palette and laid out his figures often make little masterpieces of his posters." (p. 228)
Est: $800-1000.

KENNETH SHOESMITH (1890-1939)
115. Two Southern Railway Posters.
a. Swanage
24⅞ x 39¾ in/63 x 110 cm
Waterlow & Sons Ltd., London
Cond B / Folds show; colors excellent
Southern Railway poster for the seaside resort. Flat colors of blue, aquamarine, yellow and tan. As officer in the Mercantile Marine, Shoesmith left the sea after World War I to devote himself to art: oils, watercolors, decorative paintings. He received many commissions from shipping companies.
b. Anon. South for Sunshine.
25⅛ x 40¼ in/64 x 102.1 cm
Waterlow & Sons, London
Cond A-/ Some creasing in the image
Bibl: Schackleton, 127 (var)
Photogravure with blue border, white lettering. In this photo by Charles E. Brown, the small boy talks to engineer—a very popular poster reissued many times with different lettering.
Est: $500-600 (2)

DUTCH POSTERS

116

117

118

119

a   b   121

ANON.
116. Nieuwe Sneltreinverbinding. 1905.
22¾ x 38½ in/57.9 x 97.9 cm
Cond B / Tears largely at paper edges and at folds; some staining at top; colors excellent.
Detailed scene in delicate colors shows first-class luxury compartment of train traveling from Amsterdam to Munich. The friendly scene includes young girl charming a male passenger for a mint and distracting a young woman from her view of the countryside.
Est: $300-400.

117. De Hollandsche Revue.
31½ x 26⅜ in/80 x 67 cm
Cond C / Large tears and creasing, mostly in margins and in text areas; restored losses at top paper edge, and top and bottom right corners; colors very good.
Image composed of bold forms reduced to solid shapes and shadow in light green, light yellow, brown and black. The man is so engrossed in reading this Dutch journal that he is still glancing at a few final words while ringing doorbell. Artist's name is not decipherable.
Est: $400-500.

WILLEM FREDERIK TEN BROEK (1905-   )
118. Holland-America Line. c. 1937.
24⅞ x 38⅛ in/63 x 96.9 cm
Joh. Enschede en Zonen, Haarlem
Cond A−/ Horizontal fold shows slightly; colors excellent. P.
Bibl: Dutch Posters, 199; Purvis, p. 104; Phillips II, 106; III, 33.
Exaggerated perspective, simplified shapes and the contrast of a small white sail in front of massive ship's bow create a powerful Deco image. Brown hull with red trim against solid bright blue sky and water; lettering in grey. Broek was obviously influenced by Cassandre, who produced some fine posters for Dutch companies, as well as the Normandie in 1935.
Est: $1000-1200.

HENRI CASSIERS (1858-1944)
119. Hollandsche Societeit
24⅛ x 39⅛ in/61.3 x 99.5 cm
Lith. O. de Rycker Mendel, Bruxelles
Cond A−/ Unobtrusive tears and pinholes at paper edges only; colors and image excellent.
Colorful street scene of early 19th century Amsterdam. Bright colors and patterns set against rich texture of brick buildings and cobblestone street. Scene includes both the Dutch working class in native costume and the more elegantly suited leisure class; a boat passes in the canal. Poster advertises the Dutch Society, which claims to be the first life insurance company in the world, founded in 1807.
Est: $600-700.

An early poster for an old airline: KLM was one of the first airlines in the world and is the oldest airline still in existence. Established in October 1919, it started its scheduled service (Amsterdam-London) in May 1920. Purple, blue and orange Fokker plane, landscape below in pastel colors; top text in orange—purple, blue and orange at bottom.
Est: $700-900.

121. TWO AIR SHOW POSTERS.

ANDRE GOFFIN (b. 1930)
a. **Brussel Eeuwefeest Stadion.** 1948.
23⅞ x 33⅝ in/60.5 x 85.3 cm
Litho. "Linsmo" & DeJonghe, Bruxelles
Cond A
Bibl: Phillips III, 441
Poster for air show includes stylized planes, helicopters, jets and balloons; red, yellow, blue and brown predominate.

KEES VAN DER LAAN (1903-   )
b. **Avia.** 1937.
24¾ x 32⅞ in/62.3 x 83.5 cm
Kuhn & Zoon, Rotterdam
Cond B / Tears at folds; colors excellent.
For an aviation exhibition in The Hague. Colors are blue, magenta and grey.
Est: $600-800. (2)

ALBERT HEMELMAN (1883-1951)
122. **Nordlandfahrten.** 1926.
23⅝ x 36⅝ in/60 x 93 cm
Cond B / Small tears and some creasing; unobtrusive restoration at
       top and bottom paper edges; colors excellent. Framed.
Bibl: Barnicoat, 157 (var)
Colorful deck scene, with forms reduced to flat shapes. Figures and backdrop of snow capped mountains framed by "de stijlesque" border in red, grey and black; lettering in red. Hemelman was a landscape painter, posterist and designed many calendars.
Est: $1000-1200.

See color plate 13.

GEORG RUETER (1877-1965)
123. **Bijbel Tentoonstelling.** 1937.
23⅝ x 35⅝ in/59.4 x 90.4 cm
Druk Senefelder
Cond A
For an exhibition celebrating the 300th anniversary of the official Dutch translation of the bible, we are given a primitive Dutch design in woodcut, with heraldic ornamental fountain embellished with flowers and birds, in blue and gold ink. Rueter was a painter of portraits and flowers, as well as a graphic artist. He designed book ornaments, calendars and ex-libris, elements of which appear in the poster.
Est: $600-700.

GERARD RUTTEN (1902-   )
124. **Holland and Walcheren.** 1924.
24½ x 39⅜ in/62.1 x 99.8 cm
Geuze en Co., Dordrecht
Cond B / Very small tears and light foxing, largely at paper edges;
       small stain in image background; mounted on heavy paper.
Poster, aimed at British tourists, invites them to "quaint Holland" via rail and sea. Primitive design, folkloric rendering, stylized but purely Dutch lettering in bright primary colors—red, yellow and blue, with green—create an odd, interesting and ultimately humorous design.
Est: $600-700.

JOHANN VON STEIN (1896-1965)
125. **Rotterdam Lloyd.**
24 x 40⅝ in/61 x 103.2 cm
Ned Rotograve, Leiden (name unclear)
Cond B+/ Unobtrusive restored tears and losses at right paper edge;
       colors and image excellent.
Sleek Deco design frames the steamship "Balderan" of the Rotterdam Lloyd Line, traveling from England to the Far East; the major stop in Marseille calls for French text. Ship and reflection in white; sky and water blue; framed with black border, lettering in gold.
Est: $600-800.

KAREL J. VERBRUGGEN (1871-1931)
126. **Amsterdamsche Courant.** c. 1902.
29½ x 39 in/74.6 x 99 cm
Cond A-/ Very unobtrusive tear in image; colors and image excellent
To advertise the Amsterdam newspaper that features local news and advertising. Strong image in brilliant yellow, red and black. Solid forms and roughly drawn details outlined in solid black. Man reads paper informing him of the local politics, marketing and news evolving in the street traffic beyond.
Est: $600-800.

CHARLES C. DICKSON
120. **KLM-Royal Dutch Airlines.** 1928.
25 x 39½ in/63.5 x 100.3 cm
L. Van Leer, Amsterdam
Cond A-/ Very unobtrusive folds; colors excellent. Framed.

FRENCH POSTERS – to 1914

127

128

129

130

ANON.
127. La Buveuse d'Or. c. 1899.
57¾ x 42½ in/146 x 108 cm
Imp. Paul Dupont, Paris
Cond A
Poster advertises the serialization of the novel "La Buveuse d'Or" ("The Gold Drinker") by Maxime Villemer in the *Le Petit Journal*. The stormy scene on a ship's deck is given in dramatic, darkened colors: yellow, orange and blue.
Est: $300-400.

128. Chaussures de Luxe PDC.
13⅛ x 23⅝ in/33.2 x 60 cm
J.L. Goffart, Bruxelles
Cond B+/ Small, unobtrusive tears in image at bottom; unobtrusive tear into text at top; colors excellent. Framed.
A lovely Art Nouveau image for "hand-sewn" shoes. The fashionable young woman, in elegant red gown with blue peacock pattern, examines the shoe styles. The decorative fashions, jewelry and even the rookwood vase at center express luxury, quality and haute-couture. (The woman's wear and pose seem to be unintentionally mimicked by the PDC trademark, a rooster!)
Est: $700-900.

129. Kohler Chocolat.
39⅛ x 58⅞ in/99.3 x 149.6 cm
Imp. F. Champenois, Paris
Cond B / Small tears at folds; some staining in background; colors excellent.
Brilliant, flat colors: eye-catching peacock in bright blue, green and brown; lettering bright blue; background rolls from orange to yellow.
Est: $600-800.

130. High-Life Tailor.
45¾ x 62¾ in/116.3 x 159.3 cm
Imp. P. Vercasson, Paris
Cond A−/ Small tears and light staining at bottom paper edge; colors and image excellent.
Dapper gentleman in grey outfit offers complete suits, overcoats, redingotes and dress suits, all for the reasonable price of 69.50 francs. Background in red; lettering in black.
Est: $300-400.

HUGO D'ALESI (1849-1906)
131. Lakes of Killarney. c. 1896.
30 x 42⅛ in/76.1 x 106.8 cm
Cond B+/ Small tears, largely in margins; image and colors excellent.
Bibl: 25 ans, 76 (color)
The soft colors and leisurely scene are typical of this artist's many travel posters for the French railways. We're given a buggy ride through lush green Irish countryside, with lakes and castle ruins and morning and evening scenes inset with pink dogwood blossoms. "Hugo d'Alesi, an important supplier to railway companies, was notorious for having ruined several printers, not hesitating to ask for one or two extra color

---

CONDITIONS OF SALE

We call your attention to the Conditions of Sale printed on the last two pages of this catalogue.

The Conditions of Sale in this catalogue, as it may be amended by any posted notice or oral announcement during the sale, constitutes the complete terms and conditions under which the items listed in this catalogue will be offered for sale. Please note that the items will be offered by us as agent for the consignor.

Every potential buyer should acquaint himself fully with these Conditions of Sale and it will be assumed that he or she has done so at the time of any purchase or transaction.

PL 15	Jules Chéret	No. 155

PL 16	Jules Chéret	No. 156

PL 17
Jules Chéret
No. 145

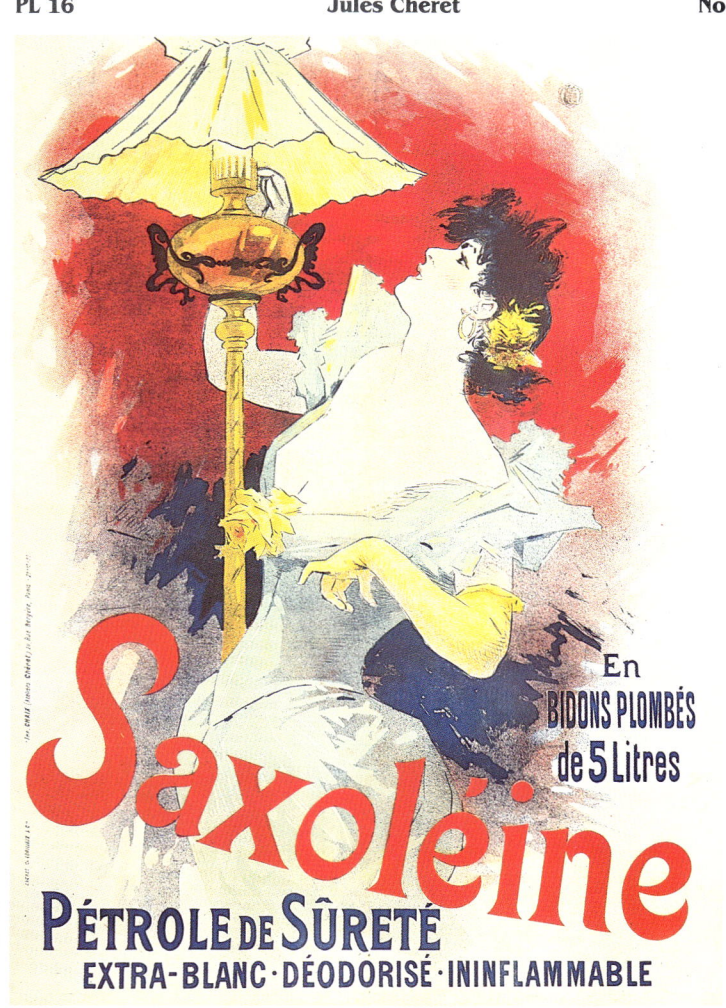

PL 18
Jules Chéret
No. 147

PL 19 Fernand Gottlob No. 165		PL 20 Eugene Grasset No. 166
PL 21 H. Gray No. 169	 	PL 22 Alphonse Mucha No. 197

PL 23　　　　　Alphonse Mucha　　　　　No. 180

PL 24　　　　　Alphonse Mucha　　　　　No. 182

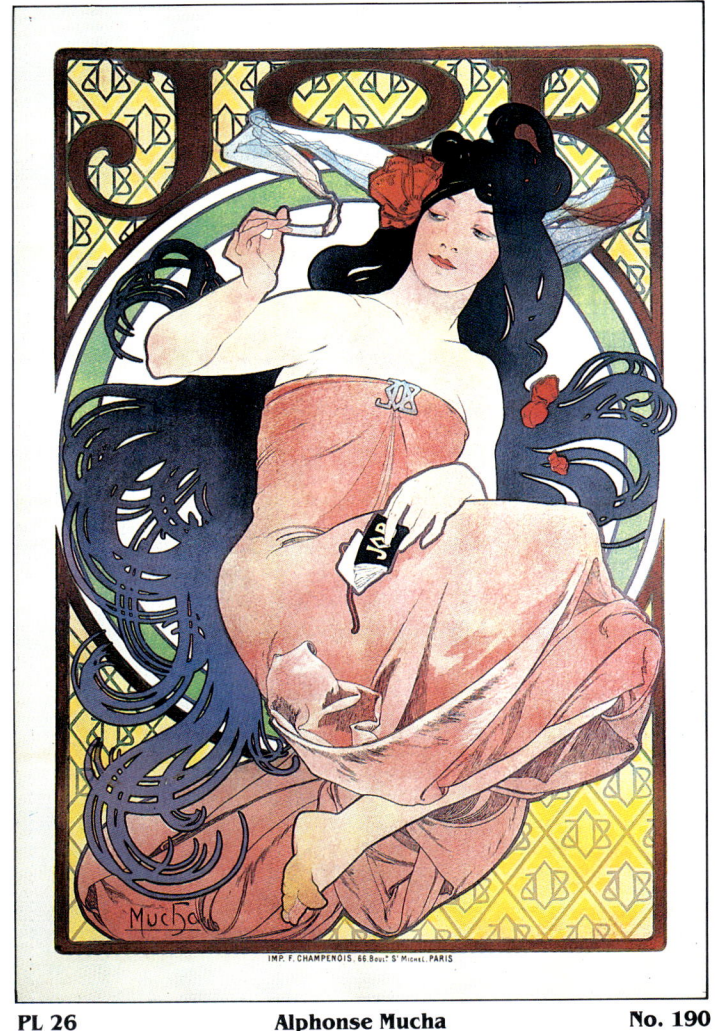

PL 25　　　　　Alphonse Mucha　　　　　No. 187

PL 26　　　　　Alphonse Mucha　　　　　No. 190

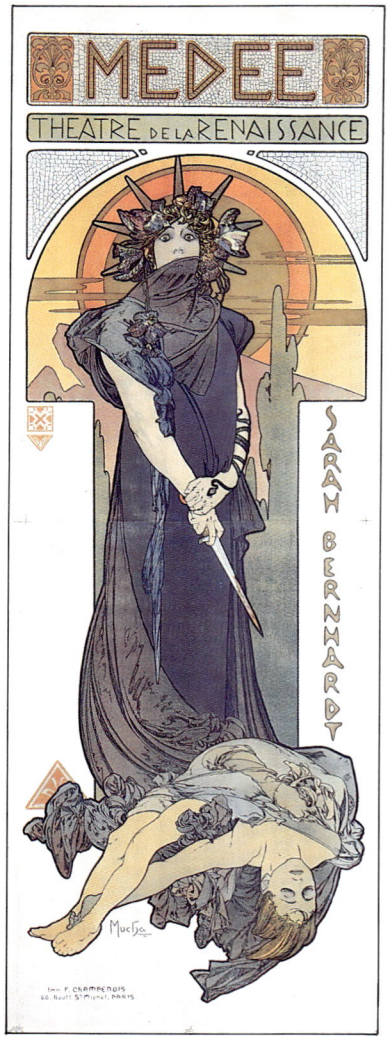

PL 27   Alphonse Mucha   No. 192

PL 28   Manuel Orazi   No. 199

PL 29   Alexandre De Riquer   No. 364

131

132

135

134a

133

134b

printings in order to obtain exactly the shadings he wanted." (Livre de l'Affiche, p. 14). Not only was he an exacting artist, he was an immensely popular and prolific one in the 1880s and 1890s. In the 1896 Reims exhibition, he was represented by 29 posters. In the St. Petersburg exhibition of 1897, there were 24 of his travel posters, more than any other French artist, including Chéret!
Est: $300-400.

PAUL BERTHON (1872-1909)

Berthon was a pupil of Eugene Grasset and was heavily influenced by him. But he did have his own definite style and he proved a tireless exponent of Art Nouveau in many writings. Victor Arwas sums up his contribution as follows: "Berthon took the imagery developed by Grasset and transformed it, creating a small but characteristic body of work which epitomizes the Art Nouveau style on paper." (Berthon & Grasset, p. 8). He produced about fifteen posters and sixty decorative panels. His subjects are all quite aloof, his designs full of softness and pastels, but he can evoke a romanticism and even a sensuousness that is all his own.

132. Le Livre de Magda. 1898.
19⅝ x 25½ in/49.7 x 64.8 cm
Imp. Chaix, Paris
Cond A. Framed.
Bibl: DFP-II, 66; Berthon & Grasset, p. 97; Phillips I, 52; II, 71; VII, 70
Muted yellows predominate in this lyrical poster to advertise a book of poetry by Armand Silvestre.
Est: $1000-1200.

133. Les Eglantines. 1900.
25½ x 19½ in/65 x 49.5 cm
Imp. Chaix, Paris
Cond A
Bibl: Berthon & Grasset, p. 106; Phillips II, 80
This panel titled "Les Eglantines" (Dog Roses, or Wild Roses) is one of a series of floral panels by Berthon. Rogers commented that "The *estampes* of Paul Berthon assimilate closely to his posters, and possess the same peculiar charm of delightfully-delicate treatment, with all the individuality that this clever young artist puts into his work." (p. 126)
Est: $400-500.

134. Two panels.
25⅝ x 19¾ in/64.6 x 50.1 cm
Imp. Chaix, Paris (not shown)
a. Les Boules de Neige. 1900.
Cond A / Pencil signed and numbered 16/100
Bibl: Berthon & Grasset, p. 106; Phillips II, 79
This Guelder Rose panel has subtle colors of yellow and olive, with light orange hair.
b. Queen Wilhelmina. 1901.
Cond A.
Bibl: Berthon & Grasset, p. 116; Phillips I, 59; II, 81.
Soft shades of gold, orange and sepia, forming rich sunset glow.
Est: $600-800. (2)

135. Sarah Bernhardt. 1901.
19⅝ x 25⅝ in/50 x 64.4 cm
Imp. Bourgerie, Paris (not shown)
Cond A. Framed.
Bibl: Berthon & Grasset, p. 90; Phillips VII, 71
Arwas calls this Berthon's "most famous lithograph" and describes it well: "Sarah is shown in three quarter profile in the role of Mélisandre in 'La Princesse Lointaine' by Edmond Rostand, a play she had originally put on in 1894 at the Théatre de la Renaissance. She wore, in the part, a crown which carried large jewelled flowers which framed her face. Berthon transformed this into a decorative conceit, large irises taking the place of the jewelled ones. Within an otherwise utterly idealized composition, he characteristically lavished the greatest care on a realistic interpretation of the lace on her dress." (Berthon & Grasset, pp 125-128). This is the state before the addition of printer's and Sarah's name at the bottom.
Est: $1000-1200.

PIERRE BONNAUD (1865-)

136. Chocolat des 3 Frères. 1901.
18 x 24⅝ in/45.8 x 62.6 cm
Societe Lyonnaise de Photochromogravure, Lyon
Cond A−/ Slight staining at paper edges; unobtrusive small tear in upper image.
One school boy distracts an unsuspecting delivery boy with a game of marbles while the other steals the bar of chocolate from his basket. Naturalistic colors; lettering in red.
Est: $300-400.

LEONETTO CAPPIELLO (1875-1942)
For other works by Cappiello, see 7, 39, 253-256.

If Chéret is the Father of the Poster, then Cappiello should be called the Father of the Modern Poster. For though the Italian-born artist, who created posters in Paris for forty years, had clear antecedents in his style, he had an entirely original approach to the means of portraying the advertising message. To arrest the attention of the passerby and to indelibly etch an image in his mind—that was Cappiello's mission. By means of wide color planes and highly exaggerated colors and situations, he shocked, surprised and moved; he made us notice and made us remember. His posters can be said to be fantastic—in the literal sense. Beginning with an ordinary caricature-style, such as the Amandines de Provence, he went on to create classics such as the Chocolat Klaus (1903), Cinzano (1910), Thermogène (1909), Kub (1931) and over 1,000 other posters.

137. Amandines de Provence. 1900.
39¼ x 55⅛ in/99.8 x 140 cm
Imp. P. Vercasson, Paris
Cond B+/ Some staining and small tears at folds; colors and image excellent.
Bibl: DFP-II, 116; Cappiello, 232; Viénot, p. 143; Abdy, p. 168; Menegazzi, 444; Phillips V, 13 (color)
A flamboyant young woman in bright yellow dress nibbles suggestively on the Biscuit—note the three glasses of champagne on the table—against a vibrant blue background. The design gains strength from the effective use of flat colors and the humor and animation from the scribble of ribbon on woman's dress which ties in with the lettering above.
Est: $1000-1200.

See color plate 39.

138. Chocolat Klaus. 1903.
44⅜ x 62½ in/112.7 x 158.3 cm
Imp. P. Vercasson, Paris
Cond B / Tears and scrapes, largely in black background; image and colors excellent. Framed.
Bibl: DFP-II, 120; Musée d'Affiche, 60; Timeless Images, 102 (color); Menegazzi, 448; Livre de l'Affiche, 25 (color); Viénot, Pl.XVIII; Weill, p. 125 (color); Wagner, 104 (color); Cappiello, 257; Phillips V, 15
It is with this poster, printed in 1903, that Cappiello firmly established himself as the master of the modern poster—if not of modern advertising—as he slowly began to leave caricature, not only in preoccupation but in its form, and with a newfound flamboyance of style and fertile imagination pursued the posterist's goal with a clarity and purpose which was to set him apart from all his colleagues. "The poster for Chocolat Klaus is incomprehensible, but so striking that it immediately assured success for Cappiello: his quest for the movement, the line, the arabesque, the dynamic of his characters in a state of weightlessness, his combinations of violent flat colors on a black background vibrate the walls like splashes of light." (Livre de l'Affiche, p. 40).
Est: $1000-1200.

139. Remington. c. 1910.
49¼ x 77¾ in/125.3 x 197.5 cm
Imp. P. Vercasson, Paris
Cond B / Unobtrusive tears at folds and paper edge; image and colors excellent.
Bibl: Cappiello, 286
Red-haired secretary types up a storm on her Remington. The usual Cappiello excess turns it into an exciting poster.
Est: $800-1000.

140. Job. 1912.
46¼ x 62⅜ in/117.5 x 158.5 cm
Imp. Vercasson, Paris
Cond B / A 10-in. tear into image at bottom; creasing and tears in background upper right paper edge; colors excellent.
Bibl: DFP-II, 124 (var); Phillips II, 114 (color)
Sultan in white, on red pillow, brown background, text in green. This is the larger of two formats.
Est: $800-1000.

141. Lampe O.R. 1912.
50¼ x 77¾ in/127.6 x 197.5 cm
Imp. Vercasson, Paris
Cond B−/ Slight tears at folds and paper edge; image and colors very good.
Green-clad lady against black background sports

headdress, necklace, earrings—and much more—composed of Auer light bulbs. An image sure to electrify the viewer.
Est: $700-900.

HENRI CASSIERS (1858-1944)
142. Red Star Line.
22³⁄₄ x 35⁷⁄₈ in/57.8 x 91.2 cm
O. de Rycker, Bruxelles
Cond A−/ Small tear in left margin; restored loss in bottom right corner; colors and image excellent.
Bibl: DFP-II, 1005 (var)
Seaman in orange, the "Belgenland" steamship in black, water is green, sky yellow and text in red and black. The hallmark of all Cassiers posters is a sympathetic and colorful rendering of native people, usually farmers, fishermen or sailors, and it is from their vantage point that we see the item being advertised. This very human touch adds a great deal to the appeal of his posters.
Est: $800-1000.

JULES CHERET (1836-1932)
Jules Chéret is unquestionably the most important individual in the history and development of the poster. He is the founder of the color pictorial poster and, most importantly, it was Chéret, the printer and designer, who showed the world how to effectively and economically use the techniques of lithography to mass-produce large and colorful posters.

The English critic, Charles Hiatt, writing in 1895, was full of praise of this artist's achievement: "It may be that men of rare, or more fascinating, talent have now and again devoted themselves to the *affiche;* but none of them can compare with Chéret in the magnitude and curiosity of his achievement. Many have produced charming wall pictures: nobody, save Chéret, has made an emphatic mark on this aspect of a metropolis." (p. 24). And commenting on Chéret's use of color, he remarks: "Blazing reds, hard blues, glowing yellows, uncompromising greens are flung together, apparently haphazard, but in reality after the nicest calculation, with the result that the great pictures, when on the hoardings, insist positively on recognition. One might as well attempt to ignore a fall of golden rain, as to avoid stopping to look at them; they are so many riots of colour, triumphant in their certainty of fascinating and bewildering the passerby." (p. 30).

143. Aux Buttes Chaumont. 1888.
41⁷⁄₈ x 106¼ in/106.5 x 269.8 cm
Imp. Chaix, Paris
Cond B+/ Some tears at folds; colors and image excellent.
Bibl: Broido, 703; Maindron, 586; Maitres, 185; Reims, 284.
Chéret produced over 40 posters, from 1879 to 1890, for this Paris department store. In this rare 2-sheet poster to announce a sale of toys, the woman and children are shown in red and yellow, background is blue, lettering is yellow. Chéret often portrayed children in his posters, largely for such toy and gift sale announcements. Hiatt speaks of his treatment of them: "The joy of the little ones in the possession of their new playthings is contagious." (p. 34).
Est: $1000-1200.

144. Ed. Sagot. 1891.
33³⁄₈ x 94½ in/84.6 x 240 cm
Imp. Chaix, Paris
Cond B+/ Small tears in text areas; unobtrusive 8 in. tear in image at bottom left edge; colors excellent.
Bibl: Broido, 528; Maindron, 427; DFP-II, 218; Reims, 406.
Originally designed for the Belle Jardinière store, the rejected maquette was quickly grabbed up by Paris' leading poster and print dealer, Edmond Sagot, who had just issued his formidable poster catalogue that year. It's one of the loveliest of all Chéret posters, with a lyrical quality, and colors that can only be described as electric. Woman in red and yellow striped dress, red stockings, yellow shoes and hat; lettering in blue; multicolored bouquet.
Est: $2000-2400.

145   **150**   **151**   **152**

JULES CHERET (continued)

145. Purgatif Géraudel. 1891.
34 1/8 x 96 3/4 in/86.8 x 245.7 cm
Imp. Chaix, Paris
Cond A−/ Very unobtrusive staining at folds; colors excellent.
Bibl: Broido, 899; Maindron, 743; DFP-II, 221; Phillips/Chéret, 122; Wagner, 38 (color); Reims, 489

A lively Chérette in yellow juggles boxes of Purgatif Géraudel against blue background; lettering is red. The product promises "fresh-looking, rosy complexion, excellent digestion, physical strength, perfect health and regular sleep"— and all for only 1.5 francs a box. A 2-sheet poster.
Est: $800-1000.

See color plate 17.

146. L'Etendard Français. 1891.
34 x 48 1/2 in/86.4 x 122.2 cm
Imp. Chaix, Paris
Cond A−/ Unobtrusive tears at top center (into woman's hat) and at paper edges; colors and image excellent.
Bibl: Broido, 998, Pl. 45 (color); Maindron, 820; Bicycle Posters, 52; DFP-II, 219; Reims, 345; Petite Reine, 52 (color)

Woman's dress red with blue details; background in turquoise and tan. Bicyclist in blue, white and red, holds the banner of the Etendard Français bicycle firm. The company (Etendard means both "banner" and "standard" and both are obviously implied in this design) offers payment plan of 50 francs down and 25 francs per month. Surprisingly enough, although his printing firm, Chaix, which was next to the large Clément Bicycle Company, produced many bicycle posters, Chéret himself designed few of them. He did a colorful one for Cleveland bicycles, as well as an earlier one for the Paris-Course-Hippodrome.
Est: $1000-1200.

146   **147**

147. Saxoléine. 1892.
34 5/8 x 49 in/88 x 124.3 cm
Imp. Chaix, Paris
Cond A−/ Vertical center fold slightly visible; colors and image excellent
Bibl: Broido, 946, Pl. 39 (color); Maindron, 785; DFP-II, 232; Maitres, 145; Affichomanie, 82; Reims, 507

Woman in green dress adorned by yellow gloves and yellow "corsage" beneath green lamp. Both the woman and lamp in green and yellow stand out against the red and blue background; lettering in red. One of the best of the Saxoléine series of posters by Chéret.
Est: $700-900.

See color plate 18.

148. Palais de Glace. 1893.
33 7/8 x 47 7/8 in/86 x 121.1 cm
Imp. Chaix, Paris
Cond B / Folds show; small related tears; colors excellent.
Bibl: Broido, 362; Maindron 292; DFP-II, 240; Reims, 455; Word & Image, p. 25; Timeless Images, 6 (color); Phillips II, 162 (color)

Woman in tan coat, red hat, blue background and lettering. One of the loveliest and rarest of Chéret's series for the ice skating rink on the Champs Elysées.
Est: $1700-2000.

148

149

153

149. Théatre de l'Opéra-Carnaval. 1893.
34-3/8 x 48-3/8 in/87.2 x 122.9 cm
Imp. Chaix, Paris (not shown)
Cond A
Bibl: Broido, 288, Pl. 17 (color; var); Maindron, 246; Schardt, p. 61 (color; var); Abdy, p. 39 (color)
In this rare version, before letters, of the Carnaval 1894 poster, we have one of Chéret's happiest and most colorful scenes: Woman in pink in foreground is pursued by a harlequin in yellow and red; light blues and reds predominate in background.
Est: $1200-1500.

150. Cacao Lhara. 1893.
34-3/8 x 96-7/8 in/87.3 x 246 cm
Imp. Chaix, Paris
Cond A
Bibl: Broido, 864; Maindron, 730; DFP-II, 241
Maiden in yellow-striped dress, red stockings and red and white flowered shawl, beckons us to celebrate with a glass of Mugnier's Cacao Lhara. The colors of this two-sheet poster are especially brilliant.
Est: $800-1000.

151. Saxoléine. 1894.
33-3/4 x 95-1/8 in/85.8 x 241.5 cm
Imp. Chaix, Paris (not shown)
Cond B / Staining in upper image and in blank text area at bottom and along paper edges; some tears at paper edges.
Bibl: Broido, 950; Maindron, 789; DFP-II, 242, Color Pl. II (var); Phillips/Chéret, 131; Abdy, p. 49; Reims, 510
An impressive two-sheet poster, before letters, with woman in blue dress with yellow trim; blue lampshade and red background.
Est: $700-900.

152. Palais de Glace. 1894.
34-1/4 x 97-1/2 in/87 x 247.2 cm
Imp. Chaix, Paris
Cond B / Unobtrusive tear across lower image; tears and creasing in text area at top; colors excellent.
Bibl: Broido, 366; Maindron, 295; DFP-II, 246; Abdy, p. 42; Weill, 29; Reims, 454; Phillips/Chéret, 71; Phillips V, 19 (color)
In this magnificent two-sheet poster, the woman is in red outfit with navy blue trim, silhouettes in background are in blue, text is royal blue. Charles Matlack Price notes that "The motion in the 'Palais de Glace' posters needs only the music to which the care-free skaters disport themselves, gracefully balanced like birds on the wing, or with tantalizing smile and beckoning arm, enticing the beholder to join them." (p. 22).
Est: $1700-2000.

153. Lidia. 1895.
34-1/4 x 48-3/4 in/87 x 123.4 cm
Imp. Chaix, Paris
Cond A-/ Light staining, largely at paper edges; colors and image excellent
Bibl: Broido, 174 (var); Maindron, 154, repro p. 48 (color); Maitres, 25; Wagner, 45 (color); DFP-II, 250; Affichomanie, 85 (var); Café-Concert, 58; Reims, 407; Phillips I, 147; II, 172
Extremely fresh colors: dress in white, mint green gloves and hat, blue background, red lettering. It was used as a stock poster by this star, with theatre name imprinted at top.
Est: $700-900.

JULES CHERET (continued)

154. Pastilles Géraudel. 1895.
34¼ x 48¼ in/87 x 122.5 cm
Imp. Chaix, Paris
Cond B / Staining at horizontal fold.
Bibl: Broido, 910, Pl. 36 (color; var); Reims, 472; Abdy, p. 38 (color)
This image of the Chérette in bright red coat with umbrella to protect her from the blizzard, undaunted by winter's chill now that she's taken her Pastilles Geraudel, is one of Chéret's most dazzling designs.
Est: $1200-1500.

155. Eldorado. 1894.
33¾ x 47⅞ in/85.8 x 121.6 cm
Imp. Chaix, Paris
Cond A-/ Faint time staining in upper and lower image
Bibl: Broido, 216, Pl. 14 (color); Maindron, 190; Wember, 180; DFP-II, 244; Schardt, 88 (color); Reims, 340; Timeless Images, 9 (color); Phillips/Chéret, 46
The red spotlight on the dancing girl at the Eldorado Music Hall adds to the impact of this vivacious work.
Est: $1500-1800.

See color plate 15.

156. Musée Grevin. 1900.
34 x 48½ in/86.3 x 122.2 cm
Imp. Chaix, Paris
Cond A
Bibl: Broido, 471 (Pl. 24 + cover); DFP-II, 267; Wagner, 49 (color); Phillips I, 153; III, 388; VII, 95 (var); Phillips/Chéret, 87; Takashimaya, 2 (color)
This is the version before letters. There were two uses for this poster: to announce a "Fête des Artistes" and another for the puppet show of John Hewelt at the Musée Grevin. Chéret's fine sense of composition and his great lithographic skill shine in this design.
Est: $2000-2200.

See color plate 16.

L. DAMARE.
157. Olympia. Vers les Etoiles. 1906.
42½ x 58¾ in/108.1 x 149.2 cm
Imp. Clemont, Leroy, Paris
Cond B / Stains and unobtrusive tears at paper edges; image and colors excellent
Little is known of Damaré, other than the fact that he had a most fertile imagination (*see* Phillips VII, 97, 98). For a dance and drama spectacle at the Olympia, he uncorks a voluptuous, soaring spirit in a diaphanous robe followed by star-bearing visions in the midnight blue sky beyond, drawing our attention "Vers les Etoiles" ("Toward the Stars").
Est: $400-500.

L. LUCIEN FAURE (1872-)
158. Claudine. 1901.
40¼ x 55 in/102.3 x 139.2 cm
Imp. Charles Verneau, Paris
Cond A
Fauré gives us a portrait of Colette, the author of the immensely popular "Claudine" series of novels—two of which are seen at lower right—in contrasting broad, flat shapes with delicately drawn, natural details in face. Colors are light red, green and black. It is a very rare—and very striking—poster. Writer, dramatist, script writer and film actress, Gabrielle-Sidonie Colette created the character Claudine in several books between 1900 and 1903, which brought her the first recognition as a writer. She was offered a drama critique column in the magazine *Gil Blas,* which was headed "Claudine en concert." Later she also did film reviews and appeared on stage as an actress in 1906. Starting in 1917, she wrote screenplays and dialogue for a number of French films, most of them adaptations of her own novels, including *Gigi* (1948), *Claudine à l'Ecole* (1937), *Minne* (1950) and *Cheri* (1950).
Est: $600-800.

159. Championnat de Lutte.
30⅝ x 46½ in/77.8 x 118 cm
Lith. G. Bataille, Paris
Cond B / Tear at lower right corner; folds show, with some related tears
For the world wrestling championship held at the Casino de Paris; colors are orange and black. Another stark but effective design by Fauré, an artist who produced about a dozen posters, but of whom little is known.
Est: $400-500.

GEORGES FAY (d. 1916)
160. Le "Quartier" Cabaret-Salon. 1897.
30½ x 46⅜ in/77.5 x 117.8 cm
Imp. P. Vercasson, Paris
Cond B / Some tears, largely at folds; colors excellent.
Bibl: DFP-II, 337; Wember, 303; Schardt, p. 103
One of the finest and rarest of the turn-of-the-century cabaret posters: actor with bright yellow hair, women with black hair, red dresses, background bright green. The color and line—a rainbow of colors at top and a sparse use of outline at bottom—are rendered with remarkable effect. Little is known of this painter and illustrator who died in World War I.
Est: $600-800.

158

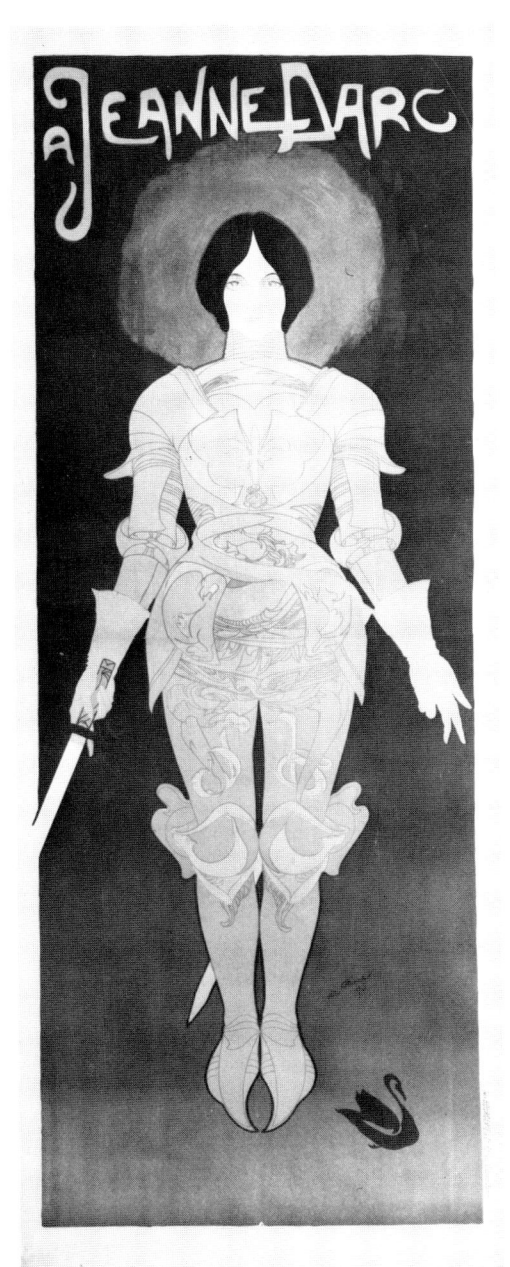

159

160

162

163

161

GEORGES DE FEURE (1868-1928)
DeFeure (whose real name was Georges Joseph van Sluijters) was a fine designer, decorator—from painter and posterist. His zest for decoration—from furniture to clothing—comes through in almost all his posters. Rogers commented: "The posters of this artist are usually well drawn and have a distinct boulevard flavour. His types of men and women are jaded, hard-featured, and worldly, and look upon us from out the glare and mysterious glamour of the gas-lights." (p. 64).

161. Salon des Cent. 1894.
16¼ x 24½ in/41.2 x 62.2 cm
Imp. Bourgerie, Paris
Cond B / Horizontal center fold shows slightly; very small tears at paper edges; tiny dirt spots in woman's hands; colors excellent. Framed.
Bibl: DFP-II, 343; Maitres, 10 (color; var); Maindron, p. 63; Hiatt, p. 124; Abdy, p. 153; Reims, 619; Phillips I, 222; II, 223; III, 431; PAI-I.
This is the version before the application of the purple stone. Hiatt states that this is DeFeure's "most characteristic effort" and finds that "This design is very modern and very fantastic."
Est: $1500-1800.

162. Le Diablotin. 1894.
23¾ x 31⅛ in/60.3 x 79.1 cm
J. Weiner, Paris
Cond A
Bibl: DFP-II, 345; Reims, 609; Affiches de Presse, 41
To advertise the Brussels-based illustrated literary journal, "Le Diablotin," DeFeure gives us a more assertive female character and adds a dash of wit as well.
Est: $500-600.

163. A Jeanne d'Arc. 1896.
36½ x 100¾ in/92.6 x 256 cm
Imp. Bourgerie, Paris
Cond A-/ Small tears, largely in margins; some staining in margins; colors excellent.
Bibl: DFP-II, 350 (var); Maitres, 130; Wember, 305 (color; var).
In this poster for the department store, Joan of Arc is seen in a suit of armor that only DeFeure's vivid decorative and symbolist imagination could create. Armor in ochre, lavender and yellow; gloves and lettering in lavender, background in brown. This is the version before advertising text in lower sheet.
Est: $2500-3000.

JEAN-LOUIS FORAIN (1852-1931)
164. Deuxième Salon du Cycle. 1894.
80¼ x 33⅞ in/203.8 x 85.9 cm
Imp. H. Herold, Paris
Cond B−/ Tears largely at corners and at paper edges, folds show, some rippling at joining of sheets. Colors excellent.
Bibl: DFP-II, 362; Maindron, p. 64; Maitres, 51; Hiatt, p. 93; Petite Reine, 80; Abdy, p. 106; Bicycle Posters, 20; Wagner, 55; Phillips I, 232; II, 238

This poster by the prolific illustrator, painter and lithographer Forain, had an immediate impact. Maindron, a year after publication, was unequivocal: "This poster is perfect." Hiatt commented: "The colour scheme is restrained and delicate, and the production, which exists in two sizes, should certainly be found amongst the treasures of every amateur of the *affiche*." (p. 95). Soft colors, delicate image and calligraphic lettering combine to create a most effective and eye-catching poster. The colors in this larger, two-sheet version, are olive, peach and beige.
Est: $600-800.

FERNAND GOTTLOB (1873-1935)
165. 2e Exposition des Peintres Lithographes. 1898.
31⅛ x 47½ in/79.1 x 120.7 cm
Imp. Lemercier, Paris
Cond A
Bibl: DFP-II, 392; Maitres, 219; Timeless Images, 31 (color); Takashimaya, 24 (color); Phillips I, 253

For the second exhibition of lithographic art held at the Salle du Figaro in Paris, Gottlob shows a young lady in a rakish chapeau looking through a display cradle of prints.
Est: $500-600.

See color plate 19.

EUGENE GRASSET (1841-1917)
Grasset did much to introduce the concept and practice of Art Nouveau in France. In fact, says Weill, Grasset "brought Art Nouveau to the aid of the poster: it was to become a worldwide vehicle of the art of advertising. In France, Grasset was the pioneer of an attempt, like that of William Morris of England, to reconcile art and industry . . . Interested as he was in all the applied arts, he came naturally to the poster." (p. 32). Price commented that "Eugène Grasset, whose work can be likened only to that of Mucha, dignified the poster almost to the grandeur of a stained-glass window, with masses of gorgeous color, heavy outlines like leads, refined conception in design, with an intricate imagination and skill over all." (p. 54).

166. Exposition Internationale de Madrid. 1893.
43⅜ x 59½ in/110.1 x 151 cm
Imp. Lemercier, Paris
Cond A−/ Some very unobtrusive tears and staining at folds; colors excellent.
Bibl: DFP-II, 407; Berthon & Grasset, p. 32; Hiatt, p. 51; Reims, 673; Phillips I, 262; II, 270.

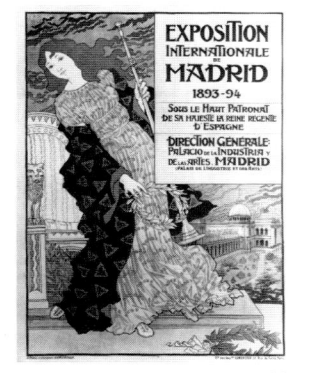

In this famous poster by Grasset, the woman in decoratively patterned yellow dress and black robe against subtle olive green background steps down from her embellished throne to announce the Madrid Exposition. In the background is the site of the exposition, the Palace of Industry and Arts.
Est: $1000-1200.

See color plate 20.

167. Abricotine. c. 1905.
42¾ x 29⅛ in/108.7 x 73.8 cm
Imp. Devambez, Paris
Cond A−/ Very unobtrusive vertical center fold; colors and image excellent.
Bibl: DFP-II, 420; Phillips II, 277

A maiden, rather impractically (but seductively) dressed, picks apricots for the Abricotine liqueur. Dress is pink, grove is green, apricots and hair are yellow-orange. This is the smaller format. A rare, late poster of Grasset.
Est: $2000-2300.

170

171

172

168. Inquiétude. 1897.
4 1³⁄₈ x 19³⁄₄ in/105 x 50.2 cm
G. de Malherbe, Paris (not shown)
Cond B / Vertical center fold shows with some breaks; image and colors excellent.
Bibl: Berthon & Grasset, pp 72-73; Phillips II, 283
The restless young woman in ochre dress rambles through a field of goldenrod. The blooms are in yellow, background and leaves in dull green. This is Plate III of "Dix Estampes Décoratives," a series of ten lithographs, paired in five different sizes, published by G. de Malherbe in an edition of 750 copies.
Est: $1200-1500.

169. Pétrole Stella. 1897.
39¹⁄₂ x 51³⁄₈ in/100.4 x 130.5 cm
Imp. Courmont Frères, Paris
Cond A
Bibl: DFP-II, 421; Affichomanie, 116; Phillips I, 274; II, 285; III, 444; V, 29 color)
A most extravagant design to advertise lamp oil, Gray's poster has three celestial nudes with butterfly wings soaring over what appears to be a finely calibrated compass rosette against a starry sky. Gray was the pseudonym of Henri Boulanger; this surrealistic flight is his very best work.
Est: $800-1000.

See color plate 21.

JULES-ALEXANDRE GRUN (1868-1934)
170. Concert de la Pépinière. 1902.
37¹⁄₄ x 51 in/94.6 x 129.5 cm
Imp. J. Thil, Paris
Cond A
Bibl: Timeless Images, 18 (color); Weill, p. 45 (color); Phillips V, 30 (color)
In his new book, Weill states that Montmartre was "the domicile of one of the most original talents of this time: Jules Alexandre Grun. If in his posters he had not treated mainly carousers and coquettes, with facility but without genius, he would be one of the greatest poster artists of the period: in fact he is the only one to use flat tints without outlines, allowing the paper itself to function as a design element, to compose scenes that are often of great graphic audacity." (pp 43-44). The joyful good humor that he displayed so well is most evident here: A rosy-cheeked woman in bright yellow-orange dress and hat is pursued by a policeman who springs from black background, threatening, "I'm going to tell your mother"—the name of the revue at the Pépinière.
Est: $800-1000.

ALBERT GUILLAUME (1873-1942)
171. A la Scala. 1908.
35¹⁄₂ x 50³⁄₄ in/90.2 x 128.9 cm
Imp. Minot, Paris
Cond B+ / Small tears and creases in upper image background and in top margin; colors and image excellent. Framed.
Bibl: Spectacle, 1333
Guillaume, a prolific illustrator, was a contributor to many journals, including *Gil Blas* and *Figaro Illustré*. He had 32 posters in the Reims exhibition of 1896. Although best known for his caricature style with heavy outlines, he could sometimes, as here, use a very fine brush and give us a painterly treatment. The debonair couple arriving at the theatre, with surrounding glow of evening lights, is rendered with soft colors, largely brown and black, with accents of yellow and red.
Est: $700-900.

PAUL CESAR HELLEU (1859-1927)
172. Ed. Sagot. 1900.
29¹⁄₂ x 41³⁄₄ in/75 x 106 cm
Imp. Chaix, Paris
Cond A
Bibl: DFP-II, 466; Affichomanie, 3; Takashimaya, 25 (color); Phillips I, 291; II, 300.
Sagot was the principal poster dealer in Paris, also handling drawings and prints. His first poster ctalogue in 1891 listed 2,233 items for sale. His sales copy indicates a great enthusiasm for the poster medium. In this poster by Helleu, the client is deeply absorbed in some detail of a print laid before her.
Est: $400-500.

173. Ed. Sagot. 1900.
29¹⁄₂ x 41³⁄₄ in/75 x 106 cm
Imp. Chaix, Paris (not shown)
Cond A
Bibl: *See* No. 172.
This is the version before letters.
Est: $400-500.

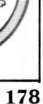

E. CHARLES LUCAS
174. Folies-Bergère. La Loïe Fuller. c. 1894
37⅝ x 57⅝ in/96 x 146.5 cm
Lith. F. Appel, Paris
Cond B / Folds show; slight creasing in margins; several unobtrusive restorations; image and colors very good.
Bibl: Reims, 819
This is one of the rarest of all the Loïe Fuller posters. When the Virginia Museum mounted its Loïe Fuller exhibition in 1979, it gathered together all the posters for this famed American dancer, but it could not locate this one. Swirls of gauzy fabric accentuated by colored lighting was Fuller's specialty dance in a nutshell, and here the artist catches the spectacle in delicate pastel tones.
Est: $1200-1500.

MARIE
175. Edmond Sagot. 1897.
25½ x 35½ in/64.8 x 90.3 cm
Afiches Ed. Sagot, Paris
Cond A
Bibl: DFP-II, 562; Affichomanie, 4; Phillips I, 381
The left panel, with a Grecian woman, advertises Sagot's poster and print gallery and the right panel, featuring a modern woman, suggests that his Paris-Almanach makes a fine gift for the ladies. In red, green and black, with gold ink.
Est: $250-300.

J. MATET
176. Fashionable House. 1910.
30½ x 46⅜ in/77.5 x 117.9 cm
Imp. Emile Pecaud, Paris
Cond B+/ Folds show; colors and image excellent.
Simple design for Rouen clothing store with a "fashionable" English name. Small boy in a dapper grey coat and hat, yellow gloves, red spats and flower in lapel; blue background, lettering in red and green.
Est: $300-400.

EDOUARD MOREROD (1879-1919)
177. Régina Badet. 1910.
47 x 63 in/119.5 x 161 cm
Imp. G. Delattre, Paris
Cond B−/ Some tears and staining, largely at folds; several scrape marks; colors excellent.
Régina Badet (1879-1949) was a ballerina and a stage and screen actress. She made her debut in the Grand-Théatre of Bordeaux, her home town, at the age of 10. In 1905, she appeared for the first time in Paris in the ballet "Lakme" by Delibes, at the Opéra Comique. She gained further recognition for her spirited performance of the part of Conchita Perez in "La Femme et le pantin" in 1910, the performance being advertised in the wild design by Morerod, an artist who studied with Steinlen (another Swiss expatriot) in Paris. Badet is shown in black and lime green, background in yellow and orange; lettering is light green.
Est: $1000-1200.

ALPHONSE MUCHA (1860-1939)

Writing in 1901, Rogers called Mucha "The apostle of the beautiful." He spoke of these posters "in which scholarly decoration, delicate colouring, repose, dignity, and a classic refinement characterize the methods of their gifted designer. . . . The basis of his designs is a draughtsmanship at once thorough and technically correct, dominated by an instinctive grace of line and a keen sense of decorative effect." (p. 54). To many, "le style Mucha" is synonymous with "le style Art Nouveau." A major retrospective of the work of Mucha will tour eight American museums for a two-year period, starting at the San Diego Museum of Art in September 1986.

178. Amants. 1895.
54 1/8 x 41 1/2 in/137.5 x 105.4 cm
Imp. Camis, Paris
Cond C / Folds show; restored tears, largely at paper edges and in border area; large restored loss at bottom right corner; small restored hole in right image; colors excellent.
Bibl: Rennert/Weill, 7 (color); Bridges A3, p. 48 (color); DFP-II, 625; Mucha/Paris A6; Reims, 896; Phillips II, 405 (color); III, 522; PAI-I, 215

"Mucha's first theatrical poster without Sarah Bernhardt was one of three projects he made at the printing firm of Camis before settling down with Champenois. The play, a comedy by Maurice Donnay, starred Jeanne Granier and Lucien Guitry, and premiered on November 5, 1895. There is very rich ornamentation in this poster which adroitly divides it into three scenes and thereby harmonizes elements which might otherwise appear quite busy: There is a Punch-and-Judy show in the upper left, a tragic commentary in the upper right, and the entire bottom section is given to the play's party scene, replete with fashionable guests, strolling violinist, dancers, flowers, champagne, and other indications of a good time had by all." (Rennert/Weill, p. 62).
Est: $2500-3000.

179. La Dame aux Camelias. 1896.
30 1/8 x 81 5/8 in/76.5 x 207.3 cm
Imp. F. Champenois, Paris
Cond B+/ Unobtrusive folds with some related staining and tears; silver very fresh; image excellent. Framed.
Bibl: Rennert/Weill 13 (color); Bridges A11, p. 54 (color); DFP-II, 627; Maitres, 144; Mucha/Paris, A9; Wagner, 70; Weill, p. 40; Philips I, 442; II, 408

"A literary and theatrical classic receives a masterful treatment at the hand of a great designer . . . Sarah Bernhardt presented the play many times in the course of her career; but the poster prepared by Mucha for the revival starting September 30, 1896 at the Théatre de la Renaissance was the only one that ever came close to expressing perfectly the rapture of the girl who loved not wisely but too well . . . With its delicate coloring, tasteful pose and exquisite design, it remains one of the all-time masterpieces of poster art." (Rennert/Weill, p. 76).
Est: $9000-10000.

180. Job. 1896.
18 x 24 3/8 in/45.1 x 61.9 cm
Imp. F. Champenois, Paris
Cond A. Framed.
Bibl: Rennert/Weill, 15 (color); Bridges A6, p. 50 (color); DFP-II, 635; Maitres, 202; Mucha/Paris, 28; Weill, p. 41; Timeless Images, 33 (color); Phillips II, 414; III, 528

"Jane Abdy called it 'a secular icon,' and indeed it is a magnificent production, considering that it advertises so prosaic an item as cigarette paper. . . . One of Mucha's all-time winners, this poster helped to popularize the 'Mucha girl' with his exquisite arabesque of luxuriant hair, which became the artist's instantly recognizable trademark over the next few years. Note the meticulous attention to detail, for example the letters JOB worked ingeniously into the purple background. . . . It was printed with two different background colors: purple and lavender." (Rennert/Weill, p. 82). It is the latter color that is featured here.
Est: $8000-9000.

See color plate 23

181. The Seasons. 1896.
Each: 6 x 18 in/15.2 x 45.7 cm
Imp. F. Champenois, Paris (not shown)
Cond A-/ Trimmed to borders at sides; mounted on board; colors and image excellent. Framed
Bibl: Rennert/Weill, 18 var. 3 (color); Bridges P306, pp 20-21 (color).

"One of Mucha's most endearing and enduring sets . . . Spring is a blonde sylph who seems to be fashioning a makeshift lyre out of a bent green branch and her own hair, with some birds as interested spectators. Summer, a brunette, sits dreamily on the bank of a pond, cooling her feet in the water and resting her head against a bush. Autumn is an auburn lady, making ready to partake of the ripe grapes. Winter, her brown hair barely visible as she is huddled in a long green cloak, snuggles by a snow-covered tree trying to warm a shivering bird with her breath." (Rennert/Weill, p. 90). In this smaller-format variant, the ornamental borders have been split into four segments.
Est: $4000-5000.

ALPHONSE MUCHA (continued)

182. Savonnerie de Bagnolet. 1897.
12⅛ x 17¼ in/30.8 x 43.8 cm
Imp. F. Champenois, Paris
Cond B+/ Restored loss at upper right and bottom left corners; two well-restored losses also at top paper edge; colors and image excellent. Framed.
Bibl: Rennert/Weill, 19, var. 7 (color); Bridges C4c; Phillips II, 413 (color)

The Zodiac image of Mucha was one of his most successful designs, undergoing no fewer than seven different uses over the years. "The regal bearing of the lady is emphasized by a tiara of bejeweled splendor, and her necklace does not lag far behind in bedizened glory. And then there is the hair, starting out tamely enough as an orderly sweep of luxuriant golden tresses, but soon acquiring a wild life of its own and turning into a plethora of curling strands that cavort merrily and pay homage to the classic beauty of the lady's face." (Rennert/Weill, p. 100). In this variant, the zodiac and all the decorations around the perimeter are gone and the 1898 calendarium has been inserted. Replacing the zodiacal symbols is the text for the soap company.
Est: $4000-5000.

See color plate 24.

183. Lorenzaccio. 1896.
30 x 82⅛ in/76.1 x 208.6 cm
Imp. F. Champenois, Paris
Cond B / Some tears and filled-in holes in margins, lettering and in decorative border. Framed.
Bibl: Rennert/Weill, 20 Var. 1; Bridges A10, p. 53 (color); DFP-II, 626; Maitres, 144; Mucha/Paris, 18, A10; Wagner, 69 (color); Phillips II, 409 (color); PAI-I, 219

Proof impression printed in brown and gold; some hand coloring in face and in background.

Sarah Bernhardt played the male lead in this new production which opened at the Théatre de la Renaissance on December 3, 1896. "The hero is a prince of the city-state of Florence, a member of the Medici family. With the city under siege by Alexander, Lorenzaccio tries to think of a way out: the poster shows the prince, as played by Sarah Bernhardt, contemplating how to kill Alexander in order to save the town and his own honor. The dragon above represents evil forces that are about to devour the city of Florence—its emblem appears by the dragon's mouth. The ornate, jeweled sword in the bottom panel above the name of the theater represents the possible solution." (Rennert/Weill, p. 107).
Est: $5000-6000.

184. Lorenzaccio. 1897.
14⅝ x 39½ in/37 x 100.4 cm
Imp. F. Champenois, Paris
Cond A−/ Two unobtrusive tears at right paper edge; colors and image excellent.
Bibl: Rennert/Weill, 20 Var. 2; Phillips I, 423
This is the smaller format.
Est: $1700-2000.

185. Biscuits Lefèvre-Utile. 1896.
17½ x 24½ in/44.4 x 61.6 cm
Imp. F. Champenois, Paris
Cond A−/ Faint staining in calendar area; colors (including very fresh gold) and image excellent. Framed.
Bibl: Rennert/Weill, 22; Bridges C5, p. 86 (color); Weill, p. 42; Phillips III, 524

"One of Mucha's most personable young ladies, her hair cascading irrepressibly in fine style, is offering a dish of wafers in this exquisite design. The calendar for 1897 is imprinted on a semi-circular base. Note the initials LU in that part of the golden ornamental border that protrudes into the picture at right. The design of the girl's dress incorporates sickle and wheat emblems, elements appropriate to the subject matter." (Rennert/Weill, p. 113).
Est: $4000-4500.

186. Société Populaire des Beaux-Arts. 1897.
18 x 24⅞ in/45.7 x 63.2 cm
Imp. F. Champenois, Paris
Cond B / Small unobtrusive tears at left paper edges; remnants of old paper tape along bottom margin; some small scrapes; image excellent, gold very fresh; laid down on board. Framed.
Bibl: Rennert/Weill, 23 (color); Bridges, A20; DFP-II, 641; Mucha/Paris, 24, A12; Phillips I, 428; II, 420

"This society was founded by a Paris lawyer, Edmond Benoit-Levy, in 1894, with the purpose of popularizing

art by holding laterna magica shows—what we would today call a slide presentation. . . . One of Mucha's traits was to personify ideas in supernatural beings who interacted with ordinary people. Here is a good example of this: the lovely female with the flamboyant crown of hair, leaning on a projection machine, symbolizes art instruction by means of slides, while the young man in the foreground is an ordinary student." (Rennert/Weill, p. 116).
Est: $3500-4000.

187. Monaco Monte-Carlo. 1897.
30 x 43 in/76.2 x 109.2 cm
Imp. F. Champenois, Paris
Cond A. Framed.
Bibl: Rennert/Weill, 31 (color); Bridges, A21, p. 59 (color); DFP-II, 639; Schardt, 126 (color); Wagner, 76 (color); Phillips I, 430; III, 529
"Mucha went all out with a most opulent design. The shy maiden, kneeling, enraptured with the tranquility of the bay of Monte Carlo, is completely encircled by the curving stalks of lilac and hydrangea, featuring some of the most intricate conflorescences ever painted by Mucha. Since the client was a railroad—Chemins de Fer P.L.M.—it is probable that the design is meant to suggest the tracks and wheels that convey the public to Monte Carlo." (Rennert/Weill, p. 136).
Est: $5000-6000.

See color plate 25.

188. L'Année Qui Vient. 1897.
12¼ x 26¼ in/31 x 66.7 cm
Framed.
Bibl: Rennert/Weill, 46 (poster).
Preliminary drawing in sepia and white conté, pencil and ink on board; pencil signed.
"L'Année qui vient" (The Coming Year) was a calendar project with an image showing a dreamy vision of a girl carrying a bouquet, in sepia monochrome, surrounded by an elaborate decorative frame. It was also produced as a print without the calendarium section and also as a postcard for Vin Mariani. The print was sold under the title of "Evocation."
Est: $4000-5000.

189. West End Review (Cover). 1897.
10¾ x 15⅛ in/27.3 x 38.3 cm
Imp. Lemercier, Paris
Cond A. Framed.
Bibl: Rennert/Weill, 50 (poster)
This is the cover of the January 1898 issue of the magazine; its image is identical to the 9-sheet poster created by Mucha and also printed by Lemercier. "One of the many small literary magazines which proliferated around the turn of the century, this one started as *The West End* in London in April of 1897, changing its name to *The West End Review* with the June number of that year, and continuing publication until its September, 1899 issue. The lady in red, an oversized portfolio on her lap, is obviously ready to jot down some interesting notes with a quill pen. The circular motif is provided this time by a huge palm frond forming a semi-circle of green to complement the color of the dress. Note the delightful touch of the two cherubs, one whispering in the girl's ear, the other sulking off by herself, apparently feeling left out of the proceedings." (Rennert/Weill, p. 202).
Est: $1500-1800.

190. Job. 1898.
41 x 60⅝ in/104.2 x 153.9 cm
Imp. F. Champenois, Paris
Cond A
Bibl: Rennert/Weill, 51 (color); Bridges A36, p. 67 (color); DFP-II, 634; Mucha/Paris, 76; Wagner, 73 (color); Weill, p. 42; Phillips II, 425; III, 532; V, 46 (color)
"This is a Mucha classic by any criterion. From the circular motif and refined composition to the bold and harmonious use of colors and type—even down to the 'deliciously designed hands,' as *L'Estampe et l'affiche* put it in 1898—it all comes together with unsurpassed grace, beauty and force." (Rennert/Weill, p. 204). The colors in this exquisite copy are especially brilliant.
Est: $6000-7000.

See color plate 26.

ALPHONSE MUCHA (continued)

191. Waverley Cycles. 1898.
42¾ x 33¼ in/108.6 x 84.3 cm
Imp. F. Champenois, Paris
Cond B−/ Some tears, largely at paper edges; small stains in woman's shoulder; folds show; colors excellent. Framed.
Bibl: Rennert/Weill, 52 (color); Bridges A25; DFP-II, 642; Mucha/Paris, A53; Bicycle Posters, 55; Phillips II, 421 (color).

"Waverley was an American brand of bicycle, manufactured at Indianapolis, but with representation in the major European countries. It was a sturdy machine, and Mucha did not bother to try to show it by drawing the cycle itself, but expressed it symbolically by having the rather resolute young lady leaning on an anvil. She is holding in her hand a branch of laurel leaves, probably to indicate the accolades and prizes won by the product. In keeping with this simple and direct message, Mucha's design is almost austere by comparison with some of his other works, but it must be admitted that here, such simplicity is effective." (Rennert/Weill, p. 206).
Est: $5000-6000.

192. Médée. 1898.
29⅛ x 80⅞ in/73.9 x 205.4 cm
Imp. F. Champenois, Paris
Cond A−/ Several unobtrusive tears, largely in bottom background and at paper edges; colors and image excellent. Framed.
Bibl: Rennert/Weill, 53 (color); Bridges A33, p. 65 (color); DFP-II, 645; Mucha/Paris 93, A34; Abdy, p. 138; Phillips V, 45 (color)

"Médée," based on the classic Greek tragedy by Euripides, was written by Catulle Mendès expressly for Sarah Bernhardt. Mucha "carefully conveys the antique origin of the play by the mosaic background and the Greek letter 'D,' as well as by the pagan spiked halo behind Medea's head, and gives the tragic scene a majestic sweep that arrests the eye and leads it to the gleaming dagger. The expression of stark horror in Sarah's eyes is a masterful stroke, as is the serpentine bracelet adorning her forearm." (Rennert/Weill, p. 210).
Est: $9000-10000.

See color plate 27.

193. Bénédictine. 1898.
29⅝ x 82⅛ in/75.4 x 208.5 cm
Imp. F. Champenois, Paris
Cond A
Bibl: Rennert/Weill, 58 (color); Bridges A8, p. 52 (color); DFP-II, 648; Mucha/Paris, A35; Phillips I, 426; II, 416.

"A rare poster for Bénédictine, showing two girls in the process of pressing flowers in a book—a reference to the variety of fine herbs which go into the preparation of the liqueur. The bottom panel shows the Fécamp Abbey in northern France; the drink is prepared by the Legrand Company in the town itself." (Rennert/Weill, p. 224).
Est: $6500-7000.

194. Eveil du Matin. 1899.
15⅞ x 41⅜ in/40.2 x 105.1 cm
Imp. F. Champenois (not shown)
Cond B+/ Very unobtrusive horizontal tear across center image; small tears in top margin and border; colors excellent. Framed.
Bibl: Rennert/Weill, 62 (color); Bridges P28-31, pp 32-33 (color).

One of the four panels in the series "The Times of Day," this is titled "Eveil du Matin" (Morning Awakening). "Each girl appears in an outdoor setting, with slender trees or tall flowers emphasizing her slim figure. . . . The borders are worked out in such an exquisite pattern that each picture appears to be mounted in an elaborate frame of its own, or else seen through a decorated window. Quite possibly Mucha's whole concept for this series was that of gothic stained glass windows." (Rennert/Weill, p. 232).
Est: $2000-2500.

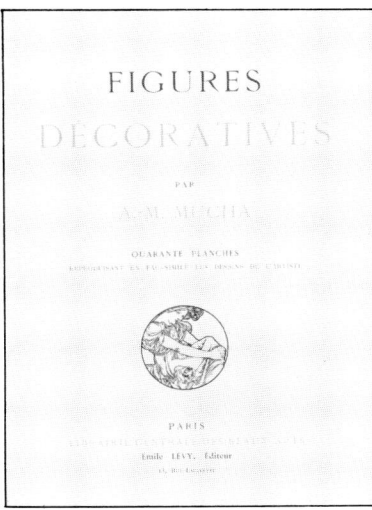

195. Repos de la Nuit. 1899.
15⅛ x 41¼ in/38.4 x 104.8 cm
Imp. F. Champenois (not shown)
Cond A. Framed.
Bibl: See No. 194
"Repos de la Nuit" (Nightly Rest) is the fourth panel in "The Times of Day" series.
Est: $2000-2500.

196. Croquis.
13⅝ x 16 in/34.5 x 40.5 cm
Framed.
Pencil drawing on board, signed in pencil.
Estate stamp lower right and that of Narodni Galerie of Prague on verso.
It is not clear what the purpose of these sketches was. As they show a woman with owl on her lap and a glass of champagne in her hand, it may well have been a preliminary drawing for a New Year's greeting card.
Est: $1800-2000.

197. Chasse (Hunting). 1894.
43½ x 62¾ in/110.5 x 159.5 cm
Imp. Camis, Paris (not shown)
Cond B-/ Restored loss at left paper edge; unobtrusive tears in image and at paper edges; shellac coated. Framed.
Bibl: Rennert/Weill, A. 1
"In 1894, Mucha designed four natural scenes for Home-Décor, a store selling decorative items, ornaments, room dividers and art reproductions for the home. The scenes were titled Flower, Fruit, Fishing and Hunting, and although lyrical in conception, they were executed in the meticulously realistic style of Mucha's book illustrations. They were offered in two different sizes as inexpensive simulations of original artwork, and were reproduced on canvas by a technique which gave them the superficial appearance of oil paintings." (Rennert/Weill, p. 378).
Est: $3000-3500.

See color plate 22.

198. Figures Décoratives. 1905.
13 x 18 in/33 x 45.8 cm
Published by Librairie Centrale des Beaux-Arts, Paris, 1905.
The binding and cover are worn, but the plates are in excellent condition (although a previous owner insisted on placing his initials in upper right border of all plates, but well removed from image.)
Total 36 of the original 40 plates (missing are No. 10, 15, 22, 29). Mucha's women are rendered with appealing grace, graphic force and decorative zeal.
Est: $3000-3500.

MANUEL ORAZI (1860-1934)
199. Ligue Vinicole de France. c. 1900.
53½ x 38¼ in/136 x 97.2 cm
Imp. Charles Verneau, Paris
Cond B+/ Small stain lower left in dress; unobtrusive folds. Framed.
Bibl: Phillips V, 49 (color)
It is often said that Orazi was a brilliant colorist; surely few of his works display that talent better than this poster for the French Wine Society. A young maiden harvests the rich nectar of the grapes in a most unusual way, by hand, while a curious cherub is dipping a tip of his arrow in it to send an intoxicating message. The soft autumnal colors, with earth tones of ever so slight gradations, add to the bacchanalian design.
Est: $4000-5000.

See color plate 28.

MANUEL ORAZI (1860-1934) and AUGUSTE FRANCOIS GORGUET (1862-1927)
200. Théodora. 1884.
34¾ x 49¼ in/88.2 x 125 cm
Imp. Delanchy, Ancourt & Cie., Paris
Cond B+/ Some tears at paper edges and at folds; unobtrusive creasing; image and colors excellent.
Bibl: DFP-II, 672; Maitres, 214; Reims, 921; Abdy, p. 131; Phillips I, 447; II, 448
Victorien Sardou wrote the play, "Théodora," expressly for Sarah Bernhardt and it was a role made to order for her: Theodora, Empress of the Byzantine empire in the 6th century, was the wife of Justinian I and an actress noted for her beauty who had great influence on the political and religious thinking at court. The mosaic design in the poster suggests the Byzantine decorative style and in particular the famous mosaics of Theodora and Justinian at Ravenna. The description of this poster in the Reims 1896 exhibition catalogue indicates that the "byzantine mosaic decor" is by Orazi, the design is by Gorguet, and the scene shows "the arrest of the insulter of the Empress." (Reims, 922). Maindron declared it "une affiche parfaite," and Sagot, in his 1891 catalogue said it was a "très belle composition."
Est: $1000-1200.

PAL (Jean de Paléologue, 1860-1942)
The Rumanian-born artist worked in England under the name of Julius Price and then went to Paris and assumed the name of Pal, creating thousands of illustrations and over a hundred posters in the period 1893-1900, the hallmark of which is always a sensuous, extremely well-endowed lady. Charles Matlack Price commented that "Pal's idea was to make drawings of a nature more commercial than those of Chéret, yet no less artistic. He was also the only designer at that time, except Chéret, who understood the technique of lithography, and was able to put his own touches on the stones." (p. 68). He apparently came to the United States with Sarah Bernhardt in 1900, settled in New York, working as portrait painter, illustrator, billboard painter, film designer and cartoon animator. He became a U.S. citizen in 1923 and lived his last two years in Miami.

201. Cléo de Mérode.
36⅞ x 50¾ in/93.5 x 128.9 cm
Imp. Chardin, Paris
Cond B / Folds show; slight staining at center of folds; colors excellent.
Bibl: DFP-II, 704
"The reigning belle of Paris . . . ballet girl at the Opéra, her carriage in the Bois . . . her diamonds are superb . . . her eyes are the toast of the clubs and the boulevards . . . she reached glory by her head, not her feet." In 1895, this is what was said of Cléo de Mérode, the fabulous beauty of the Belle Epoque. She danced not only at the Opéra, but performed at the Opéra-Comique as well. The great beauty made her farewell in Paris in 1934 in a Waltz partnered by Boris Skibine, father of the contemporary choreographer and ballet director, George Skibine. She had a romantic affair with Leopold II, King of the Belgians, whose enemies nicknamed him "Cléopold." Cléo herself died at the age of ninety-one. The dancer is shown in aquamarine blue costume, yellow background, shadow in lavender and orange, text in green. This may well have been used as a stock poster by her; the copy in cited work is without letters.
Est: $1000-1200.

PL 30 Théophile-Alexandre Steinlen No. 219

PL 31 Ettorino Andreini No. 352

PL 32 Théophile-Alexandre Steinlen No. 220

PL 33 Théophile-Alexandre Steinlen No. 222

PL 34   Henri de Toulouse-Lautrec   No. 232

PL 35   Henri de Toulouse-Lautrec   No. 237

PL 36   Henri de Toulouse-Lautrec   No. 233

PL 37   Henry de Monnnier   No. 303

PL 38 — Théophile-Alexandre Steinlen — No. 228

PL 39 — Leonetto Cappiello — No. 137

PL 40 — Leonetto Cappiello — No. 256

PL 41 George Barbier No. 244	PL 42 Jean A. Mercier No. 301
PL 43 A.M. Cassandre No. 273	PL 44 A.M. Cassandre No. 276

202. Supreme Cusenier.
45¼ x 62⅝ in/114.8 x 159 cm
Imp. Chardin, Paris
Cond B+/ Folds show slightly.
Supreme Cusenier liqueur, specially marketed in a "bouteille inviolable," a feature lending value and mystery to the product; blue background, red lettering. Pal's design enhances the image of voluptuous oriental splendor which the advertiser obviously wanted to convey. Rare.
Est: $600-800.

203. Rouart Geneste & Herscher Eau.
43⅜ x 59⅜ in/110 x 151 cm
Imp. Paul Dupont, Paris
Cond B / Folds show; tears and staining at horizontal fold in upper right image; image and colors excellent.
Water nymph oversees water dispenser (dolphin-headed fountain) while crowd eagerly waits to fill their glasses. Figures in red and yellow, blue background. This is the version before letters.
Est: $600-800.

204. Folies-Bergère.
41⅞ x 29⅝ in/106.4 x 75.6 cm
Imp. Paul Dupont, Paris
Cond A
It's a colorful and glowing scene in the boxes at the Folies-Bergère: spectators are distracted by a charming bon vivant. Red, bright blue and yellow predominate. One of the rarest and most interesting of Pal's music-hall posters.
Est: $700-900.

205. Folies-Bergère.
40 x 51 in/101.7 x 129.1 cm
Imp. Paul Dupont, Paris
Cond A-/ Small creases at paper edges; colors and image excellent.
Bibl: DFP-II, 693; Meisterplakate, 175
Dancer in light red costume with yellow veil in pastel colors; blue and yellow background and shadow suggest stage lights. Text in light orange. This was the stock poster, with right side for text as required—what a charmer!
Est: $600-800.

HERMANN PAUL (1864-1940)

206. Salon des Cent. 1895.
19¼ x 25⅝ in/48.8 x 65 cm
E. Ladam, Paris
Cond A-/ Tear at top left corner; image and colors excellent.
Bibl: DFP-II, 706; Reims, 960; Schardt, 54 (color); Color Revolution, 58; Meisterplakate, 186 (color); Phillips I, 462
Portrait of the artist, pencil and portfolio in hand, with bright orange hair, blue smock, lavender bow and light green background. One of the best in the distinguished Salon des Cent series.
Est: $1200-1500.

207. Tournoi Franco-Italian. 1895.
24⅝ x 31½ in/62.6 x 80 cm
Imp. Edw. Ancourt, Paris
Cond B-/ Small tears and stains at folds; colors and image excellent.
Bibl: DFP-II, 707; Reims, 961; Livre de l'Affiche, 122 (color)
An excellent design for a fencing tournament organized by the publication L'Escrime Française. There is a frieze of feet and formal shirts and faces framing the image; lettering is well incorporated in the design; the reserve (paper white) is used to good advantage. Colors are pink, lavender and black.
Est: $400-500.

RENE PEAN (1875-)
208. Aux Trois Quartiers. 1899.
42⅜ x 61⅞ in/107.7 x 157.2 cm
Imp. Chaix, Paris
Cond A−/ Some staining at folds; colors excellent.
Bibl: Maitres, 211; Phillips VII, 132
Péan was a student of Chéret, working under his tutelage at the Chaix plant. In this poster for a Paris department store selling oriental rugs, he shows an Arab salesman in yellow robe sitting among multi-colored, multi-patterned rugs and tapestries. The mosque and camel riders in background lend authenticity to the product.
Est: $500-600.

MAURICE REALIER-DUMAS (1860-1928)
209. Exposition Galerie G. Petit. 1895.
22¾ x 70½ in/57.2 x 179.1 cm
V. Palyart, Paris
Cond B−/ Some tears, largely in text area at top and at paper edges; restores losses in text area at bottom; colors printed slightly differently in top and bottom sheets.
Bibl: DFP-II, 734; Reims, 979; Phillips III, 575
In this two-sheet poster for the annual exhibition of the International Society of Painting and Sculpture, Realier-Dumas gives us forms reduced to flat shapes in subtle, sober colors. The mosaic design in text area lends antique quality to the poster. Maindron states that this artist gets his inspiration from Greek vases. Robe is mauve; background is dark red.
Est: $700-900.

GEORGES REDON (1869-1943)
210. Scala. Tournée des Grands Ducs. 1906.
36⅝ x 51⅛ in/93 x 129.8 cm
Imp. Minot, Paris
Cond A−/ Some very unobtrusive creases in background; image and colors excellent.
This three-act "Fantaisie" at the Scala obviously includes a grand duke who is taken with a pretty and confident young dancer. Redon uses a range of lithographic techniques—crayon in both broad and narrow strokes, India ink in bold splashes. Colors are sepia, brown, red and black.
Est: $500-600.

THEODORE VAN RYSSELBERGHE (1862-1926)
211. N. Lembrée. 1897.
19 x 26⅜ in/48.2 x 66.9 cm
Imp. Vve Monom, Bruxelles
Cond B / Unobtrusive tear into image at lower right; small tears in margins; colors excellent. Framed.
Bibl: DFP-II, 1128; Belgique/Paris, 11; Belle Epoque, 135; Schindler, p. 132; Phillips V, 67 (color)
The great Belgian artist gives us a carefully composed design in delicate tones and flat shapes enhanced by simple decorative touches of line and texture in this poster for the Brussels print dealer, N. Lembrée. In all his posters, including his famous ones for the *Libre Esthétique*, Van Rysselberghe makes the strong colors of the woman's dress (here a cape) the focal point from which the rest of the composition emanates. The telephone at left would indicate that an appointment can easily be made. Colors are orange, light orange, light green and blue.
Est: $1000-1200.

SATGE.
212. Bal Annuel. c. 1902.
26 x 34⅞ in/66 x 88.6 cm
Moullot Fils Aine, Marseille
Cond B−/ Split at folds; some small tears; colors and image excellent. Framed.
A lush, romantic poster for the annual ball for students and alumni of the Ecole des Beaux-Arts of Marseille. The graceful and romantic image is delicately drawn in subtle colors—plum and yellow, with gold border and lettering. The decorative emblem includes palette with brushes, a hammer and a triangle, symbols of studies at the school, to further embellish this image. It's a gem!
Est: $1000-1200.

213

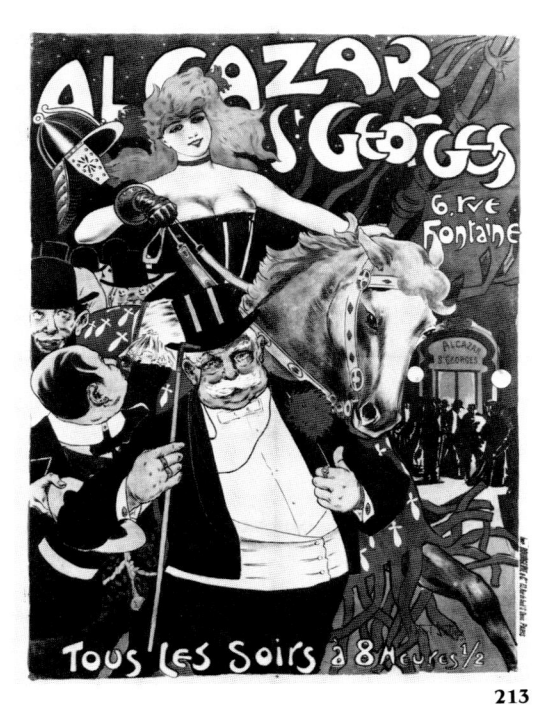

214

215

216

217

ROBERT SALLES (1871-1929)
213. Alcazar St. Georges. 1903.
46⅛ x 62½ in/117.2 x 158.7 cm
Imp. Bourgerie, Paris
Cond B / Slight staining at folds
A buxom performer on a horse attracts attention to the establishment by emphasizing the St. George and the dragon connection. A prime prospect is a portly moneyed gentleman in foreground. Colors are red, orange and black. The artist's name is not clear.
Est: $400-500.

MICHEL SIMONIDY (1870-1933)
In 1900, Simonidy created six charming posters for the newspaper *Le Figaro*. Each shows a woman from a different part of the world reading this newspaper. It is a most distinguished—and rare—series.

214. Le Figaro. 1900.
30⅛ x 47 in/76.5 x 119.5 cm
Imp. Lemercier, Paris
Cond B / Unobtrusive folds; some tears; colors excellent.
Woman in Spanish costume in blue, with yellow trim, background in violet and yellow.
Est: $500-600.

215. Figaro. 1900.
31¼ x 47⅛ in/79.4 x 119.8 cm
Imp. Lemercier, Paris
Cond B / Unobtrusive tears in image; colors excellent
Reader in costume of red, white and green—probably a lady from Holland—with blue-green background.
Est: $500-600.

216. Le Figaro. 1900.
30⅛ x 46¼ in/76.5 x 117.5 cm
Imp. Lemercier, Paris
Cond B / Unobtrusive tears and folds; colors excellent.
Bibl: Affiches de Presse, 81
Russian woman in black tunic and red blouse, with cream background.
Est: $500-600.

217. Le Figaro. 1900.
31¼ x 46¾ in/79.3 x 118.8 cm
Imp. Lemercier, Paris
Cond B / Some tears and unobtrusive folds; colors excellent.
Japanese woman in green kimono; background in mauve.
Est: $500-600.

COLLECT ALL THE BOOKS OF POSTER AUCTIONS INTERNATIONAL for an essential reference library and Price Guide to original posters.

If you do not have Volume I—PREMIER POSTERS—send $30.00, to cover book and mailing charges, to Poster Auctions International, 37 Riverside Drive, New York, N.Y. 10023. Be sure to specify you are ordering PAI-I. You may also find it at any bookstore which carries fine art books; if they don't have it, they can order it for you from Peregrine Smith Books of Layton, Utah.

THEOPHILE-ALEXANDRE STEINLEN (1859-1923)

Steinlen arrived in Paris from his native Switzerland in 1881; his first poster dates from 1885 and, in a long and extremely prolific career which saw him illustrate about 100 books and over 1,000 issues of periodicals, as well as create paintings, lithographs and bronzes, he produced about 50 posters. Abdy notes that "Steinlen was one of the four or five great poster artists of his time; all his lithographic work is distinguished by a freshness and vigour which makes it powerful, and a simplicity and sympathy which makes it appealing." (p. 94).

218. Le Journal, 1899.
46½ x 73 in/118.1 x 185.4 cm
Imp. Charle Verneau
Cond B / A few restorations, largely in top and bottom text area; a few tears and creases, largely in bottom text area; image and colors excellent. Framed.
Bibl: DFP-II, 793a; Crauzat, 503; Schardt, p. 151; Steinlen, 82 (Pl. 14, color); Timeless Images, 52 (var); Phillips I, 554; III, 587 (color); PAI-I, 245 (color).

This is the larger format and is the censored version, with full text banner, to advertise the serialization of the novel "La Traite des Blanches" ("White Slavery") in the daily Le Journal.
Est: $5000-6000.

219. Exposition à la Bodinière. 1894.
32⅛ x 23⅞ in/81.6 x 60.6 cm
Imp. Charles Verneau, Paris
Cond A-/ Several small carefully restored tears; very unobtrusive folds; image and colors excellent. Framed.
Bibl: Crauzat, 492; DFP-II, 782; Schardt, p. 135; Abdy, p. 95; Steinlen, p. 396; Takashimaya, 8 (color); Phillips I, 544; II, 539, 540.

For his own exposition, Steinlen indulges himself in one of his favorite subjects—cats. The calico female in the foreground is purring contentedly while the black, angular male is contemplating a trip down a new alley. Steinlen was correctly described at the time as a "chataphile convaincu" (A dyed-in-the-wool cat lover).
Est: $3500-4000.

See color plate 30.

220. Chocolats & Thés. 1895.
23⅜ x 31½ in/59.4 x 80 cm
Imp. Courmont, Paris
Cond B / A few tears and restorations, largely in paper edge and fold; image and colors excellent. Framed.
Bibl: Crauzat, 494; Schardt, p. 165; Steinlen, Fig. 84; DFP-II, 784; Abdy, p. 98; Wagner, 62 (color); Timeless Images, 49 (color); Phillips I, 547; VII, 140 (color)

A charming domestic scene advertises a tea importer. The cat was obviously expecting a dish of milk that would be used in the making of cocoa, the company's other most popular product. The girl is Steinlen's daughter, Colette, and the woman is probably his wife Emilie. More than any other poster artist, Steinlen seduces us by an overpowering charm and sympathetic treatment of subjects.
Est: $6000-7000.

See color plate 32.

221. Lait Pur Stérilisé. 1894.
39¼ x 54¾ in/99.5 x 139 cm
Imp. Charles Verneau, Paris
Cond B / Very unobtrusive tears and restored losses at some folds and at paper edges; colors and image excellent. Framed.
Bibl: Crauzat, 491; DFP-II, 783; Musée d'Affiche, 54; Maitres, 95; Schardt, 155; Abdy, p. 97; Affichomanie, 114; Wagner, 59 (color); Weill, p. 43; Phillips I, 545; II, 541; V, 55 (color).

There were three formats to this poster, a larger (see 222) and smaller size having been printed as well. This is the version before letters. All the warmth, humanity and affection for which he is so loved comes through

gloriously in this sympathetic treatment of his daughter Colette and three of the many cats which filled their home. The great American poster collector, Charles Knowles Bolton, writing a year after publication of this poster, called it "the most attractive poster ever made." Louis Rhead at the same time commented: "When I saw it in Paris last year, sometimes in rows of six with its bright red dress, it seemed to me the best and brightest form of advertising that had appeared." That's a judgment that remains valid today.
Est: $7000-8000.

222. Lait Pur Stérilisé. 1896.
58 x 72 in/147.4 x 183 cm
Imp. Charles Verneau, Paris (not shown)
Cond B−/ Some tears at folds; a few unobtrusive restored paper losses in dress and background; image and colors excellent. Framed.
Bibl: See 221.
This is the extremely rare (only one other copy is known to exist) two-sheet version of this poster which Steinlen redrew two years later. There are some slight changes in the design—the bowl is tilted forward, the tails of the cats are more fully shown, etc. The overpowering charm of the design remains—all the more so because of its large, six-feet high, format. This version, too, is before letters.
Est: $22000-25000.

See color plate 33.

223. Nestlé's Swiss Milk. 1895.
9⅛ x 12⅝ in/23.2 x 32 cm
Waterlow & Sons, London
Cond A. Framed.
Bibl: See 221; also: Hiatt, p. 97; Phillips II, 542.
Except for the text change and the much smaller size, this is identical to the French version. It now promotes Nestlé's Swiss Milk, which is "Richest in cream." We might speculate that this version came about this way: The original version had been printed in February 1894 by Verneau. Bella, the British manufacturer and poster promoter, was in Paris in the spring of that year to gather posters for his upcoming exhibition at the Royal Aquarium in London that October. He was so impressed with it that he bought the copyright for the British market from Verneau. He then announced in his catalogue, under the listing of this poster only, "This Copyright for Sale." In walks the head of Nestlé's, is equally impressed, bargains with Mr. Bella and reproduces it. Charles Hiatt, in October 1895, reproduced this Nestlé's version, without text, in his book.
Est: $2000-2500.

224. Chat Noir. 1896.
38⅝ x 55⅛ in/98.1 x 139.8 cm
Imp. Charles Verneau, Paris
Cond B / Folds show somewhat, with some related tears; repaired losses at top and bottom paper edges; a few unobtrusive tears in image; colors excellent.
Bibl: Crauzat, 496; DFP-II, 787; Abdy, p. 99; Timeless Images, 51 (color); Wagner, 63 (color); Phillips I, 548; II, 544; III, 590.
Salis, who owned the theatre-restaurant called "Chat Noir," was an early supporter of Steinlen. This poster went through several design changes and one smaller format. On the cat's halo are the words "Mon Joye, Montmartre." The colors are red and black on buff paper. An interesting interpretation is offered by Brian Reade: he feels that this poster was Steinlen's way of kidding Mucha by showing a cat "with its tail falling down like a lock of Mucha hair and with a halo like a black doily at the back of its head." When this "cabaret artistique" moved to larger quarters, Aristide Bruant took it over and renamed it "Le Mirliton."
Est: $4000-4500.

225. Children. c. 1919.
44¾ x 34⅝ in/113.7 x 88 cm
Imp. H. Chachoin, Paris
Cond A−/ Small creases in margins; image excellent. Framed.
A long line of children, in red, black and tan, against grey background. It is not clear if this image was intended as a poster or simply as a print. The space in the top and the large format indicate it was probably intended for an advertisement. Steinlen created many posters for the war effort and for all kinds of worthy causes; if the treatment is at times somber and harsh, it also arouses our sympathies. Without knowing the exact purpose of this design, we are nonetheless moved by it.
Est: $700-900.

STEINLEN (continued)

226. Racahout des Arabes. 1905.
16½ x 24 in/42 x 61.1 cm
Imp. Eugene Verneau, Paris
Cond A−/ Small restored tear in image. Framed.
Bibl: Crauzat, 512; Phillips I, 551; II, 547 (var)
This poster was also produced with English text: "Delangrenier's Arabian Racahout—an excellent food for children." (*See* Phillips II, 547.) Pale soft colors include pink, yellow and green.
Est: $800-1000.

227. War Series. 1915.
15 x 21⅞ in/38 x 55 cm
Cond A
Bibl: Steinlen, 160-167, fig. 44
Set of 32 lithographs from the deluxe edition of 100, each plate with remarque and pencil signed; numbered 47/100. (There was also a numbered edition of 400 without signature and remarque.) Scenes depicting soldiers, victims and refugees of World War I, in black and white, several with color highlights.
Est: $1000-1200.

228. Jean Börlin-Jenny Hasselquist. 1920.
Each: 62¼ x 90½ in/158.5 x 228 cm
Imp. H. Chachoin, Paris
Cond B+/ Small tears at paper edges, some staining; colors excellent.
Two previously unknown posters for the Swedish Ballet.
These are the largest and last of the posters created by Steinlen. They were created for the premier performances of the Swedish Ballet at the Théatre des Champs-Elysées in Paris in October, 1920.
Jean Börlin, seen here in a sailor costume in blue, yellow and white, dances a "jig" with cigar in hand. Jenny Hasselquist is shown as a Spanish dancer in green, red and gold with castenets; text in both is in gold. Börlin (1893-1930) was a radical innovator in ballet. By 1918, he was the premier dancer of his country, and formed the Swedish Ballet troupe with Rolf de Maré for the purpose of touring Europe and the United States. It gained him worldwide fame, and he appeared in two films by René Clair, *Entr'acte* (1924) and *Le Voyage Imaginaire* (1925). Hasselquist was a multi-talented Swedish performer, born in 1894, who first appeared on stage as a dancer in 1915. She joined Börlin's Swedish Ballet troupe with which she toured Europe, scoring great triumphs with her interpretations of "Jeux," "Iberia" and "La nuit de St. Jean." She also appeared in a number of Swedish and German silent films, among which Ernst Lubitsch's *Sumurun* (1920) is probably the best known. She opened her own ballet school in 1932.
Est: $3000-4000. (2)

See color plate 38.

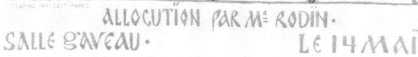

231

232

233

234

DIMITRI STELLETSKI (1875-)
229. Artistes Russes.
31¾ x 47¾ in/80.5 x 121.2 cm
I. Lapina, Paris
Cond A−/ Staining at horizontal center fold; image excellent.
Bibl: DFP-II, 802
Stelletski, who studied at the St. Petersburg Academy of Art before moving to Paris, was much influenced by the decorative style of Russian painting and icons and the Byzantine elements found in them. This poster announces a performance for the benefit of Russian students residing in France. Note that Auguste Rodin was honorary chairman and also delivered the major address.
Est: $300-400.

M. STEPHANE
230. Sadi Alardin. Vente de Collections.
34½ x 48⅛ in/87.5 x 122.1 cm
Imp. J.E. Goossens, Bruxelles
Cond B / Unobtrusive tears and stains at folds; colors and image excellent.
Bibl: Reims, 1036

A curious way of advertising a sale of antiques: a somewhat disreputable merchant, in red robe, displays one of the curios from his inventory for a lovely young treasure hunter. Colors are red, blue, yellow and olive. Nothing is known of Stéphane; this poster, which was displayed in the 1896 Reims exhibition, has a style of lettering reminiscent of posters by Mignot which were also printed at Goossens.
Est: $400-500.

HENRI DE TOULOUSE-LAUTREC (1864-1901)

Each year brings increased interest in the lithographs of Toulouse-Lautrec and it seems that the pace is accelerating. This summer the collection of Dr. and Mrs. Kurt Wagner, comprising all the posters of Lautrec, were on display at the Los Angeles County Museum of Art. The long planned exhibition of his lithographs at the Museum of Modern Art in New York should finally open the same time as this auction. And Wolfgang Wittrock's 2-volume catalogue raisonné of all Lautrec lithographs and prints will be published at the same time. I am grateful to the publisher, Philip Wilson of London, for allowing me to see advance galleys of this major work so that we could reference it in this catalogue.

Ebria Feinblatt, in an incisive introduction to the Los Angeles exhibition's catalogue which I commend to everyone interested in this subject, concludes: "Toulouse-Lautrec's greatest posters have become the classic icons of their genre. With graphically smoothened surfaces, bold, linear accents, and sprinkled enlivenment of tones, the synthesizing summariness of their images provides all that can be evoked in the passing of an instant." (Wagner, p. 34). Alain Weill, in his new book, also to be published at the time of this sale, notes that "Enchanted with Japanese engravings, like the Nabis, Lautrec loved the flat patches of vivid color, the powerful outlines and bold compositions: he made a riot of colors which can shout as they will." (Weill, p. 35).

231. Bruant au Mirliton. 1893.
22½ x 29⅞ in/57 x 76 cm
Imp. Chaix, Paris
Cond B+/ Small, skillfully repaired tears at paper edge; image and colors excellent. Framed.
Bibl: Wittrock P10c; Delteil, 349; Adhemar, 71; Adriani, 15; Wagner 11 (color); Julien XI; Phillips II, 342
The third state, in olive green and black ink only, to advertise Bruant's songbook, which was illustrated by Steinlen. For the startling back view of Bruant to work, you had to have a very confident painter and a very confident singer—both were at hand here.
Est: $3500-4000.

232. Divan Japonais. 1893.
42½ x 31¾ in/62.3 x 80.6 cm
Imp. Edw. Ancourt, Paris
Cond A. Framed.
Bibl: Wittrock P11; Delteil, 341; Adhemar, 11; Adriani, 9; DFP-II, 824; Maitres, 2; Abdy, p. 75; Julien III; Wagner, 3; Phillips I, 337; II, 337
Poster for the café-concert, Divan Japonais, showing Jane Avril and the critic Edouard Dujardin in the audience, not really looking at Yvette Guilbert, recognized by her long black gloves, on stage. Maindron declared it "le chef-d'oeuvre" of Lautrec. For an excellent appreciation of this masterful work, see Ebria Feinblatt's introduction to the Los Angeles County Museum of Art's catalogue of their recent Toulouse-Lautrec exhibition (Wagner, pp 21-22). *This is an exceedingly fresh copy.*
Est: $20000-22000.

See color plate 34.

233. May Belfort. 1895.
23⅝ x 31⅜ in/60 x 79.7 cm
Kleinmann, Paris
Cond B−/ Slight light staining; some unobtrusive tears at and near paper edges; some skinned paper pock marks at bottom. Framed.
Bibl: Wittrock P14.B.iv.; Delteil, 354; Adhemar, 116; Adriani, 136; DFP-II, 837; Abdy, p. 82; Maindron, p. 113; Julien XVI; Wagner, 16 (color)
Ebria Feinblatt points out that this is one of "three famous posters portraying solitary female figures." The other two are May Milton (*see* 235) and Revue Blanche (*see* 234). May Belfort "was a special friend of her compatriot, the entertainer May Milton . . . Her famous ditty of double entendre went:
  I've got a little cat
  And I'm very fond of that,
  But Daddy wouldn't buy me a bow-wow . . .
In the poster Belfort is framed by long black curls under an enormous cap, her hands hiding most of a yellow-eyed kitten. Lautrec presents her on a diagonal plane, her brilliant orange-red dress slanting to the left, her left shoulder brought forward in the picture plane to place her in a frontal position. The flat sweep of her gown below the frilled, green-splattered sleeves is, taken by itself, merely a red sail or banner." (Wagner, p. 27).
Est: $7000-8000.

235

236

TOULOUSE-LAUTREC (continued)

234. La Revue Blanche. 1895.
36½ x 50⅝ in/92.7 x 128.6 cm
Imp. Edw. Ancourt, Paris
Cond A. Framed.
Bibl: Wittrock P16c; Delteil, 355; Adhemar, 115;
Adriani, 108; Julien XVII, Abdy, p. 88; Maitres, 82;
Dortu, p. 145; Wagner, 17 (color); DFP-II, 838;
Phillips I, 341; II, 345; V, 38 (color).

Misia, the wife of Thadée Natanson, co-director of the *Revue Blanche*, is shown in several Lautrec drawings and paintings; here, she is portrayed at the ice-skating rink in Paris. She did much to encourage Lautrec's work, especially his early attempts at lithography. Although this poster appears to be printed in two sheets, it is in fact printed on two stones, but on a single sheet. As a result, the paper was "pinched" in the middle and there is the kind of color and registration matching which is usually associated with a two-sheet poster.
Est: $13000-15000.

235. May Milton. 1895.
23⅝ x 30⅞ in/60 x 78.4 cm
Cond C+/ Some unobtrusive tears, largely in blue background and along folds; image and colors very good. Framed.
Bibl: Wittrock P17B; Delteil, 356; Adhemar, 149;
Adriani, 138; DFP-II, 836; Timeless Images, 55;
Julien XVIII; Weill, 50; Wagner, 18; Phillips I, 342;
II, 346; III, 478; PAI-I, 254.

Feinblatt finds this poster "more intriguing" than that for May Belfort. "Emphasizing the 'horselike' jaw of the young English performer, who wanted a poster for her tour in the United States, Lautrec, influenced by Utamaro's style of pursed lips, twisted Milton's mouth in profile and portrayed her in a sacklike gown in which her body disappears completely, even under the four stripes that should have helped to define it. Since the two Mays were such great friends, Lautrec portrayed

237

240

one in red and the other in blue 'so that,' he is quoted, 'the spots (i.e., color schemes) shall be married as well'." She concludes: "The austerity of the drawing, the coloring, and the undeniable presence of the figure are arresting." (Wagner, p. 27).
Est: $5000-6000.

236. Troupe de Mlle. Eglantine. 1896.
30⅝ x 23¾ in/77.8 x 60.3 cm
Cond B+/ Expertly repaired tears at left paper edge and at upper right; colors and image excellent. Framed.
Bibl: Wittrock P21C; Delteil, 361; Adhemar, 198;
Adriani 165; DFP-II, 850; Abdy, p. 87; Wagner, 23 (color); Julien XXIII; Phillips II, 349

This poster was ordered by Jane Avril (far left) for the dancing troupe of Mlle. Eglantine (second from right) while in England. "The success of Mlle. Eglantine's company in England was ephemeral, but the poster drawn for this occasion created a style. Lautrec invented endless new compositions, and this file of dancers, all thrown into the same movement but each a portrait in itself, gave the poster a new animation and personal character; it is the joyous *chahut* of a group of friends. This cheerful yellow splash shone like a ray of sunlight on the walls." (Dortu, p. 159).
Est: $10000-12000.

237. L'Artisan Moderne. 1896.
24½ x 34¾ in/62.2 x 88.2 cm
Imp. Bourgerie, Paris
Cond C+/ Slight tears, largely at folds; 1x4 in. restored area upper right corner; image and colors excellent. Framed.
Bibl: P24A; Delteil, 350; Adhemar, 70; Adriani, 58;
DFP-II, 835; Abdy, p. 86; Julien XII; Wagner, 12 (color); Phillips II, 343 (color)

"*L'Artisan Moderne* . . . was made to advertise a designers' collective organized in 1896 by André Marty, the editor of *L'Estampe Originale*. The collective produced household objects, such as earthenware, lampshades made from color lithographs, wine jugs, and artistic jewelry, among other pieces. . . . An artisan appears at an early hour in a lady's boudoir, much to her maid's consternation. The woman herself appears pleasantly undisturbed. Humorously, Lautrec included in the picture his friend, the jeweler and medalist Henri Nocq, his head curiously small, uncertainly posed as

the artisan. On Nocq's toolbox Lautrec drew the name of the advertiser, Niederkorn." (Wagner, p. 24).
Est: $6000-7000.

See color plate 35.

238. Cycle Michael. 1896.
50 x 35 in/127 x 88.8 cm
Imp. Chaix, Paris
Cond B / Slight tears and restorations at paper edge; imge excellent. Framed.
Bibl: Wittrock P25; Delteil, 359; Adhemar, 184; Adriani, 194; DFP-II, 849; Julien XXI; Wagner, 21 (color); Phillips II, 348; III, 479

Lautrec's improper drawing of the chain resulted in this design being rejected; he did the only sensible thing, therefore, and ran off 200 copies at his own cost for the amusement of friends and collectors. The cyclist is the British champion Jimmy Michael. A tooth-pick in the mouth was his trademark. The man with the stop watch is the sports correspondent, Frantz Reichel. Bending over the bag in the background is Michael's coach, Choppy Warburton. The scene is the Buffalo track at Neuilly. It was printed in a single, olive-green color.
Est: $4000-5000.

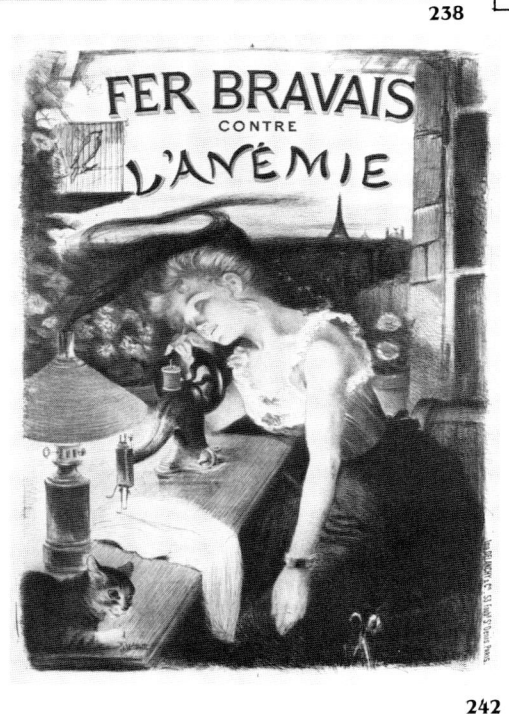

239. La Vache Enragée. 1896.
23⅛ x 32 in/58.3 x 81.2 cm
Imp. Chaix, Paris
Cond B-/ Several well-restored holes in image; some tears and small losses at paper edges and at four corners; mounted on heavy stock. Framed.
Bibl: Wittrock P27A; Delteil, 364; Adhemar, 197; Adriani, 175; Abdy, p. 85; DFP-II, 844; Julien XXVI; Wagner, 26 (color); Phillips III, 481

First state, before letters, of the poster which advertises Willette's magazine, *La Vache Enragée,* which lasted for only one year. Wittrock, who rates the rarity of this state as "uncommon," also indicates that "the image in the poster was drawn by Toulouse-Lautrec in imitation of the style of A. Willette." (p. 808). This is one of the few Lautrec posters with movement: the runaway cow is the centerpiece of a remarkable caricature depicting sheer panic in some, curious non-involvement in others—a reflection of the real world.
Est: $5000-6000.

FERNAND TOUSSAINT (1873-1955)
240. Spa. Exposition des Sports. 1904.
29¾ x 41 in/75.5 x 104 cm
O. De Rycker et Mendel, Bruxelles
Cond A-/ Restored loss at lower left corner; image and colors excellent.
Bibl: Belgique Sportives, 63 (color)

The Belgian artist Fernand Toussaint had a long and productive career as a painter, but executed few posters. He is best known in this medium for his posters for "Le Sillon" and "Café Jacqmotte." Here, three lovely women in lush setting represent the three major sports at the Sports Exposition in Liège. Each carries the appropriate sports equipment—racquet, horse quirt, hunting rifle. Modelled features in natural colors including blue-grey, green, bright blue with grey border and white text; inset at lower left shows "superb casino" and "private club."
Est: $800-1000.

WEILUC (1873-1947)
241. La Folie-Pigalle.
30⅞ x 46⅞ in/78.3 x 119.1 cm
Société Nouvelle d'Art & Décoration, Paris
Cond B+/ Very light staining at horizontal center fold; colors and image excellent.

A seductive invitation offered by a lovely reveler, to join in the extravagence and frivolity of the Folie-Pigalle. Colors are white, yellow and blue on red background. Weiluc, whose real name was Lucien Henri Weil, was a prolific illustrator whose cartoons and drawings appeared in many journals; he did few posters and is best known in this medium for the famous "Frou-Frou" poster of 1900.
Est: $500-600.

ADOLPH WILLETTE (1857-1926)
242. Fer Bravais Contre L'Anémie. 1898.
34½ x 48½ in/87.5 x 123.2 cm
Imp. Delanchy, Paris
Cond B / Upper left corner restored; small tears at top paper edge; colors and image excellent.
Bibl: DFP-II, 892; Affichomanie, 98; Meisterplakate, 239; Color Revolution, p. 64 (color)

A sensitively drawn image in subtle colors advertising an iron supplement: the pale seamstress, exhausted from work and drained by anemia succumbs to sleep while resting her head on her sewing machine. The curling smoke from the lamp, the wide-eyed cat, the yellow bird and the falling scissors are strikingly animated by comparison. *L'Estampe et l'Affiche* commented on its publication that his was "more a print than a poster," was critical of its color scheme, but concluded that "in any case, it's a beautiful lithograph." (1898; p. 98). And the public must have agreed, as it was also reproduced as a supplement to the *Courrier Français* of March 6, 1898.
Est: $500-600.

FRENCH POSTERS – post-1914

243

246

244

245

ANON.
243. Jeanne Bayle.
31½ x 47¼ in/80 x 120 cm
Cond A−/ Small, unobtrusive tears at upper edges. Nothing is known of this glamorous pianist. The colors are black in background and piano, with yellow highlights, dress in black with red details and lettering in red. It is a striking design, using an inverted spotlight effect.
Est: $800-1000.

GEORGE BARBIER (1882-1932)
244. Lyonnelle. 1917.
39¼ x 51⅛ in/100 x 129.9 cm
Atelier MN, Paris
Cond A−/ Very small, unobtrusive repaired hole at bottom center; excellent colors and image. Framed.
Barbier was a painter and illustrator whose first love was the theatre in general and dance in particular. He designed costumes and stage sets for the ballet and produced numerous fashion plates for journals such as *Vogue, Feminia* and *Gazette du Bon Ton*. In this most striking poster, he gives us an exotic dancer, emphasized with rich flesh tones in broad areas, a costume with floral pattern of dark blue ground, light blue and pink flowers. The lettering is stylized into delicate exotic forms. Extremely rare.
Est: $4000-4500.

See color plate 41.

ALFRED BALLOT-BEAUPRE.
245. Pilote d'Avions.
31¼ x 47⅜ in/79.5 x 120.3 cm
Imprimerie Nationale, Paris
Cond A−/ Small tears in lower right margin; colors and image excellent.
A recruiting poster from the Ministry of Aviation inviting young Frenchmen to fulfill their military obligations as airplane pilots. An idealized aerial view, in cheerful colors, from the bright blue biplane. An active Signac-like landscape and harbor view below in blue and yellow with accents of red and light green. This is certainly an appealing way to serve one's country. The French were among the first to realize the potential of air power, and had the first unit attached to the Army in 1910. By the outbreak of World War I in 1914, the French Air Force had 24 squadrons with a total of 160 aircraft of 14 different types—mostly Blériots, Voisins and Caudrons. By mid-1916, this total was increased to 1,500 airraft. There were many other firsts for France in this field: the first industrial production of planes; the first to employ planes for bombardment (August 14, 1914), the first to shoot down an enemy plane in an aerial battle (October 5, 1914), and the first to establish an Aviation Ministry (1915). Vive l'avion!
Est: $500-600.

G.K. BENDA
246. Mistinguett. c. 1913.
46¼ x 62⅛ in/117.5 x 152.1 cm
Philippe G. Dreyfus, Paris
Cond B+/ Several unobtrusive creases, some staining in white paper areas; colors excellent.
Bibl: Phillips I, 43
Possibly the very best poster ever done for the famous performer. Mistinguett is shown in white and green dress, with red accents, against a black background.
Est: $700-900.

PIERRE BOUCHER (1889-1971)
248. Ducretet-Thomson. 1938.
30⅞ x 46⅝ in/78.5 x 118.3 cm
Imp. Printel, Paris
Cond A−/ Slight stains at paper edges.
Bibl: Phillips VII, 152
A montage of photo-offset and lithography gives us a somewhat surrealistic treatment for the radio that is your door to the world. The motto is: "The voice of the world in every home."
Est: $500-600.

ROGER BRODERS (1883-1953)
Broders was the finest designer of French railway posters in the period between the Wars. His travel posters, almost all of which were created for the PLM railroad, show a heightened sense of perspective and linear composition, and this creates a dramatic impact in what might otherwise be an ordinary travel poster. He seems most interested in properly positioning the viewer, usually at the top of a hill or behind some foliage. We therefore never just see a place, we come upon it. This, and his use of bright, flat colors, is what makes Broders' work so distinctive.

249. Crédit de l'Ouest. 1920.
23½ x 31⅜ in/60.2 x 79.7 cm
Devambez, Paris
Cond A
One of the few Broders posters that's not for the railway. In this bank poster, the teller discreetly passes along the news of a 6% interest rate "in your interest." Flat colors—brown border, teller in black jacket, grid pattern in background and lettering in grey.
Est: $400-500.

250. Hyères.
24½ x 38½ in/62.1 x 98 cm
Lucien Serre, Paris
Cond B−/ Painted in loss at lower left corner; tears in text area at bottom; unobtrusive tear into image at top; colors excellent.
For the PLM railway's travel to the Côte d'Azur, the landscape and trees are blue, purple and green; the text area is brown; the houses are yellow and orange, reflecting the hot Mediterranean sun, which is contrasted with the cool green of the golf course and spectators in foreground.
Est: $600-700.

251. Le Tour du Cap Corse. 1923.
28⅜ x 39⅞ in/72.1 x 101.2 cm
Cond B / Small tears, and a 7- in. tear into image at top. Mountainside village and view of Mediterranean; subtle colors (blue, light yellow, gold and pine green, with pine green border) suggest sunset. The railway's excursion bus—a large open car—is seen taking vacationers to their seaside resort.
Est: $500-600.

MICHEL BOUCHAUD
247. La Plage de Monte Carlo. 1929.
30 x 47¼ in/76.1 x 120 cm
Toler, Paris
Cond A−/ Small crease in image background; colors excellent. Framed.

One doesn't see many beach scenes in true art deco style—and this is one of the best. Stylized figures in solid colors; a cubist design with decorative details and dramatic colors, including pink, blue and tan. Brown text area at bottom.
Est: $1200-1500.

CONDITIONS OF SALE

We call your attention to the Conditions of Sale printed on the last two pages of this catalogue.

The Conditions of Sale in this catalogue, as it may be amended by any posted notice or oral announcement during the sale, constitutes the complete terms and conditions under which the items listed in this catalogue will be offered for sale. Please note that the items will be offered by us as agent for the consignor.

Every potential buyer should acquaint himself fully with these Conditions of Sale and it will be assumed that he or she has done so at the time of any purchase or transaction.

By the making of a bid, the Purchaser acknowledges his acceptance of these Conditions of Sale and all terms and conditions announced at the sale.

ROGER BRODERS (continued)

252. Le Mont Blanc Chamonix.
29⅝ x 41¾ in/75.2 x 104.7 cm
Imp. F. Champenois, Paris
Cond B / Vertical tear through text area at bottom; horizontal fold shows slightly; colors and image excellent.
Broders allows us to enjoy the perspective of the hikers at left. Shaded forest frames view of sunny, green village of Chamonix and the magnificent blue and lavender peaks of Mont Blanc rising beyond.
Est: $600-800.

LEONETTO CAPPIELLO (1875-1942)
For other works by Cappiello, see 7, 39, 137-141

253. Sigrand. 1920.
45¾ x 61¾ in/116.3 x 156.8 cm
Devambez, Paris
Cond B / Unobtrusive tears at folds and paper edge; colors and image excellent.
In this poster for the Paris clothier, Sigrand, a man in formal attire manages to wear several hats and coats at once. He is seen against a yellow-orange background.
Est: $600-800.

254. Aurore.
47¼ x 62⅜ in/120 x 158.7 cm
Devambez, Paris
Cond A−/ Small tears, largely in margins; three tape-stains in bottom margin; image and colors excellent.
Woman in bright blue dress, silhouetted by number "1" for this quality shoe manufacturer; background is dark blue, letter in light blue and red.
Est: $500-600.

255. Spa-Monopole.
46¾ x 62⅝ in/118.7 x 159.3 cm
Vercasson, Paris
Cond B+/ Unobtrusive horizontal fold; slight tears at paper edge; image and colors excellent.
Nymph in green-yellow dress pours water from the Spa Monopole in a red-orange forest. Cappiello last used Vercasson as his agent in 1916, and started his long association with Devambez after World War I. The fact that Vercasson published this poster in 1922 indicates that this was based on one of the many maquettes rendered by Cappiello before 1917 to which Vercasson still had title.
Est: $600-800.

256. Dentifrices Docteur Pierre. 1923.
39 x 58½ in/99.1 x 148.6 cm
Devambez, Paris
Cond B / Slight creases and bubbles, largely at paper edge; colors and image excellent.
For the dentifrices of Doctor Pierre, Cappiello shows us teeth sparkling—literally! An inspired design. Back is red; dress is black.
Est: $600-800.

See color plate 40.

JEAN CARLU (b. 1900)
"Born in 1900, Jean Carlu gave up his architectural studies in 1918 after the loss of his right arm in an accident. After a reeducation spent in making posters for food products 'à la Cappiello,' he could at last apply the principles of cubism which he passionately studied (Gleizes and Juan Gris had a great influence on him), for *Monsavon* (1925), followed by the *Aquarium de Monaco, Dentifrice Gellé, Paris Soir,* and *Théatre Pigalle*. He stated his theories in various articles and lectures: 'The poster is a means of propaganda designed to associate a name with an image: it is necessary to reduce its role to that single ambition.' But to arrive at this, some rules must be respected. 'To stay etched in the mind of the passer-by, the poster must be a closed composition, following the rhythm of a simple geometric system, which catches the eye more easily than a limited amorphous composition.' We thus arrive at what Carlu calls 'the graphic expression of the idea' which is the basic rule of the poster." (Weill, pp. 204-06).

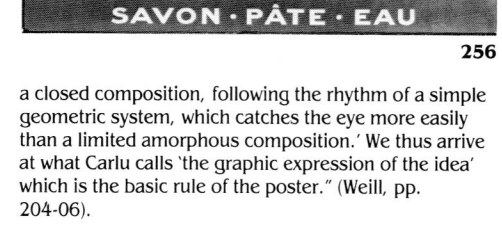

257. Birds Custard. 1933.
15⅜ x 23 in/39 x 58.5 cm
Cond C+/ Restored losses at four corners and at paper edges; creasing in image and small tears in image. Framed.
Bibl: Carlu, 24
Provenance: Collection of Jean Carlu.
Exhibited: Carlu Exhibition, Musée de l'Affiche, Paris, 1980-81, Cat. No. 24
A cubist image in simple geometric shapes and bright colors, lettering an integral part of the design. Blue, green, orange and yellow on black background. Extremely rare.
Est: $1500-2000.

258. Journées d'Espérance. 1932.
45⅞ x 61⅜ in/116.5 x 155.9 cm
Cond B−/ Two large tears into image at top and bottom right; colors and image excellent.

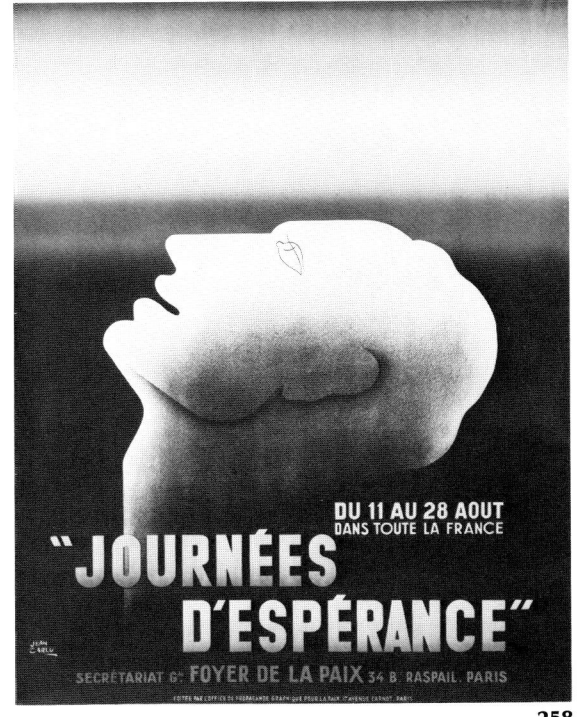

Bibl: Carlu, 32
To celebrate "Days of Hope" throughout France, organized by the Graphic Propaganda for Peace Office, Carlu gives us a dramatic image: a black and white profile looks up from dark black background to a rainbow-filled—and therefore hopeful—sky. The rainbow rolls from red to blue; text in beige and red.
Est: $700-900.

259. Grandes Fêtes de Paris. 1935.
61⅝ x 45 in/156.4 x 115 cm
Alliance Graphique, Paris
Cond B−/ Several tears at left paper edge; folds show; colors excellent
Bibl: Carlu, 39 (color); Paris Posters, 9
Provenance: Collection of Jean Carlu.
Exhibited: Carlu Exhibition, Paris, 1980-81, No. 39

Four artists were commissioned to create posters for the 1934 Fêtes de Paris: Cassandre, Colin, Domergue and Carlu. Carlu had earlier submitted a design very much like this for *Vanity Fair*, with the outlines in neon, but it was never published. So he redrew it for this occasion. The imposition of forms and the pastel treatment in vivid colors—blue, green, yellow and brown predominate—work to create a very smart poster design.
Est: $1000-1200.

260. Journée Franco-Britannique. 1939.
62½ x 46⅞ in/158.8 x 119 cm
Cond B−/ Folds show; tears, largely at folds and at paper edges.
Bibl: Carlu, 48 (var)
Profile of a French and British soldier, to celebrate the 21st Anniversary of Armistice Day and the end of World War I. It was meant to benefit those who were in the new battle. Brown, olive and black images, with red lettering. This is the larger format.
Est: $800-1000.

261. Sloan's Liniment. 1940.
20¼ x 10½ in/51.4 x 26.6 cm
Cond B / Restored losses at upper left and lower right corners; several largely unobtrusive tears at edge; colors excellent.
Bibl: Carlu, 61
Provenance: Collection of Jean Carlu.
Exhibited: Carlu Exhibition, Paris, 1980-81, No. 61
A photo-offset poster printed in the United States, showing Frosty, the snowman, who "aches from exposure." Image in black and white; text in turquoise, yellow and light orange.
Est: $500-700.

JEAN CARLU (continued)

262. Coca-Cola. 1944.
27½ x 15½ in/69.6 x 39.3 cm
Bibl: Carlu, 62. Framed.
Original, signed maquette; gouache on board.
Provenance: Collection of Jean Carlu
Exhibited: Carlu Exhibition, Paris, 1980-81, No. 62
Carlu, in an interview quoted in the exhibition catalogue, indicates that this design for a Coca-Cola poster was not in the usual style of advertising for the company and he was unable to sell it to them. The war was coming to an end, and so he used the dove to signal the coming peace.
Est: $2000-2500.

263. Pacifique 45. 1945.
38⅜ x 58⅛ in/97.5 x 147.6 cm
Havas, Paris
Cond B / Staining and crackling in image; two tears into top image background.
Bibl: Carlu, 60
Provenance: Collection of Jean Carlu
Exhibited: Carlu Exhibition, Paris, 1980-81, No. 60
This is the first poster produced by Carlu after his return from the United States. It was for a showing of a film about the American air war in the Pacific at the Paris Opéra and it became a celebration of French-American friendship. Said Carlu, "It was a kind of Victory Celebration and I very much wanted to do this poster which retains a very special place in my heart." (Carlu catalogue, No. 60). It is a dramatic, stylized design that we see: Japanese fighter plane, its wing ripped off, falls from sky, with a smoky trail, to the bright blue sea below, dotted with a navy convoy. Text in yellow, plane in grey and reserve, Japanese sun in red.
Est: $800-1000.

264. Flair. 1950.
11⅝ x 15 in/29.5 x 38.2 cm
Bibl: Carlu, 64
Original maquette: pastel on thin japan, with gouache on cellophane overlay.
Provenance: Collection of Jean Carlu
Exhibited: Carlu Exhibition, Paris, 1980-81, No. 64.
This cover design for the magazine *Flair* is a surrealist image: white bust with realist eye and red lips; background cube in light yellow, light blue, brown and black; text in yellow. Unsigned.
Est: $800-1000.

265. Perrier.
31½ x 47⅜ in/80 x 120.3 cm
Bibl: Carlu, 75 (color)
Original, signed maquette; gouache on paper.
Provenance: Collection of Jean Carlu
Exhibited: Carlu Exhibition, Paris, 1980-81, No. 75.
Carlu, in an interview quoted in the catalogue of his exhibition, indicates that he sought to approximate the sound of the slogan ("the water that goes pschitt") by means of a huge ear, completely suppressing the name of the product. "The agency and client were flabbergasted," he relates. "How can you launch a slogan without attaching it to the product name?" The secret, he discloses, is that the viewer was forced to think Perrier when he read the slogan, and "the impact was more marked if they had to think because the name remained etched in their subconscious." And the result, he states, "was an overwhelming success, the slogan being on everyone's lips." Any way you try to explain it, it is an effective message delivered with an economy of means.
Est: $1500-2000.

266. Dentifrices Gellé Frères.
20⅞ x 31¼ in/53 x 79.2 cm
Framed.
Bibl: Carlu, 15; Weill, p. 206 (color)
Maquette, gouache on board, of the 1927 poster, redrawn and signed by Carlu in 1985.

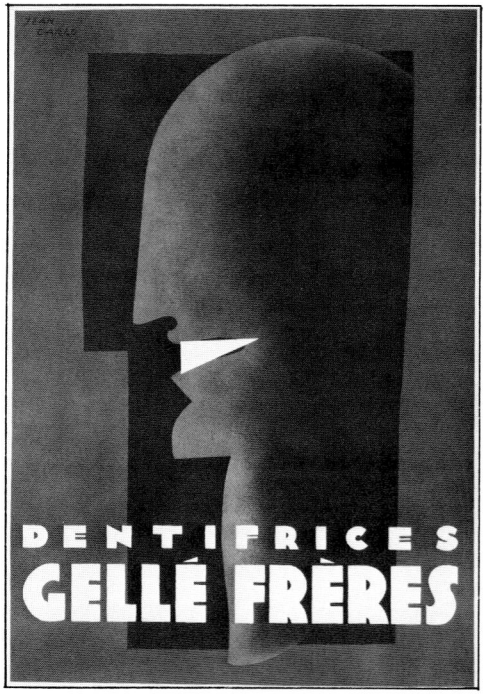

This poster is at once graphically strong and simple: the white triangle says it all.
Est: $1800-2000.

See color plate 46.

A.M. CASSANDRE (1901-1968)
For another work by Cassandre, see 41.

No artist has been able to realize the full potential of the poster as clearly, as forcefully, and, most important, as intelligently as Cassandre. "A.M. Cassandre's achievements remain unrivalled. His posters for newspapers, railways, shipping-lines, beverages, stores and so on are proof of his wealth of ideas, spirit and humour combined with a rare feeling for form and colours, an eye for fundamentals and the ability to simplify things to a sign-like design to make them more easily understandable. Cassandre combined strength with elegance, solidity with transparency and static quietness with dynamic vivacity." (Muller-Brockmann, p. 42). A major book on the posters, advertisements, covers, typography and stage designs of Cassandre, written by his son, Henri Mouron, is to be published at about the time of this auction.

267. Nord Express. 1927.
29 x 41-3/8 in/73.6 x 105.2 cm
Hachard, Paris
Cond B+/ Small tears and unobtrusive restorations largely at paper edges; image and colors excellent. Framed.
Bibl: Brown & Reinhold, 27, Pl. 9 (color); Cassandre/Japan, 85; Avant-Garde, p. 162 (color); Musée d'Affiche, 85; Cassandre, p. 20; Word & Image, p. 80; Takashimaya, 134 (color)

"With Cassandre, the machine found its herald . . . there's a powerful inducement to travel in . . . the magnified image of the train at full speed (in the Nord Express). His virtuosity with the airbrush, the rigor and geometrism of the composition, the layout of the lettering, whose details are relegated to the borders, all give (this poster) unrivaled beauty and effectiveness." (Weill, p. 200). This is one of the best examples of his use of perspective which he applies more dynamically here than in most other travel posters.
Est: $3500-4000.

268. Etoile du Nord. 1927.
29-3/8 x 41 in/74.5 x 104 cm
Hachard, Paris
Cond B/ Restored tears and losses, largely at paper edges; colors and image excellent. Framed.
Bibl: Brown & Reinhold, 28, p. 10 (color); Cassandre/Japan, 6; Cassandre, 21; Musée d'Affiche, 83; Hillier, p. 256; Avant-Garde, p. 158; Timeless Images, 105 (color); Weill, p. 199 (color); Rickards, p. 47; Takashimaya, 135 (color); Phillips III, 46; V, 77 (color)

When asked which is the world's finest poster, many a collector might name the Etoile du Nord, with its quintessential use of lines converging in infinity. Of the many testimonials of unbounded admiration for it, we can quote that of Rickards: "The Etoile du Nord design was among the first of the world's truly great posters. It had few of the statutory ingredients. Visual wit, a characteristic of the French poster of the twenties and thirties, is absent. So is the element of sex. So in fact is human interest of any kind. By standards of rule of thumb, this is scarcely a poster at all. But its visual impact, its almost hypnotic hold on the attention, its breathless directional drive to the distant point, its economy and its clarity make it all-compulsive. It is a true poster; it owes nothing to the lithographic stone or the canvas; it is not an adaptation of existing techniques and conventions—it speaks in an idiom of its own construction and it is an idiom that is instantly understood. This was the beginning of something very big in France." (p. 46)
Est: $3500-4000.

269. LMS The Best Way. 1928.
28-1/2 x 43-1/2 in/72.5 x 110.5 cm
L. Danel, Lille (not shown)
Cond A-/ Slight staining and small holes in top image and in margins.
Bibl: Brown & Reinhold, 36, Pl. 15 (color); Cassandre/Japan, 8; Cassandre, p. 26; Weill, p. 228; Phillips I, 110

Pencil-signed "AMC" and numbered "25/50"
Cassandre created an almost hypnotic fascination with his lines of gleaming rails—a motif that he used in many variations. Here the stylized switch and tracks are in black and grey; lettering in red. Another edition was printed in French, promoting "Grande Bretagne."
Est: $2500-3000.

A.M. CASSANDRE (continued)

270. Chemin de Fer du Nord. 1929.
48¼ x 78 in/122.7 x 198.2 cm
Imp. L. Danel, Lille
Cond A
Bibl: Brown & Reinhold, 44, Pl. 18 (color); Cassandre/Japan, 9; Cassandre, p. 34; Phillips I, 111; VII, 163

The larger format edition.
The format is four times the size of the usual version—twice its height and twice its width! It makes an impressive design even more forceful. Compass points, telegraph lines, railroad tracks—travel is a geometric experience, says Cassandre, and who can dispute the message when it is told with such stark impact?
Est: $4500-5000.

271. En Wagons-Lits. 1930
24½ x 39⅝ in/62.2 x 100.4 cm
Imp. L. Danel, Lille
Cond B / Folds show; unobtrusive diagonal crease at upper right corner; minor tears in margins only; colors excellent. Framed.
Bibl: Brown & Reinhold, 56, Pl. 27 (color); Cassandre, p. 32 (color); Phillips I, 113; III, 49 (var)
Red glow of railroad signal light against deep blue background; a fine way to sell railway sleeping cars. This is the rarer version, with text added to advertise second (economy) class, and the addition of "Voyagez la Nuit" (Travel at Night) at top and the company name in bottom border.
Est: $2000-2500.

272. Vinay Chocolat. 1930.
46¾ x 62⅝ in/118.7 x 159.7 cm
Les Belles Affiches, Paris
Cond A-/ Unobtrusive stains and tears at paper edges.
Bibl: Brown & Reinhold, 61; Cassandre/Japan, 42 (color); Phillips VII, 165

A pencil-signed copy.
Provenance: Atelier of the artist.
The Vinay milk chocolate is advertised by a silhouette of a cow overlaid with a section of a chocolate bar. Bottom background is green, top is chocolate brown. The message is conveyed by the most direct graphic means.
Est: $3000-3500.

273. Lawn-Tennis. 1932.
46½ x 62½ in/118.1 x 158.1 cm
Alliance Graphique, Paris
Cond B-/ Some small tears and creasing, largely at paper edges; large tear into image at top center and some unobtrusive tears into text at bottom; image and color excellent. Framed.
Bibl: Brown & Reinhold, 80, Pl. 39 (color); Cassandre, p. 68; Phillips V, 77 (color)
There were two text versions of this poster. In this one, the 15th International Lawn-Tennis match is being advertised; in the subsequent one, the Davis Cup challenge round is announced. The composition is—as always in a Cassandre poster—perfect: scale and movement are given with seemingly minimal effort and certainly minimal lines, largely by the graphic counterpoint of the close-up ball and the distant player. Remove that center line and the ball would merely be suspended; with it, it comes straight at us and makes us notice. As Cassandre knew we would.

The Alliance Graphique, founded in 1930 by Cassandre and Charles Loupot, functioned as a design studio; almost all its printing was done by the firm of L. Danel in Lille, which is the probable printer of this work as well.
Est: $4000-5000.

See color plate 43.

274. Angleterre. 1934.
91 x 122¾ in/231 x 311.5 cm
Alliance Graphique, Paris
Cond B / Some tears and losses, largely at paper
    edges; slight creasing in image.
Bibl: Brown & Reinhold, 90, Pl. 43 (var); Cassandre,
    p. 83 (color); Cassandre/Japan, 49
The large, four-sheet version.
Provenance: Atelier of the artist
*Exhibited: Cassandre Exhibition, Seibu Museum of Art,
    Tokyo, 1984, No. 49.*
Rich greens, greys and black, with text in light yellow, capture the lush green English countryside. One of two large, four-sheet billboards produced for the British railways. This one promotes England, the other Scotland. Extremely rare.
Est: $2000-2500.

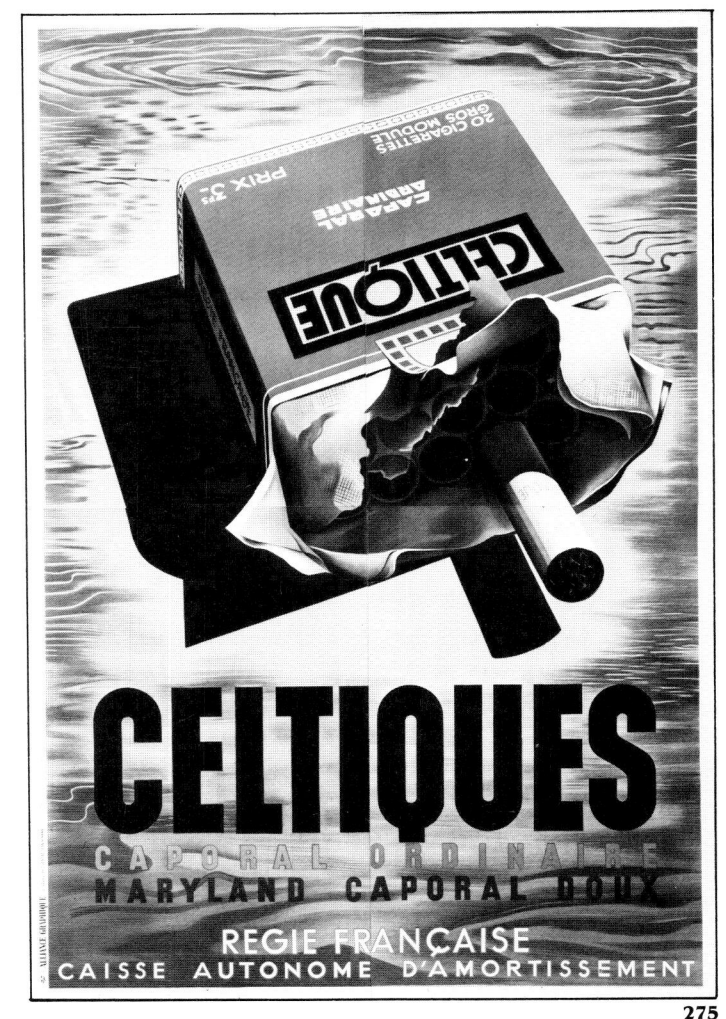

275. Celtiques. 1934.
78⅜ x 117⅜ in/199.2 x 298 cm
L. Danel, Paris
Cond A-/ Some unobtrusive tears; image and colors
    excellent.
Bibl: Brown & Reinhold, 92; Pl. 45 (var, color);
    Cassandre, p. 87; Cassandre/Japan, 29 (color);
    Phillips II, 135 (var)
The large, four-sheet version.
Provenance: Atelier of the artist
*Exhibited: Cassandre Exhibition, Seibu Museum of Art,
    Tokyo, 1984, No. 29*
This four-sheet billboard is the largest of the three sizes for this image. Close-up view and clever placement of cigarette pack deliver the design and cigarette directly. Photo-realist treatment emphasized by wood grain texture in background and strong shadow. Background tan, pack blue, text primarily in black.
Est: $1200-1500.

276. Maison Prunier. 1934.
39⅜ x 59¾ in/100 x 152 cm
Cond A-/ Unobtrusive background creases. Framed.
Bibl: Brown & Reinhold, 94, Pl. 47 (color); Cassandre,
    p. 91; Cassandre/Japan, 48 (color); Weill, p. 203
    (color); Phillips VII, 166
Austin Cooper has provided a fine appreciation of this charming work: "The problem set: a poster to announce the opening of a restaurant, already world-famous, that specialises in fishy dishes. The solution achieved: one quick glance does the trick—fish, dining-table, Prunier. The fish, belonging to no particular piscine genus, dominates the composition and gives life and movement to the scene. Its sparkling eye and the criss-cross pattern by which scales are sugggested, the isolated use of blue and gold, combine to arrest the spectators' attention at once . . . A general atmosphere of warmth and comfort is provided by the colour: the brown, of course, greatly assists in giving emphasis to the sea-green and blue that surrounds the golden fish . . . Fish, table, lobster, shell—each is epitomised rather than described." (p. 86).
Est: $5000-5500.

See color plate 44.

A.M. CASSANDRE (continued)

277. Normandie. 1938.
24⅝ x 39½ in/62.5 x 100.5 cm
L. Danel, Lille
Cond B / Folds show; small tears at paper edge; colors excellent. Framed.
Bibl (all variants): Brown & Reinhold, 101, Pl. 53 (color); Cassandre, p. 99; Musée d'Affiche, 83 (color); Weill, p. 202 (color); Phillips I, 120 (color); II, 128, 129; V, 80 (color)

The many variants of this poster began with that of the Inaugural voyage in May of 1935 and went through several text changes. This one, printed in 1938, is no doubt the last change, indicating that this proud ship will have made 60 Atlantic crossings, covered 400,000 nautical miles and carried 115,000 passengers by January 1, 1939. This ship towers above us in its design, imposing its sleek size and strength on us, and it towers over almost all other posters as well. It is one of Cassandre's finest works and it is, as always with this master, so deceptively simple in execution. The flight of the birds at bottom left gives us the right perspective and adds to the stature and movement of the ship. We, no less than those birds, feel dwarfed and awed by it.
Est: $4000-5000.

278. Dubonnet.
46¾ x 61¾ in/118.6 x 156.7 cm
Imp. Monégasque, Monte-Carlo
Cond B-/ Tears at paper edges; several larger tears at top and bottom; colors and image excellent.
Bibl: Phillips II, 134

"One is so enchanted by the immediately grasped idea—'Dubious—it's good—the name of the wine'—that the subtleties of the conception may go unnoticed. But it is precisely the rolling eye (simply rendered as a disc within a circle), the warm color suffusing the drinker by stages as the word fills out with color, and the immobility of the body in contrast to the shifts in position of hand, head, and eye that bear the imprint of Cassandre's genius as a poster designer." (Word & Image, p. 60).

The famous 1935 Dubo/Dubon/Dubonnet poster went through several editions and was widely used by Dubonnet in posters, menus, advertisements and all sorts of promotional tie-ins for many years. This later version, in red, white and blue, based on his design ("d'après Cassandre") is probably a post-World War II edition.
Est: $1000-1200.

MARC CHAGALL (1887-1985)

Born in 1887 in Vitebsk, Russia, Chagall came to Paris in 1910 for a four-year stay. At the start of World War I, he returned to Russia and got caught up in the Revolution until 1922, becoming a comissar of culture in his native town. He returned to France in 1923, spent World War II (1941-46) in New York and after that returned to France, where he died earlier this year. This master of 20th century art is frequently thought to have created many posters—there is even a book about them. But, in fact, they are almost all reproductions of his paintings and drawing, used for a variety of exhibitions and events. This fact was brought home to me when, in Spain in 1974, I had wanted to commission Chagall to do a poster. He replied that he was too old to learn a new trade! And, sensing my shock, he explained that he had never really sat down to consciously create a poster as a poster and, having a lot of respect for the medium, did not think he could do it justice at this late date! Nonetheless, his lyrical art work and strong colors lend themselves to fine poster usage.

279. Metropolitan Opera Opening. 1966.
25¼ x 40¾ in/64.2 x 103.5 cm
Imp. Mourlot, Paris
Cond A. Framed.
Bibl: Sorlier, p. 108; Lincoln Center Posters, 14 (color); Phillips I, 125; II, 139

This is a detail from "The Triumph of Music," one of the two large decorations at the entrance to the Metropolitan Opera in New York which was used for the inaugural poster in 1966. According to Sorlier, the subject is the opera Carmen and it is Rudolf Bing, the Opera's director, who had commissioned the works, who is portrayed as the central character. Sorlier lists the edition as 3000 proofs with text on poster paper and 100 proofs with text and 200 without text on Arches vellum, numbered and signed.
Est: $800-1000.

282

283

284

285

280. Die Zauberflöte. 1966.
26 x 39¾ in/65.7 x 101 cm
Mourlot, Paris
Cond A /P.
Bibl: Sorlier, p. 106; Phillips I, 126; II, 140
This poster was prepared from a detail from one of two large decorations which Chagall was commissioned to make for the Metropolitan Opera in New York under the title "The Sources of Music." It was used for the opening performance of "The Magic Flute" of Mozart, with sets and costumes by Chagall, on February 19, 1967. Sorlier lists 3000 proofs with text on poster paper, 100 proofs with text and 200 proofs without text on Arches vellum, numbered and signed.
Est: $600-800.

281. Four Seasons. Chicago. 1974.
25 x 36⅞ in/63.5 x 93.6 cm
Mourlot, Paris
Cond A /P.
Bibl: Sorlier, p. 62
For the unveiling of a Chagall mural at First National Plaza, on Monroe Street, between Dearborn and Clark, in Chicago. Poster in light washes of color; primarily blue, pink and green. There is a fine description of this work in Bach and Lachritz's *A Guide to Chicago's Public Sculpture:* "More than 3,000 square feet of hand-chipped stone and glass fragments from all over the world, including bits of Chicago common brick, cover this massive, five-sided architectural mosaic. The work incorporates 250 soft color shades into the 128 panels approximately 5 by 3 feet each that make up the great monolith measuring 70 feet in length, 10 feet in width, and 14 feet in height. The vertical sides depict six fantasy views of Chicago in all four seasons, which Chagall also sees as representing all of life itself . . . Chagall donated his design for *The Four Seasons* to the people of Chicago."
Est: $300-400.

282. Paris Opera. 1965.
38⅞ x 24⅞ in/98.8 x 63.1 cm
Imp. Mourlot, Paris
Cond A /P.
Bibl: Sorlier, p. 96; Weill, p. 358
This poster was published by the Office of French Tourism, and is a detail from a preliminary sketch for Chagall's design for the ceiling of the Paris Opera.
Est: $300-400.

CHOPPY.
283. Les Soeurs Lungla. 1926.
46¼ x 62⅞ in/117.5 x 159.2 cm
Cond B / Small tears and staining at paper edges; folds show; colors excellent.
A Josephine Bakeresque duo in feathers and baubles of magenta, turquoise and red, strike a seductive and playful pose. Stylized figures of musicians at bottom further remind us of Paul Colin's "Revue Nègre" poster of the previous year. Border is red, with yellow lettering. Nothing is known of the artist or the Lungla sisters.
Est: $1700-2000.

PAUL COLIN (1892-1985)
Paul Colin's life was immersed in that of the French music hall and theatre. Beginning with his appointment as decorator at the Théatre des Champs Elysées in 1925, he launched a distinguished and prolific career as posterist, designer, as well as subsequently a painter and illustrator. It was his poster for the Revue Nègre, featuring Josephine Baker, in 1925, that launched his career as a posterist, and he went on to create about 1,400 posters after that. In many ways, the history of Paris can be traced through the posters of this talented man. He died this summer.

284. Maya. 1927.
46¾ x 63 in/118.5 x 160 cm
Imp. H. Chachoin, Paris
Cond B / Small tears, largely at paper edges and in background.
Bibl: Colin, 22 (color; var); Musée d'Affiche, 78 (var); Phillips I, 169
This is one of several designs for the play "Maya" drawn by Colin. The poster was given much credit for the play's success at the time. Colin has perfectly captured the heroine, a streetwalker. The sharp delineation of the progressively disrobed heroine, with a night/day slash, in which Colin actually uses two reds and two blacks, one each for the "daytime" and "nighttime" personality, makes a very strong, effective poster, one of his best.
Est: $1200-1500.

285. Pierre Meyer. 1926.
47¼ x 62¾ in/120.1 x 159.3 cm
Imp. H. Chachoin, Paris
Cond B–/ Tears and staining, largely at paper edges and at folds; colors and image excellent.
Bibl: Colin, 50 (color; var)
This poster, printed in 1926 and in 1930, is one of Colin's fine cubist images, in red, grey and black. Pierre Meyer's music-hall career was brief and entirely unmemorable. Pierre's parents, department store owners, could refuse their son nothing. So when he decided to appear in music-halls, they commissioned a separate poster for him. He was, by all accounts, a snob, but at least in Colin's poster, he is an elegant and interesting snob.
Est: $1000-1200.

PAUL COLIN (continued)

286. Loterie Nationale. 1936.
23 x 31 in/58.5 x 78.7 cm
Cond B / Tears largely in text at top and bottom, with some related staining. Framed.
Bibl: Colin, 81 (poser)
Signed maquette, gouache on paper.
In this charming poster for the National Lottery, Colin turns the spectators into numbers. As he put it, "In a lottery, it's all a question of numbers. Everybody thinks about the winning number. They have numbers on their brain, the winning number, of course, and the winning sum." The poster can be regarded as a pun, or simply a comment, on the lottery buyer's natural greed. Lettering is white; background is green.
Est: $800-1000.

287. Transatlantique. c. 1948.
24 x 39½ in/61 x 99.8 cm
Imp. S.A. Courbet, Paris
Cond A
Bibl: Phillips I, 176; II, 191; IV, 55
For the French Line, Colin gives us a black and white ship sailing through shimmering blue, white and red "flag" colors.
Est: $600-800.

FRANÇOIS DAUDE

288. Pianos Daudé. 1926.
45⅝ x 60⅝ in/116 x 153.9 cm
Publicité PAG, Paris
Cond A-/ Staining in upper right corner, largely in margin; image and colors excellent.
Bibl: Phillips I, 27; II, 27
It can finally be revealed: the artist of this stunning poster for the piano store on Avenue Wagram in Paris (still there today) is none other than the former president of that company, M. François Daudé. His son tells me that he dabbled in design work—and what inspired dabbling this is: the overhead shot of the baldheaded pianist is a stroke of genius. Colors are red, orange and black.
Est: $600-800.

JEAN-GABRIEL DOMERGUE (1889-1964)

289. Hiver à Monte-Carlo. 1937.
25 x 39½ in/63.5 x 100.3 cm
Lucien Serre, Paris
Cond B / Small tears at bottom paper edge into black text area; creasing in image; colors excellent. Framed.
Bibl: Phillips II, 215 (var)
An impression of this poster with text includes a reference to the "gens chic" who spend their winter in Monte-Carlo—a message that is clear even without this remark. The blonde is in pink dress with olive green gloves; he is in navy suit, against a snow-filled, bright midnight blue sky.
Est: $600-800.

290. L'Eté à Monte-Carlo. 1937.
24⅜ x 39⅛ in/62 x 99.2 cm
Lucien Serre, Paris
Cond A. Framed.
This is the companion poster to the previous work. The text announces that the most beautiful women in the world spend their summer in Monte-Carlo. The golden brown skin of these tanned beauties stands out against white background. The girl on the left, hair drawn in blue, is in a white suit; the blonde on the right in a light green one.
Est: $500-600.

MAURICE DUFRENE (1876-1955)
291. Rayon des Soieries. 1930.
31½ x 47 in/79.8 x 119.3 cm
Imp. Chaix, Paris
Cond A
Bibl: French Opera, 17; Timeless Images, 116; Phillips I, 210; II, 220
One of the most spectacular and yet restrained art deco posters was created for the 1930 opening of an operetta by Manual Rosenthal involving intrigues in the silk department of a department store, Dufrène also designed the sets and costumes for this operetta.
Est: $600-800.

RAOUL DUFY (1877-1953)
292. Primavera. Au Printemps.
45⅝ x 61⅛ in/115.8 x 155.3 cm
Cond B / Horizontal folds show; faint staining at folds; light grey smudges, largely in top text area; colors excellent.
Dufy first began painting under the influence of impressionism and Vincent Van Gogh, but in 1905, when he saw Matisse's famous canvas *Luxe, Calme et Volupté*, his painting style was dramatically affected. By 1906, he had exhibited with the Fauves and in the following years carefully studied Cézanne and cubism. It was not until the early 1920s, however, that Dufy truly arrived at his own style of painting—a style at once elegant, decorative and inventive. In this poster for the decorative arts fair at the Au Printemps department store, the vivid flat colors, simplified forms and calligraphic lines add to the charm of the scene. Colors are pink, turquoise, red and green, with text in brown.
Est: $2000-2500.

GEORGES FAIVRE
293. Remington.
45⅝ x 71⅞ in/115.6 x 157.2 cm
Testa, Neuilly s/Seine
Cond B-/ Tears and small holes at folds; folds show; slight restorations; colors excellent.
Remington was the first commercially produced typewriter. There were several dozen tinkerers on both sides of the Atlantic who designed various mechanical devices for typing, but the machines were clumsy, slow, hard to work, and plagued by breakdowns. The man who cut through all this was Charles L. Sholes of Milwaukee, who built the first machine to use the now standard keyboard (with all the letters that spell TYPEWRITER in the top row) in 1868. Realizing the need to build a sturdy machine that would work reliably, he took his prototype to the Remington Armory at Ilion, New York, known for their guns, in 1870, and they put it into commercial production. Portables came into use after World War I. And it is the Remington portable, "the truly portable machine," that is advertised here, with typist in red dress, blond hair, being held in orange hand; lettering is green and background is black.
For another Remington poster, see 139.
Est: $700-900.

SANDY HOOK
294. Messageries Maritimes. 1922.
28⅜ x 40¾ in/72.1 x 103.5 cm
Imp. Max. Cremnitz, Paris
Cond A
Shipping company advertises cargo transport from the Mediterranean to India, Indo-China and the Far East. The ship being loaded is the "Yang-Tse." Colors in this dawn scene are primarily orange and blue.
Est: $400-500.

295. Messageries Maritimes.
28½ x 41 in/72.4 x 104.2 cm
E. Dauvissat, Paris
Cond A
Another maritime scene, with French freighter unloading cargo. Service from Antwerp and Dunkirk to the Far East and Indo-China is advertised at bottom. Colors are orange, brown and pale blue with lettering in red.
Est: $400-500.

COLLECT ALL THE BOOKS OF POSTER AUCTIONS INTERNATIONAL—for an essential reference library and Price Guide to original posters.

If you do not have Volume I—PREMIER POSTERS—send $30.00, to cover book and mailing charges, to Poster Auctions International, 37 Riverside Drive, New York, N.Y. 10023. Be sure to specify you are ordering PAI-I. You may also find it at any bookstore which carries fine art books; if they don't have it, they can order it for you from Peregrine Smith Books of Layton, Utah.

ADRIEN KARBOWSKY (1855-)
296. XIme Salon des Artistes Décorateurs. 1920.
29⅝ x 43⅛ in/75.2 x 109.1 cm
Imp. H. Chachoin, Paris
Cond A-/ Unobtrusive tears in lower right corner.
A delicately drawn image in sepia and royal blue for an exhibition of decorative arts. Karbowsky was a designer of ornamental decorations, furniture, tapestries and textiles.
Est: $300-400.

CHARLES KIFFER (b. 1902)
297. Théatre Maurice Chevalier. 1948.
39¼ x 59¾ in/99.7 x 151.7 cm
Imp. Bedos, Paris
Cond A-/ Slight soiling; colors excellent
Bibl: Phillips II, 326; Folies-Bergère, 101.
From 1925, Kiffer designed almost all of Chevalier's posters for a period of 40 years. In a few strokes, Kiffer made the Chevalier silhouette and straw hat easily recognizable trademarks of France's most popular music-hall figure. Here the hat is bright yellow against blue background.
Est: $800-1000.

JULIEN LACAZE (1886-)
298. Evian-les-Bains
30¾ x 42¼ in/78.2 x 107.2 cm
Robaudy, Cannes
Cond A-/ Very small tears at paper edges
Twilight scene in blue, brown and black, in this photo-offset poster for the resort city on Lac Léman, at the Swiss border across from Lausanne. Lacaze produced many fine travel posters for the French railways from 1910 to 1930.
Est: $300-350.

G. LECORNU
299. Exposition de l'Habitation. 1939.
39⅝ x 59 in/100.5 x 149.8 cm
Ed. de l'Architecture d'Aujourd'hui, Boulogne.
Cond A-/ Small, unobtrusive tears and staining, largely at paper edges; image and colors excellent.
Strong graphics for a home show at the Grand Palais in Paris which features an exhibition of modern architecture: red and white striped sun shade, blue facade, white terrace; text in red, blue and black expertly used to balance the composition and frame the design. Very striking.
Est: $800-1000.

CHARLES MARTIN
300. Chaussures F. Pinet.
39¼ x 52⅛ in/99.8 x 135 cm
H. Schnerb, Paris
Cond B-/ Tears and staining at folds; colors excellent.
Deco image in pink, yellow and black, featuring an elegant couple in theatre dress, for the Pinet shoe company. Text reads: "Elegance, Fashion, Quality," a boast inherent in the design.
Est: $1000-1200.

JEAN A. MERCIER (b. 1899)
301. Foire de Marseille. 1927.
89⅞ x 116¼ in/228.4 x 295.3 cm
Les Affiches Lutetia, Paris
Cond B / Some tears at folds; colors excellent.
Bibl: Phillips III, 508 (var)
Mercier was a prolific posterist, creating hundreds of fine film posters in the Twenties and Thirties, as well as several for the Transatlantique company. Here he touts—and toots—the Marseille Fair for businessmen. Both this large two-sheet and the smaller format of it are indicated as being "from a design of" ("d'après") Mercier. It's a simple yet very impressive design, with ship's smokestack in red and white against blue sky—the colors of the French flag. The background

HENRY DE MONNIER
303. Valisère. 1924.
45 x 60½ in/114 x 153.7 cm
Affiches Lutetia, Paris
Cond B / Some tears, largley at folds; colors excellent.
In a humorous pose, the model is dressed from head to toe in Valisère gloves (which are everywhere but on her hands), underwear and stockings. This attention-getting design shows Cappiello's influence on this artist. The woman is dressed in red slip, red and tan stocking and gloves, with background in dark green.
Est: $800-1000.

See color plate 37.

ORSI (1889-1947)
304. Columbia Records. 1928.
92⅛ x 123⅜ in/234.2 x 313.3 cm
Cond B−/ Staining and some tears at folds; colors excellent.
A cubist image in painterly strokes for Columbia Records in France. Colors include magenta, red, ochre, purple and black. Its large size makes it all the more impressive. Orsi was a prolific artist, producing hundreds of posters, many for the theatre. Very rare.
Est: $2500-3000.

See color plate 45.

MAURICE ROMBERG
305. Foire de Saint Sulpice. 1917.
35⅜ x 47 in/89.8 x 119.6 cm
Imp. F. Champenois, Paris
Cond B+/ Small tears and creases at paper edges; a 2-in. scrape in image at left; folds show slightly.
Poster for the Franco-American fair at the Church of Saint-Sulpice, organized by "merchants and guardians of peace of the 6th and 14th arrondisement" for war relief fund to aid refugees, soldiers and disabled veterans. Sepia drawing of allegorical figures, including liberty and justice, French and American flags in the sky; Saint Sulpice, the famous baroque church in the St. Germain district, at lower right.
Est: $400-500.

silhouette of buildings, including the minaret, give dimension and power to the massive form in the foreground.
Est: $1500-2000.

See color plate 42

302. Cursky Kummel Cointreau. c. 1928.
46 x 61¼ in/116.8 x 155 cm
M. Valotaire, Angers
Cond B−/ Tears and staining, largely at folds; several restored losses; colors excellent.
Character in bright blue with white collar, orange cheeks, against black background, holds a green bottle of the Cursky Kummel, a liquor flavored with caraway seed. It's a delightful image in bright, solid colors.
Est: $800-1000.

ROGER SOUBIE (b. 1898)
306. Lolita. 1962.
47-3/4 x 63 in/121.2 x 160 cm
Cinemato, Paris
Cond A
For the French release of "Lolita," directed by Stanley Kubrick and starring James Mason, Shelly Winters, Peter Sellers and Sue Lyon. Text at top: "How does anyone dare to make a film of Lolita?" Well, one of the ways is by changing the age of the nymphet who seduces her mother's lover from 12 to 17, thereby losing most of the poignancy of the original Nabokov novel. Soubie, who created over 1,000 film and travel posters from 1924 to 1972, when he retired, gives a seductive close-up in pastel colors. Lolita, in red, heart-shaped glasses, sucks a red lollipop. Powerful composition and large scale rendering are the stylistic trademarks of Soubie.
Est: $700-900.

J. SPRING
307. Cognac Sorin. 1930.
47 1/4 x 63 in/120.3 x 160.1 cm
Imp. Vercasson, Paris
Cond A-/ Small, unobtrusive tears in image background at lower left
In a design obviously influenced by Cappiello, the playful Pierrot figure in green costume toasts the star-filled sky with a glass of Cognac Sorin. Background is bright blue, lettering in yellow. Odd perspective adds interest and gives image a mysterious, capricious quality.
Est: $700-900.

J.D. VAN CAULAERT (1877-1979)
308. Mistinguett. Théatre Mogador. 1937.
46 1/8 x 61 1/2 in/117.3 x 155.6 cm
Atelier Girbal, Paris
Cond A-/ Some very small tears at paper edges; image and colors excellent.
Bibl: Phillips I, 586; III, 608; IV, 443
Mistinguett is seen in her rags-to-riches costume for her

role in the revue "Ça c'est Parisien" ("That's Parisian!") at the Théatre Mogador. She is in brown and black with red scarf, green hat; lettering in red, brown and black; background is paper white.
Est: $500-700.

RENE VINCENT (1879-1936)
For other works of Vincent, see 59-61.

"The world of this artist was one of car races, fashionable watering holes, casinos and elegant automobile shows. He designed a great number of the posters for the department store, Au Bon Marché, and for many other diverse products. To convey his message, René Vincent used smiling faces, small children, elegant or athletic people who projected a love of life which, between the wars, was the hallmark of a particular segment of the French people. Color, form, composition—everything is imbued with a sense of carefree cheerfulness." (Weill).

309. Au Bon Marché.
77¾ x 58½ in/97.5 x 48 cm
Imp. Duval et Bedos, Paris
Cond A−/ Some tears, largely in top margin and top text area; colors excellent
For a Christmas sale of toys and gifts at the Bon Marché store. Little girl in red dress, with yellow hair, blue and green doll, white teddy bear, and yellow goose; background is black.
Est: $1000-1200.

310. Au Bon Marché. 1930.
74 x 55¾ in/188 x 141.6 cm
Imp. Duval et Bédos, Paris
Cond B / Small, unobtrusive tears in image background and in text area at bottom; some staining; colors excellent.
Another two-sheet poster for a toy and gift sale at the Bon Marché department store. Boy in red jacket; yellow-haired girl in green dress hugs doll. A joy-filled scene.
Est: $1000-1200.

311. Golf de Sarlabot. c. 1930.
44¾ x 60 in/113.6 x 152.4 cm
Imp. Fr. Reunies, Paris
Cond B+/ Unobtrusive, well-restored loss with related tears in figure's hands; margin made up at top; colors and image excellent.
Bibl: Weill, 328 (color); PAI-I, 327 (var)
Chic woman golfer in brown and gold tees off at a stylish resort; background in greys and black. This is the larger and more impressive of the two formats. Rare.
Est: $5000-6000.

RAOUL VION
312. La Bicyclette Sanpene. c. 1925.
31 x 47 in/78.6 x 119.4 cm
Affiches Gaillard, Paris
Cond A−/ Tear in bottom margin
Bibl: Bicycle Posters, 91
This comical scene, in primary colors, shows clown shaving while pedaling along rocky, closed road. "Sans peine" means without difficulty, or easily, and the Sanpene Bicycle is meant to connote this. The poster announces that it is equipped with shock absorbers and springs that will eliminate all vibrations. Everyone seems quite happy and satisfied—except the incredulous dog who's just been run over.
Est: $500-600.

ANDY WARHOL (b. 1930)
313. Perrier. 1983.
135½ x 117½ in/342.7 x 299.8 cm
Imp. S.A. Lalande-Courbet, Paris
Cond A
This six-sheet billboard is the largest poster ever created by the celebrated Pop Art master, Andy Warhol. It was used only once, and only in the subways of Paris, in 1983. Perrier bottles are shown against hot pink background; colors are aqua, pink, red, yellow and black. Extremely rare.
Est: $1800-2000.

See color plate 55.

ZIG (d. 1936)

314. Casino de Paris. Mistinguett. 1931.
30½ x 85½ in/77.8 x 217.2 cm
Centrale Publicité, Paris
Cond B+/ Light overall foxing; some small tears and
  unobtrusive creasing, largely in upper text
  area; image and colors excellent. Framed.
Bibl: Phillips I, 618; II, 604a (var); IV, 454 (var); PAI-I, 330
At the death of Gesmar in 1928, Mistinguett entrusted all her design work—from costumes and sets to programs and posters—to Zig, whose real name was Louis Gaudin. Black background spotlights the bejewelled Mistinguett—a feather in one hand, the reins of her playful team in the other. A dazzling poster; the larger of two formats.
Est: $1000-1200.

315. Lina Tyber. 1926.
47⅜ x 62⅝ in/102.4 x 159 cm
Imp. Richier & Laugier, Paris
Cond B / Some tears and staining, largely along
  vertical fold, in background.
Portrait of Lina Tyber in lavender and green. Rare.
Est: $700-900.

GERMAN POSTERS

ANON.

316. Two Bicycle Posters.
a. Naumanns Germania
16⅞ x 30¼ in/42.2 x 76.8 cm
W. Hagelberg Akt. Ges., Berlin
Cond A
Soft, natural colors: one woman in brown, the other in dark blue, lettering in bright blue.
b. Real-Pneumatic.
20⅜ x 30⅝ in/51.6 x 77.8 cm
Kunst. Anst. Richard Burger Nachf.
Cond B-/ Tears largely in background; colors
  excellent.
Delicate image, natural colors for bicycle tires claiming to be "first class and insurpassable." Woman in white outfit with red trim.
Est: $600-800. (2)

317. Nederland.
24⅞ x 39⅝ in/63.2 x 100.6 cm
George Pullman, London
Cond A-/ Small tear barely into text at bottom; colors
  excellent. Framed.
A colorful scene and interesting composition: the viewer is placed neither on ship's deck nor over the water. Advertisement for Germans to travel by the Nederland line from Amsterdam to the Mediterranean. Black border with text in yellow.
Est: $900-1100.

318. Roverkönig.
30⅝ x 46 in/77.8 x 116.9 cm
Fabersche Buchdruckerei Magdeburg
Cond B / Some unobtrusive tears and staining in
  image and at paper edges; colors excellent.
Belle Epoque models pedal their "Rover King" bicycles down a birchlined path. Woman in lavender and red—birch trees in black and white form part of the grey border and frame the image. The bicycle is manufactured by W. Staby. A charming design!
Est: $1200-1500.

319. Coca-Cola.
46⅝ x 66⅛ in/118.3 x 167.7 cm
Cond A
A refreshed Fräulein in pink outfit against bright blue background; text in brown background at bottom. This is a Coca-Cola classic!
Est: $500-700.

318

319

321

320

322

OTTO AMTSBERG (1877-)
320. Norwegen-Fahrt. 1913.
38 x 28¾ in/96.5 x 73 cm
Arno Kypke, Berlin
Cond B–/ Folds show, with some related tears; several small tears in image; colors excellent.
Bibl: DFP-III, 21
For travel to Norway via the Norddeutscher Lloyd line home-ported in Bremen, we are shown a design in flat, solid colors. Man in royal blue with rust trim enjoys pipe; moose in beige chews on green grass; mountain range beyond in blue and green. A strong design, expertly composed in horizontal format, creating a sense of depth and wide space.
Est: $600-700.

ANTON
321. Hamburg-American Line.
25½ x 39⅝ in/64.7 x 100.6 cm
Langebartels & Jurgens, Altona
Cond A

A dramatic nighttime scene contrasting majestic passenger ship with its twin yelow, orange and blue stacks and massive black hull against a tiny tugboat in the foreground. Sky and water in dark blue; lettering in tan and yellow.
Est: $500-600.

PETER BEHRENS (1868-1940)
322. Darmstadt. 1901.
17¼ x 50⅛ in/43.8 x 127.2 cm
Jos. Scholz, Mainz
Cond B–/ Restored losses at lower left and lower right paper edges and at upper corners; horizontal folds show with some related tears; colors excellent. Framed.
Bibl: DFP-III, 90; Wember, 20; Internationale Plakate, 206; Weill, p. 99
For the exhibition "A Document of German Art" in Darmstadt, by the influential industrial and graphic designer, Peter Behrens.
Est: $5000-6000.

See color plate 48.

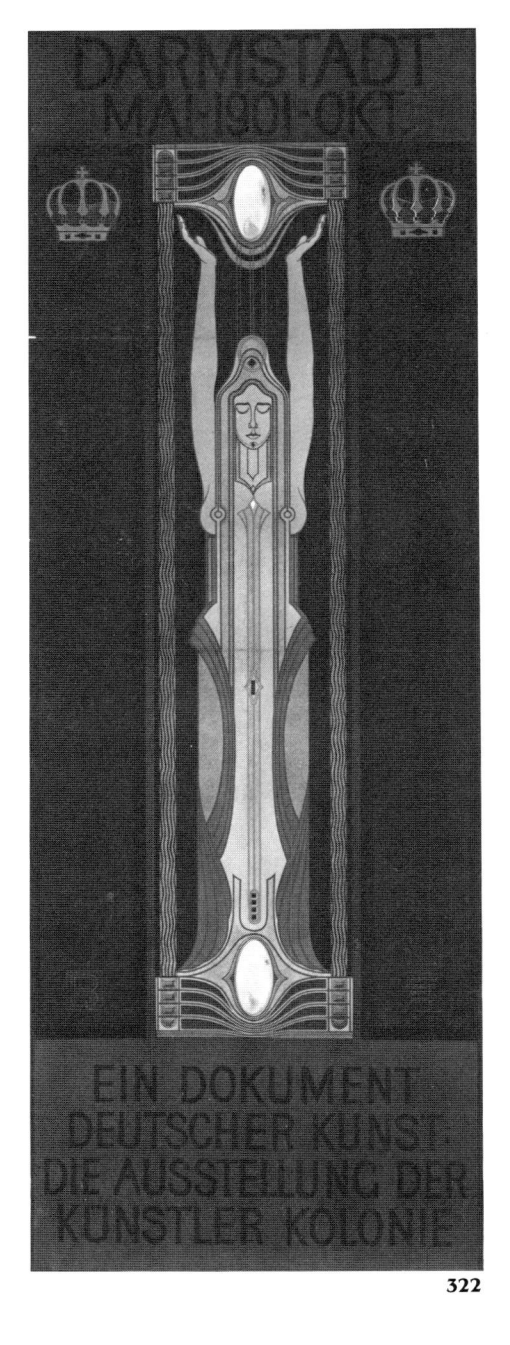

LUCIEN BERNHARD (1883-1972)
For another work by Bernhard, see 6.

323. Diehol. 1911.
18½ x 27½ in/47 x 69.9 cm
Hollerbaum & Schmidt, Berlin
Cond A-/ Unobtrusive scrape; colors excellent; on heavy stock. Framed.
Bibl: DFP-III, 209 (var)
For a medication which will heal distemper and skin disease of dogs, Bernhard gives us a not too menacing bulldog in flat brown and blue colors. Bernhard was probably the most influential designer of the early decades of the century; Klinger called him "the father of advertising." He was not only a poster artist, but an innovative interior designer, and he also created several type faces. Almost all his work was done at the Hollerbaum & Schmidt firm in Berlin. "His 'Sach Plakat' (Object Poster) brought a true revolution to advertising and overturned established ideas. This new approach required an absolute mastery of drawing, of stylization, and of composition. Bernhard added to this the science of color and an unusual talent as a typographer." (Weill, p. 100). He left for the United States in 1923 where he set up his studio and taught at N.Y.U. and the Art Students League.
Est: $700-900.

JOSEPH BINDER (1898-1972)
324. Austria.
24⅞ x 37⅜ in/63.2 x 94.9 cm
Christoph Reisser's Sohne, Wien
Cond A-/ Very unobtrusive tears at top; small stain at top left paper edge; colors and image excellent.
Bibl: Phillips I, 66; III, 21 (color)
One of Binder's finest poster designs, it went through several language changes. Bright, flat colors heighten interest: skier in red sweater waves to a companion on the slope; sky is blue, mountains purple and white, lettering in black.
Est: $400-500.

325. L'Austria Invita.
24¾ x 37⅜ in/62.7 x 94.9 cm
Waldheim-Eberle, Wien
Cond A-/ Small tears at paper edges; a 2-in. tear into text at top center; colors excellent.
Another Austrian tourist poster by Binder in flat, bright colors, this one for the Italian market. The welcoming Fräulein stands before a lake and view of the Austrian Alps.
Est: $400-500.

330

331

HANS RUDI ERDT (1883-1918)
Rademacher refers to Erdt as "the interpreter of the modern way of life." He points out that Erdt "brought something new to the Berlin poster, emphasizing a sporting element—the gentleman rider, the racing driver, the tennis champion, or globetrotter. He depicted society, luxury restaurants and upper-class entertainment, fashionable magazines and the world of privilege, employing satire and caricature." (p. 21). Erdt was one of the great German graphic artists, working in Munich and, after 1908, in Berlin for Hollerbaum & Schmidt. Born the same year as Bernhard, who had been at that firm for five years before Erdt arrived there, he was greatly influenced by him.

326. Excelsior. 1911.
13½ x 18⅝ in/34.3 x 47.3 cm
Hollerbaum & Schmidt, Berlin
Cond A
Bibl: DFP-III, 807
In this poster for Excelsior, the maker of "rubber heels that are worn everywhere," Erdt thrusts the subject advertised through the cameo he has created. Skirt and shoe are bright orange, face and oval shape grey, background black.
Est: $700-900.

327. Mazeppa. Engelhardt. 1913.
37⅜ x 27½ in/94.9 x 69.9 cm
Hollerbaum & Schmidt, Berlin
Cond B / Vertical folds show; small tears at paper edges; colors excellent
Bibl: DFP-III, 822; Wember, 284
A determined-looking "native" smoker, dark brown complexion, black hair; lettering in red and black; cigarette smoke and rings in lavender. It's sure to attract attention.
Est: $700-900.

328. Müller Extra. 1908.
46⅛ x 69⅝ in/117.2 x 176.9 cm
Hollerbaum & Schmidt, Berlin
Cond B-/ Tears and breaks at folds; small tears at paper edges; colors excellent
Bibl: DFP-III, 764; Wember, 258
In this two-sheet poster for a champagne, the man is in yellow vest, maroon jacket; text and design in grey.
Est: $700-900.

ALBERT FUSS (1889-)
329. Hamburg-Amerika Linie.
25⅝ x 39⅝ in/65 x 100.1 cm
Cond A
We are drawn into this beautiful scene by Fuss's fine design: passenger ship glides through still, icy blue fjord filled with sailboats, rowboats and the mint green and purple reflections of the mountains; tan border, lettering in white. Fuss created several posters for this steamship firm in the 1930s.
Est: $400-500.

WILHELM HARTZ
330. Internationale Photographische Ausstellung. 1909.
24 x 38 in/61 x 96.5 cm
Cond B+/ Tear at horizontal fold; colors and image excellent.
Bibl: DFP-III, 1187.
Hartz won first prize for this poster for the photographic exhibition in Dresden in 1909. Dull green, with gold ink.
Est: $1200-1500.

LUDWIG HOHLWEIN (1874-1949)
"While Bernhard triumphed in Berlin, Munich produced the greatest and most prolific German poster artist: Ludwig Hohlwein . . . Beginning with his first efforts, Hohlwein found his style with disconcerting facility; it would vary little for the next forty years. The drawing was perfect from the start: if he was particularly at ease with animals, horsemen, or hunters, still nothing seemed alien to him, and in any case, nothing posed a problem for him. His composition was simple and rigorous: one, two figures at the most, placed in the foreground against a uniform background to make them stand out. Hohlwein, who had no doubt seen the experiments of the Beggarstaff Brothers, used colors in flat tones, seldom outlined. But, unlike the Englishmen, he paints images that are not flat. His figures are full of touches of color and a play of light and shade that brings them out of their background and gives them substance." (Weill, pp 107-110). A major retrospective of Hohlwein's posters was shown at the Staatsgalerie of Stuttgart earlier this year.

331. Hermann Scherrer. 1907.
48¾ in/91 x 123.9 cm
Vereinigte Druckereien & Kunstanstalten, Munchen
Cond B/ Small tears and stains in margins; unobtru-

332

333

LUDWIG HOHLWEIN (continued)

sive diagonal crease at upper left corner; one horizontal fold; colors excellent. P.
Bibl: DFP-III, 1329; Hohlwein/Stuttgart, 2
In one of his very first posters—Scherrer was to become one of his regular clients—Hohlwein portrays a well "suited" sportsman returning from the hunt with an armload of ducks. Figure in brown and black against twilight background; lettering in lavender. Rare.
Est: $2500-2800.

332. PKZ. Burger-Kehl. 1911.
37⅝ x 50¾ in/95 x 128.3 cm
Gebr. Fretz, Zurich
Cond A−/ Horizontal folds show slightly; tiny tears and light staining at paper edges only; mounted on heavy paper.
Bibl: DFP-III, 1396; Hohlwein/Stuttgart, 53
One of several posters Hohlwein produced for the Swiss men's clothier. With an absolute minimum of detail, Hohlwein captures the handsome sophistication and elegance of his subject. Odd colors and bold determinate shapes add to the impact. Colors are olive, magenta and beige.
Est: 2500-3000.

333. Isidor Bach. 1912.
35½ x 47¼ in/90.3 x 120 cm
Kunstanstalt Graphia, Munchen
Cond B+/ Folds show; several tears at lower left corner; colors and image excellent. P.
Bibl: Hohlwein/Stuttgart, 78
Group of alpine travelers standing before train engine form solid design of shapes, patterns and colors—a composition unusually loaded for Hohlwein, but well-balanced with subtle colors (light blue, pine green, cream, brown and khaki) and pleasing forms. Two figures viewed from behind and the small dachshund at right add humor and interest to the image. Rare.
Est: $1500-1800.

334

334. Turnier. 1913.
37⅞ x 27⅝ in/96.2 x 70.1 cm
Vereinigte Druckereien, Munchen
Cond A−/ Unobtrusive tears at paper edges; image and colors excellent.
Bibl: DFP-III, 1461; Wember, 427 (var); Hohlwein/Stuttgart, 138
Steeplechase with tan background, brown horse and fence, riding jacket in bright red, details in white. Design carefully balances text with image.
Est: $1000-1200.

335. Tekrum. 1914.
30⅞ x 43⅝ in/78.5 x 110.7 cm
Reichhold & Lang Lith., Munchen
Cond A−/ Tiny tears at paper edges; colors and image excellent.
Bibl: Hohlwein, 124a; DFP-III, 1480; Hohlwein/Stuttgart, 146
Elegantly dressed woman poses with a box of Tekrum macaroons. Outfit is brown, accented with pink; text in pink and grey; the tiny box of macaroons is distinguished in blue.
Est: $1200-1500.

336. Marco Polo-Tee. c. 1914.
30⅞ x 21½ in/78.4 x 54.8 cm
Reichhold & Lang Lith., München
Cond B / Tears and creasing at bottom corners; small tears at paper edges; very unobtrusive staining in background; colors and image excellent.
Bibl: Hohlwein, 75; Hohlwein/Stuttgart, 148
Uniformed waiter delivers a tray of Marco Polo Tea. Colors are ochre, beige, brown and grey, with two attention-getting blue tea cups.
Est: $800-1000.

337. Die Rache im Goldtal. 1920.
34¼ x 48¼ in/87 x 122.8 cm
Kunst im Druck, München
Cond B / Folds show slightly; unobtrusive loss at lower right corner; tears in top and bottom paper edges background only; colors excellent.
Bibl: Hohlwein/Stuttgart, 321
An American cowboy on bucking horse advertises the Munich-based Wild West Film company's "Revenge in Gold Valley." Colors are red, black and grey. The German western is a strange hybrid. There was a writer, Karl May, who was enormously popular with German youth, who wrote dozens of western tales without ever getting further west than Stuttgart-Unterturkheim. It was basically under his influence that a small outfit calling itself WIWEFCO (Wild-West-Film Company) opened in Munich, probably around 1919, with Alfred and Fred Paster, who alternately directed and acted in their adventure epics. They used the Alpine country for exteriors, and the sand dunes of the north shore of Pommern served nicely as the American desert. They continued producing until the early 1930's, then quietly faded away when the Nazi regime came in. Rare.
Est: $700-900.

338. Prinz der Hosenfalter.
34⅛ x 49 in/86.7 x 124.5 cm
Kunst im Druck, Munchen
Cond B/ Folds show slightly; unobtrusive loss at lower right corner; tears in top and bottom paper edges background only; colors excellent.
There is no record of Hohlwein falling out of favor with the Third Reich as a result of using a figure based on Charles Chaplin, who would later star in the relentlessly anti-Nazi film, "The Great Dictator." It's a most striking and humorous image, as the Chaplinesque figures display the benefits of wearing these special suspenders. Figures in black and white silhouette, with red faces. Patent is indicated at top right; bottom text says it's "available everywhere." Extremely rare.
Est: $1500-2000.

JOSEPH ADOLPH LANG (1873-1936)
339. Düsseldorf Exposition. 1904.
25¼ x 38⅛ in/64 x 96.8 cm
Druck A. Bagel, Düsseldorf
Cond B / Folds show; colors excellent
Bibl: DFP-III, 1943
A simple Art Nouveau design, suggestive of Klimt, aimed at the French audience, announcing a Fine Arts and Horticultural Exhibition organized under the auspices of "his highness and crown prince of the empire of Germany and Prussia"—that would be Wilhelm II. Colors are sepia and red, with lettering in black and gold.
Est: $1000-1200.

ROBERT LEONARD (1879-   )
340. Grammophon Tanz Orchester.
37¼ x 54¾ in/94.6 x 139.1 cm
Cond B / Folds show; small tears and creases at top paper edge and at joining of sheets. P.
Nicu Vladescu was an orchestra leader from Rumania who led a popular dance band in Germany. Woman in

green dress, man in black, beige skin tones, with lettering in black, green and red.
Est: $500-600.

JOHANN B. MAIER
341. Sporthaus Schuster. 1913.
31½ x 43 in/79.8 x 109.2 cm
Reichhold & Lang Lith. Kunstanstalt, Munchen
Cond A−/ Very small tears at paper edges; folds show slightly; colors excellent.
Bibl: DFP-III, 2165
The Munich artist, Johann Maier, gives us a confident skier, well equipped and fashionably dressed by Sporthaus Schuster. Strong, flat colors include red, gold and brown.
Est: $1000-1200.

See color plate 52.

CARL MOOS (1878-1959)
For other work by Carl Moos, see 389.
342. Fritz Schulze. c. 1907.
33⅝ x 46⅞ in/84.4 x 119.1 cm
Vereinigte Druckereien & Kunstanstalten, Munchen
Cond B−/ Folds show; some tears at folds and a paper edges; colors excellent.
Bibl: DFP-III, 2233
For the sports clothing firm of Munich, we are given a skier in a handsome outfit, with blue jacket and cap, brown knickers with pattern, beige socks. Background in lavender, grey and tan. Grid pattern in knickers (in the style of Hohlwein) and offbeat colors add interest to a solid design.
Est: $1000-1200.

343. C. Wagner. 1907.
35½ x 48⅞ in/87.6 x 124.2 cm
Vereinigte Druckereien & Kunstanstalten, Munchen
Cond B−/ Folds show; some tears at folds and at paper edges; colors excellent
Bibl: DFP-III, 2234; Muller-Brockmann, 57 (color)
For the C. Wagner sporting goods store in Munich, Moos presents us with a design of strong, solid colors and forms simplified into broad flat shapes. Woman in white peplum jacket with carmine bow and buttons, brown skirt with green trim, green stockings, sled, lettering and background beige and brown.
Est: $1200-1500.

WALTER SCHNACKENBERG (1880-1969)
344. Die Jahrmarkts-Orgel. 1933.
33⅝ x 46½ in/85.4 x 118.2 cm
Kunst im Druck, Munchen
Cond A−/ Very small tape stain at left paper edge.
Bibl: Purvis, p. 127 (var)
Finding any poster by this German master is so difficult that the opportunity to see one becomes an occasion! Here, for an Annual Fair Evening Gala to benefit a winter relief charity, he shows us a young lady with rifle and targets. Colors are flat: pink and white dress, with lime green apron, black and yellow background. The same Hotel Vierjahreszeiten used this design also for an event titled "Cherubin-Redoute."
Est: $800-1000.

KARL SCHULPIG (1884-1948)
345. W. Hoffman Pianos. c. 1912.
18¾ x 27¼ in/47.5 x 69.2 cm
Adolf Simmel, Berlin
Cond B+/ Small tear and some creasing at paper edge; on heavy stock.
Bibl: Muller-Brockmann, 131 (color)
In a design owing much to Bernhard and Erdt, the colors are subtle, yet striking: piano in black with purple details, background in grey, lettering in white.
Est: $600-800.

EUGEN GUSTAV STEINHOF
346. Musik u Theaterfest der Stadt Wien. 1924.
24⅝ x 37⅛ in/62.5 x 94.4 cm
Staatsdruckerei, Wien
Cond B+/ Folds show slightly; colors excellent.
Bibl: Tagebuch der Strasse, 147 (color; var)
On September 14, 1924, the City of Vienna opened the second Music and Theater Festival and it was quite a memorable event. The brass section of the State Opera played a fanfare composed for the occasion by Richard Strauss. Arnold Schönberg's "The Lucky Hand," Arthur

PL 45　　　　　Orsi　　　　　No. 304

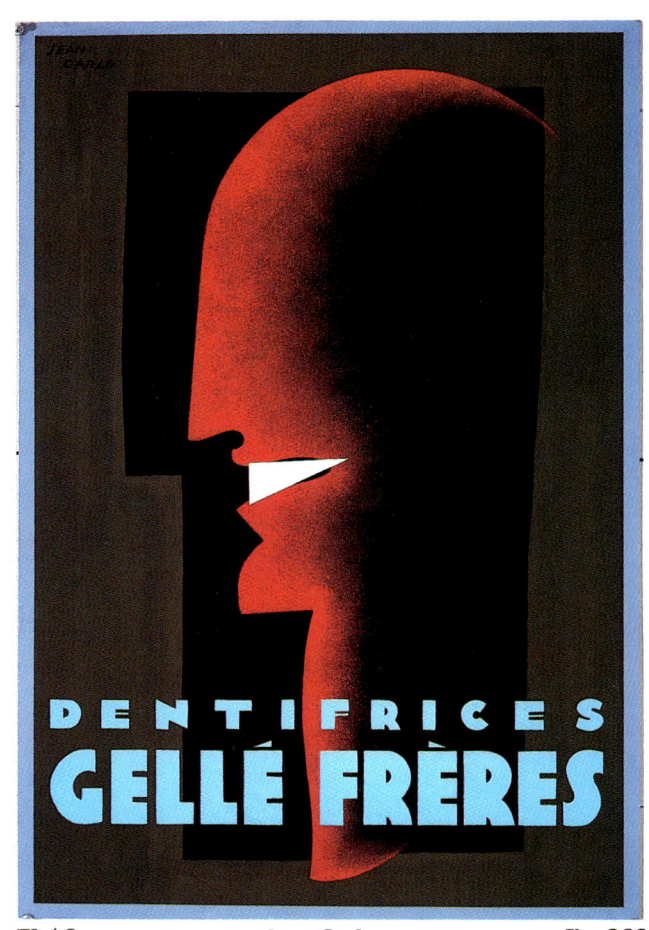

PL 46　　　　　Jean Carlu　　　　　No. 266

PL 47　　　　　Giorgio Muggiani　　　　　No. 359

PL 48　　Peter Behrens　　No. 322

PL 49　　　Charles Loupot　　　No. 383

PL 50　　　Charles Loupot　　　No. 384

PL 51　　　Emile Cardinaux　　　No. 372

PL 52　　　Johann B. Maier　　　No. 341

Burkhard Mangold

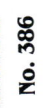

PL 54 — Jean Carlu — No. 262

PL 55 — Andy Warhol — No. 313

Schnitzler's "Comedy of Abduction" and Franz Werfel's "Maximilian and Juarez" were all presented for the first time. Steinhof's stylized portrait of a musician and actress is drawn in almost primitive manner. The musician is in white shirt, actress in pink costume and background is light green. It was also published with French text.
Est: $400-500.

MAX STERN (1872-1943)
347. Ausstellung Duesseldorfer Kuenstler.
33⅞ x 26 in/86 x 66 cm
A. Bagel, Düsseldorf
Cond B+/ Slight creases and stains in background. Framed.
An interesting composition, showing museum goers in black against red floor, orange walls, looking at art work both on the far wall and directly at us as well.
Est: $800-1000.

FRANZ VON STUCK (1863-1928)
348. Ausstellung Renaissance (Secession).
14⅝ x 30⅞ in/37.2 x 78.3 cm
Lith. Dr. C. Wolf u. Sohn, München
Cond B+/ Unobtrusive restored tear at upper left paper edge; very small losses and tears at right paper edge; tiny hole in text area; image and colors excellent; gold very fresh.
Bibl (all variants): DFP-III, 3213; Affichomanie, 151; Wember, 745; Hiatt, p. 341; Plakate Munchen, p. 53; Phillips II, 563
Stuck's classical "Athene in Gold" head, with its gold mosaic background and octangular frame, was the standard Secession poster for almost all its exhibitions for many years, including the first one in 1893. Rogers noted: "The best example of an all-mosaic poster on paper is one designed by F. Stuck for the *Munich Exhibition*, which is admirable in its classic simplicity and rich colour effect, enhanced, as it is, by the gold ground-work." (p. 116)
Est: $800-1000.

349. International Hygiejne. 1911.
23½ x 35⅛ in/59.7 x 89.4 cm
Leutert & Schneidewind, Dresden
Cond B/ Some tears, largely at paper edges; restored loss along lower right paper edge and image border; folds show. Framed.
Bibl (all variants): DFP-III, 3221; Rademacher, p. 60; Plakate München, p. 32; Internationale Plakate, 180; Phillips I, 567
Stuck's eye motif became so popular that this design was subsequently used for State Express cigarettes in 1912, for the *Lustige Blätter,* and for the same show in 1930. The stylized eye is seen in midnight blue sky with stars, Greek architecture in beige frames text below—an interesting surrealist image. This version, with text in Danish, is the rarest of all.
Est: $1200-1500.

A. THERSTAPPEN (1882-   )
350. 7tes Hallen Sport Fest. 1913.
37 x 27⅜ in/93.9 x 69.5 cm
Kunstanstalt Gebr. Hartkopf, Berlin
Cond A-/ Folds show slightly; unobtrusive tears at top left paper edge; colors excellent.
Bibl: DFP-III, 3258
Strong graphics, combining image and text—red background with lettering and figure in white, tan and brown; details in green. Figure vaults over pole—and lettering—to announce indoor sports festival including such events as relay race, cycling race, gymnastics, pole-vaulting, wrestling and hockey.
Est: $500-600.

ITALIAN POSTERS

ANON.
351. Tramvie del Governatorato. Roma. 1927.
27¼ x 39⅜ in/69.2 x 100.1 cm
Barabino & Graeve, Genova
Cond A−/ Small tears at paper edges; horizontal fold shows slightly; colors excellent.
"Take a Tramway Tour in Luxury Cars" says this poster for the Italian Tourist Board. And it is a colorful, as well as luxurious, interior of the Italian tram that we see here, as it passes along ancient walls of Rome. Brown border with yellow lettering.
Est: $300-400.

ETTORINO ANDREINI
352. Sapho—Détersif.
31¾ x 94¾ in/80.6 x 240.8 cm
Stabilimento Armanino, Genova
Cond B / Unobtrusive tears, largely at paper edges, image and colors excellent.
This colorful two-sheet poster advertises two products: Sapho tooth polish at the top and Détersif soap at the bottom. A decorative Art Nouveau image in flat colors and strong outline framed by textile-like floral border.
Est: $800-1000.

See color plate 31.

UMBERTO BRUNELLESCHI (1879-1949)
353. Trouville.
26⅜ x 38½ in/67 x 97.8 cm
La Martinella, Milan
Cond B+/ Upper right corner torn and restored
 unobtrusively; light staining in white towel;
 image and colors excellent.
Bathing beauty in orange suit grasps her windblown white towel against the bright blue Trouville sky; lettering in yellow. Brunelleschi's stylized drawings appeared regularly in *Gazette du Bon Ton, Le Rire, Vie Parisienne, Fémina* and other fashion journals of the day. Born in Tuscany, Brunelleschi moved to Paris around 1900 and established himself within the circle of writers and artists of the Latin Quarter. His modernism showed influences of Florentine color and 18th century Italian design.
Est: $600-700.

ARDUINO COLATO
354. Circuit of the Lake of Garda. 1930.
38½ x 54⅞ in/97.6 x 139.3 cm
F.I.C.I.S. Milano
Cond B+/ Small tears and staining, largely at paper
 edges and at folds; colors excellent.
Italian travel poster advertises motor excursions around the Lake of Garda from Bonomini to Verona. Bright transparent colors and sharp angular shapes broken into stripes of colors in varying intensity add interest to the design. At the same time, the zooming car, approaching those impossible zig-zag mountainside roads, portends some danger for the passengers. Car is magenta, lake is blue, sky and sun are yellow, green hills, purple mountains; black tunnel outline frames view; text in black.
Est: $800-1000.

MARCELLO DUDOVICH (1878-1962)
355. Borsalino. c. 1932.
39¼ x 55½ in/99.8 x 140.8 cm
Edizioni Star, IGAP, Milano
Cond B+/ Folds show slightly.
Bibl: Dudovich, catalogo 274.
The greatest of all Italian posterists, Dudovich created several posters for the Borsalino hat company over a 20-year period. His most famous was the hat-on-chair motif for Borsalino's Zenit brand in 1911. In this handsome design, the hats are in brown on lemon-yellow background, lettering in dark brown. He perfectly illustrates the company's slogan: "Like the sun among the stars." Rare.
Est: $700-900.

ADOLFO HOHENSTEIN (1854-)
356. Dover-Ostend Line.
24½ x 38½ in/61.6 x 97.8 cm
Chromolith. J.L. Goffart, Bruxelles
Cond B-/ Restored losses at corners and in border
 areas; folds show; several tears and some
 staining in image; colors excellent.
Bibl: Menegazzi, 106 (color)
Colorful bon voyage in sunset hues—orange, beige and brown with highlights in light blue and lime green—lettering in white. Flat color planes and rich ornamentation combine with dramatic lighting—chiaroscuro and shadow-to form a charming yet dynamic design. Weill, calling Hohenstein the "father of the Italian poster," states: "His figures were treated with impeccable photographic realism, and colored with a palette of dazzling richness which plays with the effects of light and shade. From the beginning, the boldness of his compositions left the French poster artists far behind." (p. 84).
Est: $1500-1800.

LEOPOLDO METLICOVITZ (1868-1944)
357. La Colonia Libera. 1899.
20½ x 27¾ in/52 x 70.5 cm
Ricordi, Milano
Cond B-/ Tears into text area at lower right;
 horizontal crease across image into
 woman's face; colors excellent. Framed.
To advertise the music of the opera by Floridia, its publisher, Ricordi, uses the talents of one of their best posterists working in their printing department. Metlicovitz gives us a delicate rendering: woman with red flowers in hair, ornamental frame of blossoms in white and gold, green circle of leaves behind text in green. Pietro Floridia (1860-1932) came to the United States in 1904; he was conductor of the Italian Symphony Orchestra and also wrote the music for Oscar Wilde's "A Florentine Tragedy."
Est: $600-800.

ALBERTO MICHELI (1870-1905)
358. Paneraj.
36½ x 48⅞ in/92.2 x 124 cm
Arti Grafiche, Bergamo
Cond B+/ Small tears at folds; colors excellent.
 Framed.
Stylish women in an autumn scene: woman in red at left offers sniffling woman wrapped in blue at right a Pastiglie Paneraj—a lozenge to fight her cough and cold. Light autumn colors and falling leaves suggest the oncoming cold weather and, of course, the flu season. Lettering in black is well integrated with image.
Est: $1200-1500.

GIORGIO MUGGIANI (1887-1938)
359. Recoaro. 1928.
54¾ x 77¾ in/139.1 x 197.5 cm
Edizioni Muggiani, Milano
Cond B+/ Some tears and staining in image; colors
 excellent.
"As the thirties dawned, two conflicting tendencies began to create a stir: the official fascist art, tinged with pompous memories of classical Rome, and avant-garde art . . . In this hostile environment, the avant-garde laid foundations that would carry Italian design to the front rank. It was mainly the work of a few matchless personalities." (Weill, p. 275). One such artist was Muggiani, who belonged to a group of avant-garde artists in Italy who drew their inspiration from both the German Bauhaus and the French post-cubist school. He gives us a cubist image characteristically heightened by dramatic perspective as couple toast with Recoaro table water. Woman in blue, chair is yellow, man in black, bright red background, text area red with yellow lettering.
Est: $1000-1200.

See color plate 47.

SPANISH POSTERS

360

361 a, b

363

FRANCISCO DE CIDON
360. La Tribuna. 1903.
42 x 57⅝ in/106.8 x 146.4 cm
Talleres Barral, Barcelona
Cond A−/ Small tears and losses in margins; colors excellent
For the newspaper *La Tribuna,* an allegorical figure in red gown gestures toward the sea as if to indicate the source of her message. Background in blue, yellow and olive green, text in blue and white.
Est: $500-600.

361. Exposiciones de Turin y Roma. 1911.
Two posters:
a. EDUARD JENER (1882-1967)
18⅜ x 25⅝ in/47.2 x 65.1 cm
Cond A
For the International Expositions in Rome and Turin, we are offered a montage, including travelers, train and view; colors are predominately blue, with red and yellow.
b. ANON.
18¼ x 25¾ in/46.4 x 65.5 cm
Cond A−/ Small tears at paper edges
Colors are brown and red.
Est: $600-800. (2)

RIBAS
362. Fleuves de la Galice.
24¼ x 38⅝ in/61.4 x 98.1 cm
Rivadeneyra, Madrid
Cond A−/ Small, unobtrusive tears, largely into text areas at top and bottom; colors and image excellent.
Spanish travel poster inviting French tourists to explore the rivers of Galice in northwestern Spain. Couple in blue automobile in foreground on road overlooking lush river scene filled with sailboats and cruise ship. Blue, green and yellow predominate; black border with yellow lettering. It does indeed look like one of the "Dream Spots." The artist is most probably Frederico Ribas Montenegro, born in Vigo in 1890.
Est: $400-500.

ALEXANDRE DE RIQUER (1856-1920)
363. Four Seasons. 1900.
Each: 21⅞ x 45⅜ in/55.4 x 115.2 cm
Cond A−/ Small tears, largely in margins (Winter panel has large, but unobtrusive, tear into lower image); colors and images excellent. Framed.
A set of four lithographs depicting four seasons.

Figures take on much more human, mundane air than Mucha's "The Seasons," whose figures are nymphlike and ethereal. These are involved in more ordinary tasks and they strike more realistic poses and are dressed more lifelike. DeRiquer's treatment and soft colors are fine examples of Spanish Art Nouveau. Writing the year after the publication of this set, the British critic Rogers commented on this artist: "Of Spanish placardists, undoubtedly A. de Riquer stands first. He has produced more work than any other of his countrymen, and that all of the best quality. His posters have the important qualities of strong decorative effect, cleverness and originality in colour-scheme, and of delicate and pleasing line." (p. 71). And commenting on this set, he reports that "In Spain, deRiquer has executed some charming decorative panels, which are worthy to rank with the best efforts of Mucha. The set representing the four seasons, of which 'Spring' is undoubtedly the best, are single-figure studies in the open air, and treat the subjects from an original and unconventional point of view." (p. 127).
Est: $4000-5000. (4)

See color plate 29.

362

ENRIQUE ROMERA
364. Cordoba. 1907.
106½ x 47⅝ in/270.5 x 120.9 cm
Lit. E. Portabella, Zaragoza
Cond B / Tears, most unobtrusive, at left and right paper edges; colors excellent.
This large, eight-sheet poster features a colorful and seductive image of two Cordoba beauties. Rose and green predominate. The week-long Cordoba fair it advertises features bullfights, music concerts, dancing, theatre and exhibitions.
Est: $500-600.

SWISS POSTERS

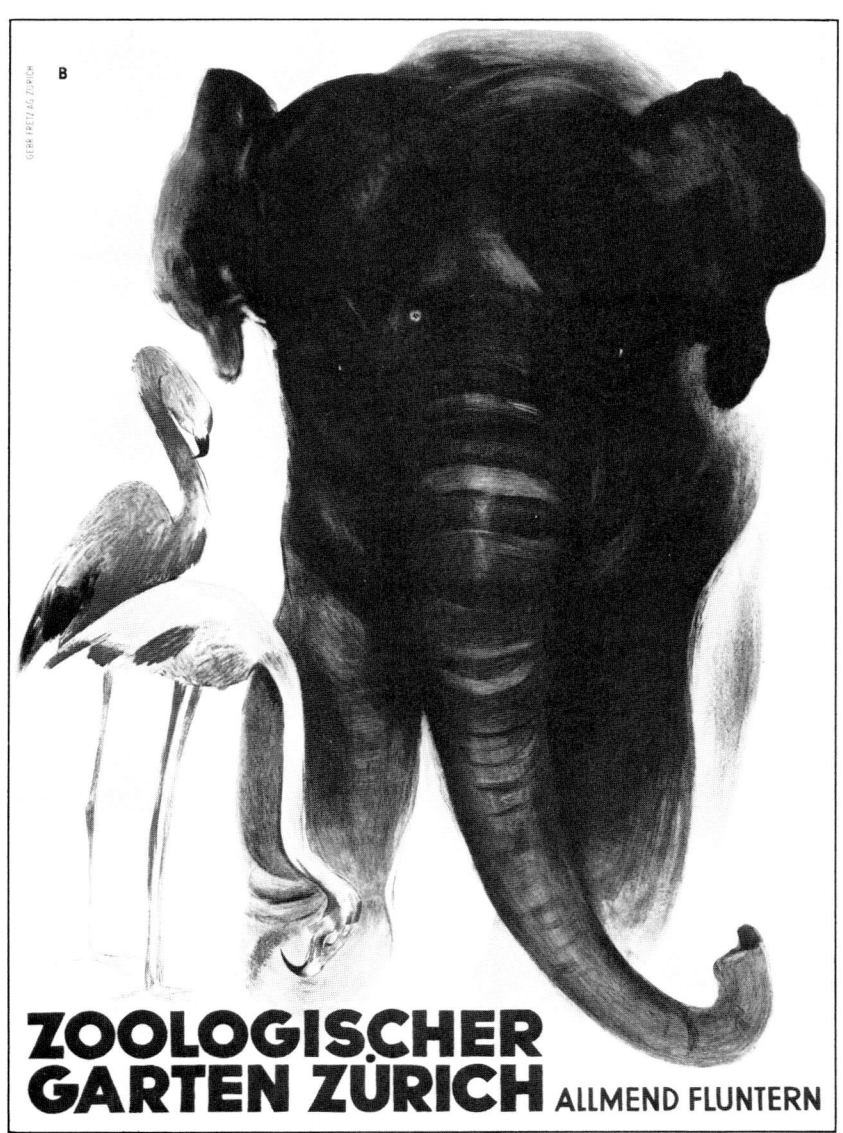

ANON.
365. Allegro. 1930.
26⅝ x 38¼ in/67.7 x 97.2 cm
Creation Publivox, Geneve
Cond A– / Diagonal crease at lower right corner; mounted on heavy paper.
The Allegro (meaning "lively" in Italian) motorcycle zooms along lightning path, sun blazing behind. Sharp angles and strong flat colors add to a striking design.
Est: $500-700.

OTTO BAUMBERGER (1889-1962)
Baumberger may well have been the most versatile posterist of all time. He had an incredible range of styles, each beautifully tailor-made to his client's purpose. Along with Emile Cardinaux, Burkhard Mangold and Niklaus Stoecklin, he is responsible for the founding of the Swiss school of graphic design and its distinctive poster image at the beginning of this century.

366. Zoologischer Garten Zurich. 1929.
35½ x 50⅜ in/90 x 128 cm
Gebr. Fretz, Zurich
Cond B / Several small tears and folds at paper edges; image and colors excellent.
Bibl: Margadant, 138; Phillips II, 60; V, 74 (color)
An unlikely yet humorous juxtaposition in a design for the 1929 opening of the Zurich zoo: the massive grey-brown elephant and the delicate pink flamingo, both on view, share a common characteristic—long appendages.
Est: $1200-1500.

OTTO BAUMBERGER (continued)

367. Simplon Line. 1934.
25⅛ x 39⅞ in/63.7 x 101.2 cm
Fretz Bros., Zurich
Cond A−/ Small unobtrusive tears at paper edges; colors and image excellent
In Baumberger's many travel posters, one sees the painter's sensitive use of colors and broad strokes to give a lyrical beauty to the lake or city being publicized. Here, Baumberger, who considered himself primarily a painter and regarded the design of posters as a means toward his livelihood, gives a colorful impressionistic trackside view of a Swiss town for the Simplon electric railway. Orange, yellow, blue and green predominate.
Est: $400-500.

368. Lucerne-Interlaken. 1936.
24⅝ x 39¼ in/62.5 x 99.7 cm
Lith. Sauberlin & Pfeiffer, Vevey
Cond A−/ Very small tears in margins only; colors and image excellent
Another impressionistic view by Baumberger: lake view with mountain scenery, in cool blues, green and grey.
Est: $500-600.

ARNOLD BRUGGER (1888-1975)

369. Kunstsalon Wolfsberg. 1914.
29 x 38¾ in/73.5 x 98.5 cm
J.E. Wolfensberger, Zurich
Cond A−/ Small handling creases in image; colors excellent
Brugger, a painter and graphic artist, exhibited with three other artists, including Otto Morach, at the gallery (still there) of the Wolfensberger printing plant. He gives us an expressionistic, painterly treatment in bold strokes of violent color—yellow, ochre, dark red, brown and black.
Est: $600-700.

EMILE CARDINAUX (1877-1936)

Cardinaux ranks as one of the best and most innovative of Swiss posterists. "Cardinaux, who had learned lithography in Munich, produced functional designs in keeping with the limits of the technique he was utilizing: the colors are simplified, the layout and composition firm, the lettering arranged at the bottom . . . (He) had the luck to find a peerless printer, Wolfensberger, to render his compositions." (Weill, p. 122). Margadant notes: "In Cardinaux's works, posters promoting tourism take pride of place. The austere beauty of the landscapes is matched by the homespun individuals, close to their native soil, he depicted in his political and commercial posters. With over one hundred posters to his credit, he became the recognized poster artist of these early years." (p. 53). A retrospective exhibition of Cardinaux's posters is being shown now in Zurich.

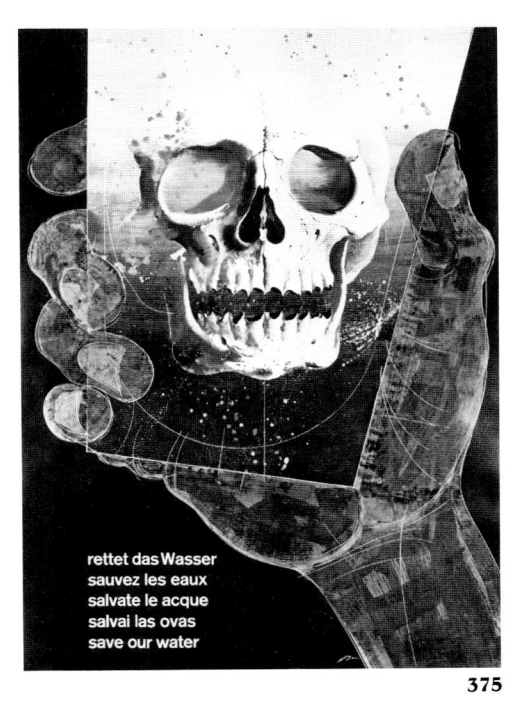

370. Rhätische Bahn. 1914.
29⅛ x 41 in/73.8 x 104.1 cm
J.E. Wolfensberger, Zurich
Cond A
In this railway poster, blues and greens predominate.
Est: $700-900.

371. Bally. 1927.
35¾ x 50½ in/90.8 x 128.3 cm
Wolfsberg, Zurich
Cond A−/ Small, very unobtrusive tears, largely at paper edges; colors and image excellent.
Stylish, but practically dressed group (woman at left in red skirt and brown and white sweater; man at center in brown knickers, white shirt and blue tie; woman at right in bright yellow dress) cleverly arranged on embankment with legs dangling and Bally shoes falling at center of poster. Cardinaux uses painterly treatment with black outline to add dimension. Background in bright blue, white cliff, red lettering. A fine composition.
Est: $800-1000.

372. Palace Hotel St. Moritz. 1922.
35⅜ x 49¾ in/90 x 126.5 cm
Wolfsberg, Zurich
Cond A
Bibl: Phillips VII, 284
A pastel-like rendering, in cool alpine colors, green predominating, showing an idyllic outing among the Swiss mountains enjoyed by a golf-playing group of picknickers.
Est: $800-1000.

See color plate 51.

373. Jungfrau Bahn.
35⅝ x 50 in/90.4 x 127 cm
Cond A
Bibl: Phillips VII, 286
View of alps and glacial valley in light purple and blue with skiers in foreground in gold jackets. Border is light yellow, lettering in red and blue. Advertises cable car to the Jungfrau—a high peak near Berne. This design was produced, with varying text, in 1921, 1925, 1927, 1930 and 1931. This probably dates to 1927.
Est: $600-700.

374. St. Moritz. 1917.
35⅞ x 50⅛ in/91 x 127.2 cm
J.E. Wolfensberger, Zurich
Cond A
Bibl: Wobmann, 45 (color)
Raw umber trees contrast with white snow, lavender shadows, and red, green and yellow colored skiers.
Est: $800-1000.

HANS ERNI (b. 1909)
375. Save Our Water. 1961.
35⅜ x 50 in/90 x 127 cm
Conzett & Huber, Zurich
Bibl: Swiss Posters, 61.8 (color); Phillips III, 421
The great painter and designer, Hans Erni, occupies a unique position in the history of Swiss posters, and his style, often consisting of scratchy lines that give shape to bold objects—surrealist in some, decorative in others—is quite distinctive and ultimately entirely his own. His humanitarian instincts have led him to create many posters for causes in which he believes, including this stark, five-language message to "Save Our Water." Brown hand holds glass of blue-green water containing skull.
Est: $400-500.

**COLLECT ALL THE BOOKS OF POSTER AUCTIONS INTERNATIONAL
for an essential reference library and Price Guide to original posters.**

If you do not have Volume I—PREMIER POSTERS—send $30.00, to cover book and mailing charges, to Poster Auctions International, 37 Riverside Drive, New York, N.Y. 10023. Be sure to specify you are ordering PAI-I. You may also find it at any bookstore which carries fine art books; if they don't have it, they can order it for you from Peregrine Smith Books of Layton, Utah.

ESBE
376. Liberty Cigarettes. 1947.
35¼ x 50 in/89.6 x 127 cm
Fiedler, La Chaux de Fonds
Cond B / Restored tears in image background at lower left; colors excellent.
A girl in a typical Ann Miller pose sells us a Swiss cigarette called "Liberty." The colors are, naturally, red, white and blue. An outrageously captivating design.
Est: $700-900.

HANS FALK (b. 1918)
377. Telephon. 1951.
35½ x 50⅛ in/90.1 x 127.3 cm
J.C. Muller, Zurich
Cond A−/ Tiny tears at paper edges; colors and image excellent. P.
Bibl: Swiss Posters, 51.20 (color)
Falk is a fine painter who has been able to use his easel technique to suit his clients' message in numerous posters. Muller-Brockmann speaks of him as "a sublime illustrator with graphic means." (p. 41). Woman in grey and white coat; beige background; lettering at top white against red. To encourage us to use the public phones.
Est: $600-800.

ALBERT HOPPLER (1890-1919)
378. P. Jecklin Sohne. 1918.
35⅝ x 50¼ in/90.4 x 127.2 cm
Mentor Verlag, Zurich
Cond A−/ Very small tears at paper edges; image and colors excellent.
Strong, painterly image of chanteuse in brown and black with white chiaroscuro highlights; black Jecklin piano accompanies her; dramatic red background and hint of lighting suggest opera or concert hall stage; lettering in black.
Est: $800-1000.

IWAN EDWIN HUGENTOBLER (1886-1972)
379. Globus. 1915.
35¼ x 50⅛ in/89.5 x 127.3 cm
Art Institut Orell Fussli, Zurich
Cond A−/ Small tears and losses at paper edges only; colors and image excellent.
Poster for the Zurich department store, Globus, shows man in tan suit; colors are brown, black, tan, with beige background.
Est: $1500-2000.

WALTHER KOCH (1875-1915)
380. Wintersport in Graubünden. 1907.
27⅞ x 39¼ in/71 x 99.7 cm
Lith. Gebr. Fretz, Zurich
Cond B+/ Expertly restored tears at upper left and upper right paper edges; colors and image excellent; mounted on heavy paper.
Bibl: Wobmann, 36; Margadant, 267 (var)
Broad treatment in cool, pastel colors: skier in blue and brown, snow in lavender, sky in light blue, text in dull orange, border in blue and plum. Skier overlooks mountain vista—possibly searching for his missing ski pole. "In 1898 Walther Koch came to Davos from Hamburg with tuberculosis. On leaving the sanatorium in 1902 the young painter settled down to live in the place of his enforced sojourn. Koch designed a series of posters for Davos which are among the best of his time. (This poster) is one of the first truly modern posters ever produced in Switzerland." (Margadant, p. 56).
Est: $700-900.

CHARLES KUHN (b. 1903)
381. Wegmann. c. 1928.
35⅝ x 50⅜ in/90.4 x 128 cm
Wolfsberg, Zurich
Cond A / P.
Possibly inspired by Loupot's 1922 poster for J.G. Weith, Kuhn gives us a gentleman in white shirt and red bow tie, which pops out from brown figure and background. Lettering in red and white. For a Zurich men's shirt shop.
Est: $1000-1200.

CARL KUNST (1884-1912)
382. Bazar Nürnberg. 1912.
36⅞ x 27⅜ in/93.7 x 69.6 cm
Reichhold & Lang, Munchen
Cond B / Tears and staining in margins only; verticle center fold; colors excellent.
Bibl: DFP-III, 1914
A painterly treatment, showing skier in dark outfit adjusting equipment, set against light blue snow and snow covered trees, pink sky. Soft pastel shades capture the glowing quality of alpine light. Lettering, also in light blue, is well integrated with the design.
Est: $800-1000.

CHARLES LOUPOT (1892-1962)
"Charles Loupot began his work in Switzerland during the First World War, where he made his first posters, and rapidly became a master lithographer. His first works . . . could be called 'mannerist'." (Weill, p. 207). The posters of his Swiss period (1916-1923) show him to be a sensitive painter, who can work magic with colors, but who is at all times aware of the posterist's need to make the client's product look enticingly good. These Swiss posters have become extremely rare. Loupot moved to Paris in 1923 and in 1930 he joined Cassandre to form the Alliance Graphique.

383. Plantol. 1919.
35⅜ x 50⅜ in/89.5 x 128 cm
Cond B+/ Horizontal folds show somewhat, with some related tears; colors excellent. Framed.
Bibl: Phillips I, 357; II, 362
One of Loupot's first posters, executed on his arrival in Switzerland, in pastel colors punctuated by the deep maroon-red of lady's hair, for a cosmetics firm.
Est: $5000-6000.

See color plate 49.

384. PKZ. 1921.
35½ x 50¾ in/90.2 x 129 cm
Wolfsberg, Zurich
Cond A-/ Tears at paper edges in margins only; unobtrusive horizontal fold; image and colors excellent. Framed.
Bibl: Loupot, 14; Phillips I, 360 (color)
Rich, splashy painter's colors, largely autumnal in tone, result here in a classic poster, one of the very best for the Zurich-based men's clothier who inspired so many fine posters.
Est: $4000-5000.

See color plate 50.

BURKHARD MANGOLD (1873-1950)

"The most highly individual poster pioneer was the Basel easel and glass painter Buckhart Mangold. In his glass painting he contrasted his clearly patterned surfaces with a predominant idealizing pseudo-naturalism, and in a similar manner he sought to rouse the poster from its romantic slumbers. . . . He worked quite independently of Cardinaux and his artistic roots. Mangold's posters—delicately perceived, humane, sometimes witty and then almost lyrical again but always profoundly painterly—had a different background. He drew his sustenance from Basel, a city with its own language and culture, a city of cosmopolitan local patriots." (Margadant, p. 54).

385. Zugerberg Wintersport. 1907.
43¼ x 32½ in/109.8 x 82.5 cm
J.E. Wolfensberger, Zurich
Cond A−/ Tiny tears in margins; mounted on heavy paper.
Bibl: Mangold, 17
For the train that takes you to the Zugerberg winter sport resort, Mangold gives us an image of eager travelers rendered in broad strokes, using several textures of lithographic crayon. Colors are beige, brown, and tan.
Est: $800-1000.

386. Davos. 1917.
Each: 28¼ x 39½ in/72 x 100 cm
J.E. Wolfensberger, Zurich
Cond A−/ Small tears at paper edges; restored loss at lower right corner of "S" panel; colors and images excellent. P.
Bibl: Mangold, 85-89.
A poster image comprised of five sheets, each containing a letter from the name Davos which frames the winter sporting scene shown in each: sleigh riding, skiing, skating and sledding. As it is a continuous image which makes no sense when broken up, it is not clear why—other than printing press limitations—it was not printed as a single sheet. Mangold gives this panoramic view a pastel treatment, with stylized images drawn in a cool, blue-grey with contrasting details in vibrant yellow, orange and pink, the lettering and border in black. Most effective, and most rare.
Est: $6000-8000. (5)

See color plate 53.

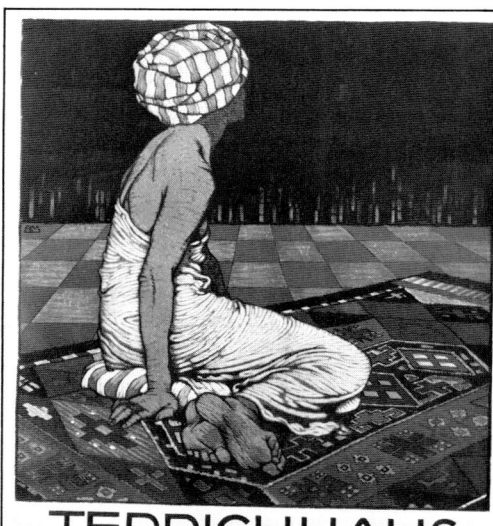

387. Teppichhaus Forster. 1911.
36⅝ x 49 in/93 x 124.5 cm
J.E. Wolfensberger, Zurich
Cond B+/ Two horizontal creases in image background at upper left; colors and image excellent. P.
Bibl: Margadant, 374 (color); Mangold, 44
A colorful poster for a Bern carpet dealer. It's interesting to compare this with another such poster for a rug sale: *See* 208.
Est: $600-700.

APPRAISALS

If you need an appraisal for insurance, estate or other purposes, please write to us. The fee varies, depending on the size of the collection and the location of it. We can inspect your posters at your premises anywhere in the world. A partial or complete rebate of the appraisal fee will be made if posters are consigned to one of our auctions within a six month period. Please write to: Mr. Jack Rennert, Poster Auctions International, Inc., 37 Riverside Drive, New York 10023.

MARTIN PEIKERT (1901-1975)
390. Globus. 1925.
35½ x 49¾ in/90.2 x 126.4 cm
Art Institut Orell Füssli, Zurich
Cond A-/ Unobtrusive handling crease in image; colors excellent.
Peikert produced many posters in a long and productive career; he is best known for travel posters which use sharp, flat colors. Here, in a design for the Globus department store, the colors are dark blue, light blue, green and bright yellow.
Est: $600-800.

JULES DE PRAETERE (1879-1947)
391. Kaller's. 1918.
32¾ x 46¾ in/83.1 x 118.8 cm
Kunstanstalt J.C. Muller, Zurich
Cond B / Some unobtrusive creasing in image; a few small tears at paper edges; colors excellent.
Painterly, yet graphic still life in bright green, carmine red, black and white of men's fashions and accessories. Lettering in tan and white; text background in black; border is carmine red. For a Zurich men's wear store.
Est: $1300-1500.

HANS THONI (1906-1980)
392. Chemin de Fer. 1958.
36 x 49⅞ in/91.6 x 126.7 cm
Impr. J.C. Muller, Zurich
Cond A
Bibl: Margadant, 293 (var); Swiss Posters, 58.12 (color; var); Phillips III, 134 (var)
Placing the passenger in a comfortable red chair against the Swiss train timetable is more than clever; it's a superb collage effect—collage in red, blue and purple with grey overlay of train schedule—which makes its point with immediacy and impact. In this French-language version of the poster, the text proclaims: "The railroad is the business road."
Est: $700-900.

ALFRED MARXER (1876-1945)
388. Zürcher-Oberland. 1905.
30¾ x 38⅛ in/78.1 x 96.3 cm
J.E. Wolfensberger, Zurich
Cond A / P.
Bold brush strokes add textured effect to the impressionistic treatment in this poster advertising winter sports in the Zurich area. Greens, gold and brown are highlighted with bright red details. Very impressive.
Est: $600-700.

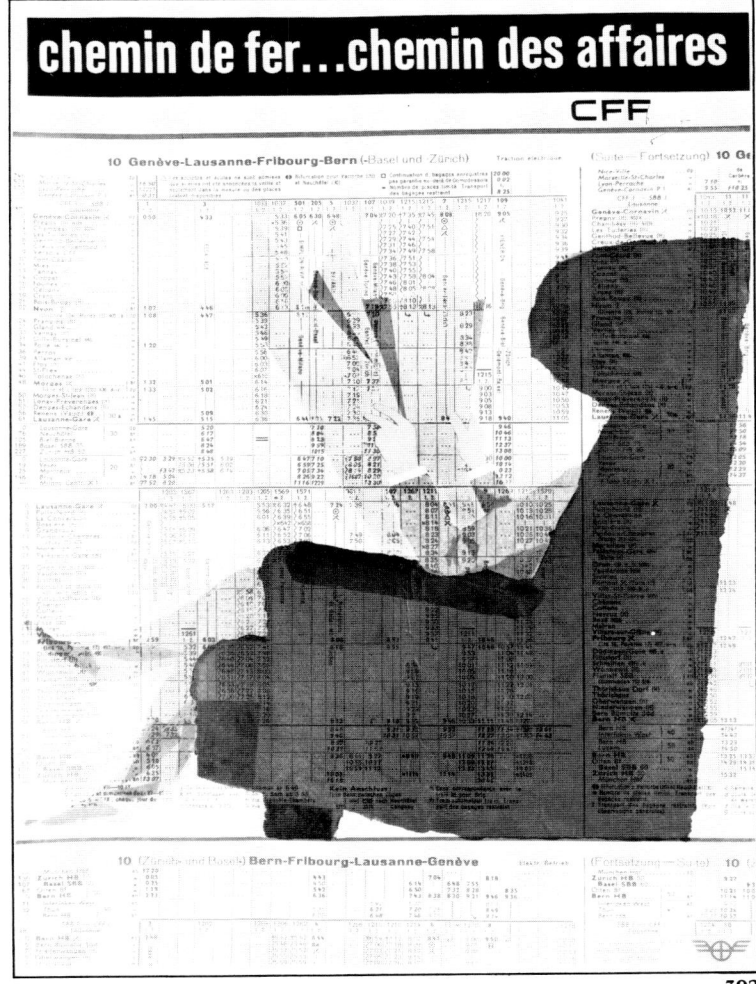

CARL MOOS (1878-1959)
For other works by Moos, see 342, 343
389. Kandersteg. 1932.
25⅛ x 40 in/64.9 x 101.5 cm
Art. Institut Orell Füssli, Zurich
Cond A
Glowing child—bronze skin, yellow hair, gold dress—in a field of bright flowers in blue, red, yellow and green. During World War I Moos moved from Munich to Zurich, where he remained the rest of his life. From 1928 to 1933 he was art director for the printing firm of Orell Füssli in Zurich.
Est: $500-600.

BIBLIOGRAPHY

The following is a list of books used in the preparation of this catalogue. In the interest of brevity, these works have been abbreviated in the Bibliography ("Bibl:") section of the description of each lot. The abbreviations used can be found below in the heading preceding the listing. It should be noted that we have made no reference to the many magazines and annuals which are essential research tools in this area, such as *The Poster, Estampe et Affiche, La Plume, Arts et Metiers Graphiques, Gebrauchsgraphik* and *Graphis Posters*.

Abdy
The French Poster by Jane Abdy. Clarkson N. Potter, New York, 1969.

Adhemar
Toulouse-Lautrec. Lithographies—Pointes Sèches—Oeuvre Complet by Jean Adhemar. Arts et Metiers Graphiques, Paris, 1965. (English language edition, *Toulouse-Lautrec—His Complete Lithographs and Drypoints*, published by Harry N. Abrams, New York, 1965)

Adriani
Toulouse-Lautrec, Das Gesamte graphische Werk by Gotz Adriani and Wolfgang Wittrock. Dumont Buchverlag, Cologne, 1976.

Affiches Etrangères
Les Affiches Etrangères Illustrées by M. Bauwens, T. Hayashi, La Forge, Meier-Graefe, J. Pennel. Boudet, Paris, 1897.

Affiches de Presse
Affiches de Presse. Catalogue of the exhibition held February-March 1984 at the Musée-Galerie de la Seita, Paris.

Affichomanie
L'Affichomanie. Catalogue of the exhibition on the subject of the Postermania of the period 1880-1900 held at the Musée de l'Affiche, Paris, 1980. Text by Alain Weill, curator.

Auto Show I
1er Salon de l'Affiche Automobile. Catalogue of the exhibition, compiled by M. Jacques Perier, and sponsored by the Automobile Club de France, Paris, October, 1978.

Auto Show II
2eme Salon de l'Affiche Automobile. Catalogue of the exhibition at the Musée de l'Affiche, Paris, September to October 1979. Edited by M. Jacques Perier.

Auto & Publicité
L'Automobile et la Publicité. Catalogue of the exhibition at the Musée de la Publicité, Paris, 1984.

Automobile & Culture
Automobile and Culture, by Gerald Silk, et al. Catalogue of the exhibition at the Museum of Contemporary Art, Los Angeles and published by Harry N. Abrams, New York, 1984.

Avant Garde
The 20th Century Poster—Design of the Avant Garde by Dawn Ades. The catalogue-book of the exhibition which opened at Walker Art Center, Minneapolis, 1984. Abbeville Press, New York, 1984.

Barnicoat
Posters: A Concise History, by John Barnicoat. Softcover edition reprinted by Thames and Hudson, London, 1985.

Belgique/Paris
L'Affiche en Belgique 1880-1980. Catalogue of the exhibition at the Musée de l'Affiche, Paris, 1980. Text by Alain Weill.

Belgique Sportives
Affiches sportives en Belgique 1890-1940. Catalogue of the exhibition in Brussels, 1981-82.

Belle Epoque
La Belle Epoque—Belgian Posters. The catalogue-book of the touring exhibition of the Wittamer-DeCamps collection. Text by Yolande Oostens-Wittamer. Grossman Publishers, New York, 1971.

Berthon & Grasset
Berthon & Grasset by Victor Arwas. Academy Editions, London; Rizzoli, New York, 1978.

Bibliothèque Nationale
Inventaire du Fonds Français Après 1800. Th 14-volume listing of all the works in the print department of the Bibliothèque Nationale, arranged alphabetically. Started in 1930, the last volume, going only to the leter L, appeared in 1967.

Bicycle Posters
100 Years of Bicycle Posters by Jack Rennert. Harper & Row, New York, 1973.

Bridges
Alphonse Mucha: The Complete Graphic Works, edited by Ann Bridges. Academy Editions, London, 1980; Harmony Books, New York.

Broido
The Posters of Jules Chéret: 46 Full Color Plates and an Illustrated Check List, by Lucy Broido. Dover Publications, N.Y. 1980.

Brown & Reinhold
The Poster Art of A.M. Cassandre by Robert K. Brown and Susan Reinhold. E.P. Dutton, New York, 1979.

Cappiello
Cappiello. Catalogue of the exhibition which opened at the Galerie Nationale du Grand Palais in Paris, April 3, 1981.

Carlu
Jean Carlu. Catalogue of the exhibition of the Posters of Jean Carlu at the Musée de l'Affiche, Paris, 1980.

Cassandre
A.M. Cassandre. Introduction by Maximilien Vox. 1948. Printed in three editions, with German, French and English text. Subtitle of English-language edition is *Posters* and published by Zollikofer, St. Gall, Switzerland.

Cassandre/Japan
Cassandre. Catalogue of the exhibition at the Seibu Museum of Art, Tokyo, 1984. Organized by Alain Weill.

Colin
100 Posters of Paul Colin by Jack Rennert. Images Graphiques, New York, 1977.

Color Revolution
The Color Revolution. Catalogue of the exhibition at Rutgers University Art Gallery, Boston Public Library and Baltimore Museum of Art. Edited by Philip Dennis Cate and Sinclair Hamilton Hitchings. 1978.

Cooper
Making a Poster by Austin Cooper. The Studio, London, third printing, 1949.

Crauzat
L'Oeuvre Gravé et Lithographie de Steinlen by E. de Crauzat. Société de Propagation des Livres d'Art, Paris, 1913.

Dance Posters
100 Years of Dance Posters by Walter Terry & Jack Rennert. Avon Books, New York, 1975.

Delteil
Le Peintre-Graveur Illustré. (Volume X and XI devoted to Lautrec.) Paris, 1920. Reprinted by Collectors Edition Ltd.-Da Capo Press, New York, 1969.

DFP-I
Das Fruhe Plakat in Europa and den USA. Volume I. British and American Posters. Edited by Ruth Malhotra and Christina Thon. Mann Verlag, Berlin, 1973.

DFP-II
Das Fruhe Plakat in Europa und den USA. Volume II. French and Belgian Posters. Edited by Ruth Malhotra, Marjan Rinkleff and Bernd Schalicke. Mann Verlag, Berlin, 1977.

DFP-III
Das Fruhe Plakat in Europa und den USA. Volume III. German Posters. Edited by Helga Hollmann, Ruth Malhotra, Alexander Pilipczuk, Helga Prignitz, Christina Thon. Mann Verlag, Berlin, 1980.

Die Bugattis
Die Bugattis. Book on the automobile, furniture, bronzes and art of the Bugattis, with various editors and contributors, published by Christians Verlag, Hamburg, 1983. The chapter on posters is edited by Ruth Malhotra.

Dortu
Lautrec by Lautrec. Ph. Huisman and M.G. Dortu. Galahad Books, New York, 1976.

Dudovich
Marcello Dudovich—Cartellonista—1878-1962, by Roberto Curci. Edizioni Lint, Trieste, 1976, 1979.

Dutch Posters
A History of the Dutch Poster 1890-1960 by Dick Dooijes and Pieter Brattinga. Scheltema & Holkema, Amsterdam, 1968.

Folies Bergère
100 Years of Posters of the Folies Bergère and Music Halls of Paris, by Alain Weill. Images Graphiques, New York, 1977.

French Opera
French Opera Posters 1868-1930, by Lucy Broido. Dover Publications, New York, 1976.

Gallo
The Poster in History, by Max Gallo. American Heritage Publishing, New York, 1974.

Hardie & Sabin
War Posters by Martin Hardie and Arthur K. Sabin. A. & C. Black, Ltd., London, 1920.

Hiatt
Picture Posters by Charles Hiatt. George Bell and Sons, London, 1895.

Hillier
Posters by Bevis Hillier. Weidenfeld and Nicolson, London, 1969; Stein & Day, New York, 1969; Spring Books, The Hamlyn Publishing Group, New York, 1974.

Hohlwein
Ludwig Hohlwein: Plakate der Jahre 1906-1940. Catalogue of the Hohlwein exhibition at the Staatsgalerie Stuttgart in Germany, March-April

Hohlwein/Stuttgart
Ludwig Hohlwein: Plakate der Jahre 1906-1940. Catalogue of the Hohlwein exhibition at the Staatsgalerie Stuttgart in Germany, March-April 1985. Text by Christian Schneegass.

Images of an Era
Images of an Era: The American Poster, 1945-1975. Catalogue of the exhibition of the Smithsonian Institution, Washington, D.C., 1975.

Internationale Plakate
Internationale Plakat, 1871-1971. Catalogue of the exhibition at the Haus der Kunst, Munich, 1871-71. Edited by Dr. Heinz Spielmann.

Jones
Posters & Their Designers, by Sydney R. Jones. The Studio, London, 1924.

Julien
The Posters of Toulouse-Lautrec. Introduction by Edouard Julien. Boston Book & Art, Boston, 1966 (Andre Sauret, Monte Carlo, 1966).

Kauffer/MOMA
Posters by E. McKnight Kauffer. Catalogue of the exhibition at the Museum of Modern Art, New York, 1937.

Keay
American Posters of the Turn of the Century by Carolyn Keay. Academy Editions, London & St. Martin's Press, New York, 1975.

Kow
A. Kow. 40 Ans de Création Publicitaire Automobile. Editions de l'Automobiliste. Arté, Adrien Maeght, Paris, 1978.

Lincoln Center
Lincoln Center Posters, by Vera List and Herbert Kupferberg. Harry N. Abrams, New York, 1980.

Livre de l'Affiche.
Le Livre de l'Affiche, by Réjane Bargiel-Harry and Christophe Zagrodzki. A publication of the Musée de la Publicité, Paris, Editions Alternatives, Paris, 1985.

Loupot
Charles Loupot. Catalogue of the exhibition at the Musée de l'Affiche, Paris, 1978.

Maindron
Les Affiches Illustrées, 1886-1895 by Ernest Maindron. G. Boudet, Paris, 1896.

Maitres
Les Maitres de l'Affiche 1896-1900 edited by Roger Marx. Imprimerie Chaix, Paris, 1896-1900. Reprinted as *Masters of the Poster 1896-1900* by Images Graphiques, New York, 1977.

Mangold
Burkhard Mangold (1873-1950). Catalogue of the exhibition held at the Kunstgewerbemuseum in Zurich, September-November, 1984, and the Gewerbemuseum in Basel, January-March, 1985.

Margadant
Das Schweizer Plakat/The Swiss Poster, 1900-1983, by Bruno Margadant. Birkhaus Verlag, Basel, 1983.

Margolin
American Poster Renaissance by Victor Margolin. Watson-Guptill Publications, New York, 1975.

Meisterplakate
Franzosische Meisterplakate un 1900. Catalogue of the exhibition of the posters of the Sammlung der Folkwangschule fur Gestaltung at the Villa Hugel, Essen, West Germany, held November-December 1968.

Menegazzi
Il Manifesto Italiano by Luigi Menegazzi. Electa Editrice, Milan, c. 1976.

Meunier
Georges Meunier, affichiste 1869-1942. Catalogue of the exhibition held May-July 1978 at the Bibliothèque Forney, Paris.

Modern American Poster
The Modern American Poster by J. Stewart Johnson. Catalogue of the Japanese exhibition of the posters from the N.Y. Museum of Modern Art collection, 1983-84. Little Brown, Boston, 1983.

Mucha/Paris
Mucha 1860-1939. Peintures—Illustrations—Affiches—Arts Décoratifs. Catalogue of the exhibition at the Grand Palais, Paris, held February 5 to April 28, 1980. Editions des Musées Nationaux, Paris, 1980.

Muller-Brockmann
History of the Poster by Josef and Shizuko Muller-Brockmann. ABC Edition, Zurich, 1971 (In German, French and English).

Musée d'Affiche
Musée de l'Affiche. Catalogue for the inaugural exhibition titled *Trois Siècles d'Affiches Françaises.* Paris, 1978.

PAI-I
Premier Posters. Book of the auction held at the Essex House Hotel, New York City, March 9, 1985, and organized by Poster Auctions International. Text by Jack Rennert.

Paris Posters
Paris Posters. Catalogue of the exhibition at the Musée de l'Affiche et de la Publicité, Paris, 1983.

Penfield
Designed to Persuade—The Graphic Art of Edward Penfield. Catalogue of the exhibition at the Hudson River Museum, Yonkers, New York, 1984. Text by David Gibson.

Petite Reine
La Petite Reine. Le Vélo en Affiches à la fin du XIXeme. Catalogue of the exhibition of bicycle posters of the end of the 19th century held at the Musée de l'Affiche, Paris, May to September, 1979.

Phillips I
A Century of Posters 1870-1970. The catalogue of the Phillips Auction, held November 10, 1979 in New York. Text by Jack Rennert.

Phillips II
Poster Classics. The catalogue of the Phillips Auction, held May 10, 1980 in New York. Text by Jack Rennert.

Phillips III
The World of Posters. The catalogue of the Phillips Auction, held November 15, 1980, in New York. Text by Jack Rennert.

Phillips IV
Poster Pleasures. The catalogue of the Phillips Auction, held April 11, 1981 in New York. Text by Jack Rennert.

Phillips V
100 Poster Masterpieces. The catalogue of the Phillips Auction, held May 2, 1981 in New York. Text by Jack Rennert.

Phillips VII
Rare Posters. The catalogue of the Phillips Auction, held November 12, 1983, in New York. Text by Jack Rennert.

Phillips/Chéret
The Posters of Jules Chéret. Supplement to the Broido book used for the Phillips sale of Chéret posters on October 24, 1980.

Plakate Munchen
Plakate in Munchen 1840-1940. Catalogue of the exhibition at the Munchner Stadtmuseum, 1975-76.

Posters/Designers
Posters and their Designers. Special Autumn Number of The Studio, London, 1924.

Poulain
L'art et l'automobile, by Herve Poulain. Les Chefs du Temps, Zoug (Switzerland), 1973.

Purvis
Poster Progress. Introduction by Tom Purvis. Edited by F.A. Mercer & W. Gaunt. The Studio, London and New York, London and New York, c. 1938.

Rademacher
Masters of German Poster Art, by Hellmut Rademacher. October House, New York, 1966 (Original German edition published in 1965 by Edition Leipzig).

Reims
Exposition d'Affiches Artistiques Francaises et Etrangères. The catalogue of the November 1986 exhibition held in Reims. Reissued, in a numbered edition of 1,000 copies, by the Musée de l'Affiche in 1980.

Rennert/Weill
Alphone Mucha: The complete Posters and Panels by Jack Rennert and Alain Weill, G.K. Hall, Boston, 1984.

Rickards
Posters of the Nineteen-Twenties, by Maurice Rickards. Evelyn, Adams & Mackey, Ltd., London, 1968.

Rogers
A Book of the Poster by W.S. Rogers. Greening & Co., London, 1901.

Schackleton
The Golden Age of the Railway Poster, by J.T. Shackleton. Chartwell Books, Secaucus, New Jersey, 1976.

Schardt
Paris 1900 by Hermann Schardt. G.P. Putnam's Sons, New York, 1970. (Originally published as *Paris 1900: Franzosische Plakatkunst,* Belser Verlag, Stuttgart, 1968.)

Schau
J.C. Leyendecker by Michael Schau. Watson-Guptill Publications, New York, 1974.

Schindler
Monografie des Plakats by Herbert Schindler. Suddeutscher Verlag, Munich, 1972.

Shahn
The Complete Graphic Works of Ben Shahn by Kenneth W. Prescott. Quadrangle/New York Times Book Co., New York, 1973.

Sorlier
Chagall's Posters, edited by Charles Sorlier. Crown, New York, 1975.

Sparrow
Advertising and British Art, by Walter Shaw Sparrow. John Lane—The Bodley Head, London, 1924.

Spectacle
Les Arts du Spectacle en France—Affiches Illustrées, 1850-1950, by Nicole Wild. The catalogue of the Bibliothèque de l'Opéra (part of the Bibliothèque Nationale), Paris, 1976.

Steinlen
Théophile-Alexandre Steinlen by Phillip Dennis Cate and Susan Gill. Gibbs M. Smith, Salt Lake City, Utah, 1982.

Swiss Posters
Swiss Poster Art (Schweizer Plakatkunst). The best posters of 1941-1965. Edited by Wolfgang Luthy. Verlag der Visualis AG, Zurich, 1968.

Tagebuch der Strasse
Tagebuch der Strasse—Geschichte in Plakaten, edited by Bernhard Denscher. Publikation der Winer Stadt-und Landesbibliothek. Osterreichischer Bundesverlag/Jugend und Volk, Vienna, 1981.

Takashimaya
The Poster 1865-1969. Catalogue of the exhibition which opened at the Takashimaya Art Gallery, Nihonbashi, Tokyo, April 18, 1985, and consisted largely of posters from the Deutsches Plakat Museum of Essen, Germany.

Theofiles
American Posters of World War I by George Theofiles. Dafran House, New York, 1973.

Timeless Images
Timeless Images. Catalogue of the touring exhibition of posters in Japan, 1984-85. Text by Jack Rennert; in English and Japanese. Exclusive American distributor: Posters Please, Inc., New York.

25 ans
25 ans d'affiches d'une imprimerie, 1912-1937. Librairie de la Galerie du Luxembourg, Paris, 1979.

Viénot
L. Cappiello by Jacques Viénot. Editions de Clermont, Paris, 1946.

Wagner
Toulouse-Lautrec and His Contemporaries: Posters of the Belle Epoque from the Wagner Collection. Book of the exhibition at the Los Angeles County Museum of Art, 1985.

Weill
The Poster: A Worldwide Survey and History, by Alain Weill. G.K. Hall, Boston, 1985.

Wember
Die Jugend der Plakate 1887-1917 by Paul Wember. Scherpe Verlag, Krefeld, 1961.

Wittrock
Toulouse-Lautrec: The Complete Prints, by Wolfgang Wittrock. 2 volumes. Sotheby's, London, 1985.

Wobmann
Touristikplakate der Schweiz (Tourist Posters of Switzerland) by Karl Wobmann; introduction by Willy Rotzler. AT Verlag, Aarau, 1980.

Word & Image
Word & Image. Catalogue of the exhibition at the Museum of Modern Art, New York, edited by Mildred Constantine. New York Graphic Society, Greenwich, Connecticut, 1968.

INFORMATION, PLEASE
Every effort has been made to make the descriptions as correct and complete as possible. However, readers are invited to submit any additions, corrections and comments they may have on any of the individual items offered in this sale. If received in time, such new data will be included in the Prices Realized *listing to be issued after the sale. Please send all information to Mr. Jack Rennert, Poster Auctions International, Inc., 37 Riverside Drive, New York, N.Y. 10023.*

CONSIGNMENTS WELCOME!

Consignments are being accepted for our Spring 1986 auctions, which includes a major sale of Belgian posters and maquettes.

Please send information regarding any possible consignments to us as soon as possible. If any questions, don't hesitate to call. Thank you.

Jack Rennert
President
Poster Auctions International, Inc.

CONDITIONS OF SALE

The Conditions of Sale in this catalogue, as it may be amended by any posted notice or oral announcement during the sale, constitutes the complete terms and conditions under which the items listed in this catalogue will be offered for sale. Please note that the items will be offered by us as agent for the consignor.

Every potential buyer should acquaint himself fully with these Conditions of Sale and it will be assumed that he or she has done so at the time of any purchase or transaction.

1. Authenticity and Terms of Guarantee.
For a period of five years from the date of this sale, Poster Auctions International, as agent, warrants the authenticity of authorship of all lots contained in this catalogue as described in the text accompanying each such lot.

This warranty and guarantee is mande only within the five year period and only to the original purchaser of record who returns the purchased lot in the same condition as when sold to him and it is established beyond doubt that the identification of authorship, as set forth in the description in this catalogue, as may have been amended by any posted signs or oral declarations during the sale, is not substantially correct based on a reasonable reading of the catalogue and the Conditions of Sale herein.

In such case, the sale will be rescinded and the original purchase price, including the buyer's premium, will be refunded. In such case, Poster Auctions International and the purchaser shall be deemed released of any and all claims that each may otherwise have had against the other arising out of the sale of such item.

The benefits of any warranty granted here are personal to the purchaser and are not assignable or transferrable to any other person, whether by operation of law or otherwise. Any attempted assignment or transfer of any such warranty shall be void and unenforceable. The purchaser refers only to the original buyer of the lot from Poster Auctions International and not any subsequent owner or other person who may have or acquire an interest therein.

It is understood that in the event of disputed authenticity of authorship of any lot results in a rescission of the sale and restitution of the original price and premium paid by such purchaser, that this is purchaser's sole remedy and that Poster Auctions International disclaims all liability for any damages, incidental, consequential or otherwise, arising out of or in connection with any sale to the purchaser.

Poster Auctions International has tried to provide as much background information for each item listed in this catalogue as possible and has made all reasonable effort to insure the accuracy of the descriptions provided, but Poster Auctions International disclaims any warranty with regard to such descriptions and statements which accompany the listings in this catalogue, including, but not limited to, the year of publication, the size, the condition, the printer, the references or any other background information or fact, and the buyer is on notice that any such information and descriptions cannot and will not be considered as material and will not effect the outcome of any sales herein.

All items are sold AS IS.

Any statements made by Poster Auctions International, whether in this catalogue or by its officers, agents or employees, whether oral or written, are statements of opinion only and not warranties or representations of fact.

The consignor warrants good title to the purchaser and Poster Auctions International and the consignor make no representations or warranty that the purchaser acquires any reproduction rights or copyright in items bought at this sale.

2. Auctioneer's Discretion.
Poster Auctions International has the absolute discretion to divide any lot, to combine any of them, to withdraw any lot, to refuse bids and to regulate the bidding. Poster Auctions International reserves the right to withdraw lots at any time prior to or during the sale. The highest bidder acknowledged by the auctioneer will be the purchaser of the lot. Any advance made on an opening bid may be rejected if the auctioneer deems it inadequate. In the event of any dispute between bidders, or in the event of doubt as to the validity of any bid, the auctioneer will have the final decision either to determine the successful bidder or to re-offer and re-sell the lot in dispute. If any dispute arises after the sale, the auctioneer's sale record shall be final and conclusive.

3. Transfer of title and property.
On the fall of the auctioneer's hammer, title to the offered lot shall pass to the highest bidder who may be required to sign a confirmation of purchase and pay the full purchase price. The purchaser shall assume full risk and responsibility for the lot purchased on the fall of the auctioneer's hammer. Poster Auctions International, at its option, may withhold delivery of the lots until funds represented by check have been collected or the authenticity of bank or cashier checks has been determined. No purchase shall be claimed or removed until the conclusion of the sale. In the event that Poster Auctions International shall, for any reason whatsoever, be unable to deliver lots purchased, its liability therefore shall be limited to the rescission of the sale and refund of the purchase price and purchaser's premium.

Poster Auctions International disclaims all liability for damages, incidental, consequential or otherwise, arising out of its failure to deliver any lots purchased.

Poster Auctions International does not charge extra or sell separately any frame if a poster is so offered; but it is clear that it is the poster and not the frame which is being offered for sale and Poster Auctions International cannot be responsible for any damage to the frame or to the poster within the frame. For the most part, framed posters were received framed and photographed that way and Poster Auctions International can make no warranty or representations regarding the condition of the poster in unseen areas of any such frame. **All items are sold strictly "as is" and as these Conditions of Sale of sale clearly indicate, the purchaser assumes full risk and responsibility for the purchased lot on the fall of the hammer.**

All lots shall be paid for and removed at the purchaser's risk and expense by noon of the second business day following the sale. Lots not so removed will, at the sole option of Poster Auctions International and at purchaser's risk and expense, be stored at Poster Auctions International's offices or warehouse or be turned over to a licensed warehouse for storage. Purchaser agrees, in either case, to pay all shipping, handling and storage fees incurred. In the case of lots stored at Poster Auctions International's own warehouse, the handling and storage fee shall be an amount equal to 2% of the purchase price for each such lot, per month, until removed, with a minimum charge of 5% for any property not removed within thirty days from the date of the sale. In addition, Poster Auctions International has the right to impose a late charge, calculated at a rate of 1 1/2% per month, based on the purchase price, if payment has not been made in accordance with these Conditions of Sale. Poster Auctions International may, on the day following the sale, remove all unclaimed lots to its offices or warehouse.

Unless purchaser notifies us to the contrary, purchaser agrees that Poster Auctions International may, at its discretion, use purchase's name as buyer of the item sold.

If the purchaser fails to comply with one or more of these Conditions of Sale then, in addition to all other remedies which it may have at law or in equity, Poster Auctions International may, at its sole option, either cancel the sale, retaining as liquidated damages all payments made by the purchaser, or sell the item and all other property of the purchaser held by Poster Auctions International without notice. Such sale will be at our standard commission rates, without any reserve. The proceeds of such sale or sales shall be applied first to the satisfaction of any damages occasioned by the purchaser's breach, and then to the payment of any other indebtedness owing to Poster Auctions International, including, without limitation, commissions, handling charges, the expenses of both sales, reasonable legal fees and collection agency fees and any other costs or expenses incurred hereunder. The purchaser hereby waives all the requirements of notice, advertisement and disposition of proceeds required by law, including those set forth in New York Lien Law, Article 9, Sections 200-204 inclusive, or any successor statute, with respect to any sale pursuant to this section.

4. Buyer's Premium.
A premium of 10% will be added to the successful bid price of all items sold by Poster Auctions International. This premium will be paid by all purchasers without exception.

5. Order bids.
Poster Auctions International will make every effort to execute bids for those not able to attend and act on the prospective purchaser's behalf to try to purchase the item desired at the lowest price possible up to the limit indicated by purchaser as if the purchaser were in attendance, but Poster Auctions International cannot be responsible for any errors or omissions in this matter. Poster Auctions International may reserve the right not to bid for any such party if the order is not clear, does not arrive in sufficient time, or the credit of the purchaser is not established, or for any other reason in its sole discretion. An Order Bid Form shall be provided on request.

6. Sales Tax.
Unless exempted by law, the purchaser will be required to pay the combined Illinois and local sales tax or any applicable compensating use tax of another state on the total purchase price.

7. Packing and shipping.
Packing and/or handling of purchased lots by Poster Auctions International and its staff is undertaken solely as a courtesy for the convenience of clients. Unless otherwise directed by purchaser, packing and handling will be undertaken at the sole discretion of Poster Auctions International, which may also, at its sole discretion, as agent of the purchaser, instruct an outside contractor to act on its behalf. If requested by purchaser, Poster Auctions International may, at its sole option and

as purchaser's agent, arrange for the transportation of purchased lots by an outside contractor. Charges for packing, handling, insurance and freight are payable by the purchaser. Poster Auctions International will make every reasonable effort to handle purchases with care, but assumes no responsibility for damage of any kind. Poster Auctions International hereby disclaims all liability for loss or damages of any kind arising out of or in connection with the packing, handling or transportation of any items purchased at this sale.

8. Reserves.
All lots are subject to a reserve which is the confidential minimum below which the lot will not be sold. Poster Auctions International may implement the reserve by bidding on behalf of the consignor. The consignor shall not bid on his property.

9. Notices and jurisdiction.
If the purchaser claims that any of these Conditions of Sale have been violated, such claim must be delivered to Poster Auctions International's offices via certified mail, return receipt requested, within twenty days of the date of sale or the claim shall be deemed waived.

These Conditions of Sale as well as the purchaser's and our respective rights and obligations hereunder shall be governed and construed and enforced in accordance with the laws of the State of New York. By bidding at an auction, whether present in person or by agent, order bid, telephone or other means, the purchaser shall be deemed to have consented to the jurisdiction of the state courts of, and the federal courts sitting in, the State of New York.

By the making of a bid, the Purchaser acknowledges his acceptance of these Conditions of Sale and all terms and conditions announced at the sale.

DESCRIPTION OF THE POSTERS

1. Artist's Name.
Unless otherwise indicated, the artist's name, mark or initials appear on the poster.

2. Year of the Poster.
The year given is that of the publication of the poster, not necessarily the date of the event publicized or the year that art for it was rendered.

3. Size.
Size is given in inches first, then centimeters, width preceding height. Size is for entire sheet, not just the image area.

4. Printer.
Unless otherwise indicated, the name of the printer is that which appears on the face of the poster. It should be kept in mind that frequently the establishment credited on the poster is, in fact, an agency, studio or publisher.

5. Condition of the Poster.
We have attempted a simplified rating of all the posters in this sale.
It should be kept in mind that we are dealing, in many cases, with 50 to 100 year old advertising paper. The standards of the print collector cannot be used. Prints were, for the most part, done in small format, on fine paper, and meant to be immediately framed or stored in a print sleeve or cabinet. A poster, for the most part, is printed in a large format, on the cheapest possible paper, and meant to last about eight weeks on the hoardings.
Most important to the condition of a poster—not eight weeks but often eighty years later—is the image of the poster: Is that image (the lines, the colors, the overall design) still clearly expressed? If so, it is a poster worth collecting.
While details of each poster's condition are given as completely and accurately as possible, blemishes, tears or restorations which do not detract from the basic image and impact should not seriously impair value.
All posters are lined, unless otherwise indicated.
All photos are of the actual poster being offered for sale. A close look at the photo and a reading of the text should enable the buyer who cannot personally examine the item to make an intelligent appraisal of it.

The following ratings have been used.:

Cond A *Designates a poster in very fine condition.* The colors are fresh; no paper loss. There may be some slight blemish or tear, but this is very marginal and not noticeable. A + is a flawless example of a poster rarely seen in such fine condition. A − indicates there may be some slight dirt, fold, tear or bubble or other minor restoration, but most unobtrusive.

Cond B *Designates a poster in good condition.* There may be some slight paper loss, but not in the image or in any crucial design area. If some restoration, it is not immediately evident. The lines and colors are good, although paper may have yellowed (light-stained). B+ designates a poster in Very Good condition. B− is one in fairly good condition. The latter may be caused by heavier than normal light-staining or one or two noticeable repairs.

Cond C *Designates a poster in fair condition.* The light-staining may be more pronounced, restorations, folds or flaking are more readily visible, and possibly some minor paper loss occurs. But the poster is otherwise intact, the image clear, and the colors, though possibly faded, still faithful to the artist's intent.

Cond D *Designates a poster in bad condition.* A good part of such poster may be missing, including some crucial central image area; colors and lines so marred that a true appreciation of the artist's intent is difficult, if not impossible.
There are no Cond D posters in this sale!

The above condition ratings are solely the opinion of Poster Auctions International, and are presented only as an aid to the public. Prospective purchasers are expected to have satisfied themselves as to the condition of the posters. Any discrepancy relating to the condition of a poster shall not be considered grounds for the cancelation of a sale.
Some other notes and designations relating to condition of poster:

Frame Where a poster is framed, this is indicated. In many cases, we have photographed the poster in the frame and the dimensions given are those which are visible within the matting or edges of the frame.

Paper All posters in this sale are linen-backed unless the designation "P." appears.

6. Bibliography.
An abbreviation for each reference is given and can be found in the complete Bibliography. The reference is almost always to a reproduction of that poster. If a "p." precedes it, it means the reproduction or reference is on that page; if number only, it refers to a poster or plate number. Every effort has been made to refer to books that are authoritative and/or easily accessible.

7. Pre-Sale Estimate
These estimates are guides for prospective bidders and should not be relied upon as representations or predictions of actual selling prices. They are simply our best judgment of the fair market value of that particular poster in that condition on the date it was written.